# Finding Truth

Journey of a Christian and His Church

William G. Chipman

# Finding Truth: Journey of a Christian and His Church

*©2021 by William G. Chipman. All rights reserved. No part of this book may be reproduced or transmitted in any form or by any means, electronic or mechanical, including photocopying, recording, or by any information storage and retrieval system, without permission in writing from the copyright owner.*

*Published by Your Online Publicist: August, 2021*

ISBN: 978-1-63892-104-2 (sc)

YOUR ONLINE PUBLICIST

Suite 337 7950 NW, 53rd St.
Miami, Florida 33166 USA
www.youronlinepublicist.com
(800) 419-3014

Printed in United States of America

This book is printed on acid-free paper

# CONTENTS

Introduction .................................................................................. 5

1 Christian Learns To Survive .................................................... 7
2 Christian Finds Christ ............................................................ 17
3 Christian Devours The Bible ................................................. 31
4 Spring ...................................................................................... 39
5 Elders ...................................................................................... 49
6 Jacob And Esau ...................................................................... 63
7 Sunday's Sermon ................................................................... 73
8 Asking For Advice ................................................................. 81
9 Fall ........................................................................................... 99
10 Bursting At The Seams ....................................................... 111
11 Romans ................................................................................ 123
12 The Bank Robbery .............................................................. 133
13 Living By Faith .................................................................... 147
14 Romans 9 ............................................................................. 155
15 United In Christ .................................................................. 163
16 Mr. Friendly And Mr. Evangelist ...................................... 169
17 Bible School ........................................................................ 179
18 Christian's First Sermon .................................................... 193
19 Afterward ............................................................................ 203

Appendix A - Christian Explains Scripture ........................... 215
Appendix B - Version Confusion ............................................ 223

# INTRODUCTION

In America of 1883, people were respected for their ability. Age was of little consequence. Amazing though it may seem to a modern reader, the young hero of this story would indeed be allowed to live on his own, even treated as an adult, as long as he could support himself. And he did. Orphaned and alone, resourceful nine-year-old Christian learned to survive.

Becoming a follower of Christ at age eleven, he brought his survival skills and inquisitive "can do" spirit into his new life. With a conviction that God deeply loves each one of us, Christian persevered and brought an understanding of God's awesome love into a stodgy, tradition-bound church.

Although the setting is 1883 America, I did adapt it somewhat to develop the message of the book. For example, in 1883, the seventy-two–hour work week left little time for anything else. I borrowed from a modern forty-hour work week, which enabled the church in my story to have home Bible studies and even do things on Saturday.

Though the Bible used in 1883 was the King James Version, for the benefit of modern readers, all Bible quotations are from the New King James Version unless otherwise noted.

I also did not take into account 1880's clothing customs. In those days, men always wore a vest over their shirt and usually a jacket as well, women wore bustles, and everyone wore a hat when outside the house. In this story, I assume that the fashion is simple and similar to what we might find today.

At the cusp of the modern era, the 1880s were an exciting time of change and invention. There were a few automobiles, and electric power was about to become widespread. Soon, electric motors would replace water to power the industrial revolution. The telephone was recently invented. The transcontinental railroad was completed in 1869, and by 1883, railroads were common. Still, there were few laws regarding children, and Christian, my young hero, would be free to live and work as he chose.

# 1 CHRISTIAN LEARNS TO SURVIVE

Christian lived two miles beyond the edge of town with his mother and father in a small rented house. From the time he could walk, his mother gave him chores that he could do. The silverware drawer was low so he could reach it. When his mother opened the drawer, he knew it was time for him to set the table. His mother set the plates out because she was afraid he might drop one. She also taught him to help with the garden and the washing. They did everything together, and she was constantly teaching him new things to do. At a very young age, Christian was learning how to work.

While they were working, his mother used to sing, and as soon as Christian could talk, he would sing with her. One of the songs she taught him was the sounds of the alphabet letters. It was a very silly song that made Christian laugh, but when he was almost three, his mother began to teach him to sound out a written word. She said reading was important, and he needed to learn to read well. Christian was thrilled to discover that the pages of books could talk. He saw how his parents loved reading. On his mother's birthday or Christmas, she was always happy to receive a new book.

Though Christian's parents believed in God and the Bible, it wasn't something they took seriously. The family occasionally went to church, and they were sure to be there on Christmas and Easter. Once, a few days after an Easter service, Pastor Caring came for a visit. Christian heard him say to his parents, "God wants us to live in a way that He can have us as friends. If that's what you want, He would find pleasure in changing your life, to make you the kind of person He can live with forever."

Christian's father said, "We try to do what's right. I think we're already pretty good people."

Looking very serious, Pastor Caring responded, "Yes, Christ died for good people and He died for bad people. But living as a Christian is really about receiving Christ into your life and growing in your relationship with Him."

After the pastor left, Christian's father commented, "That

pastor is a little bit pushy." But Christian was thinking, *I wish I could hear more about what it would be like to know Jesus.* The thought stayed with him for a few weeks before it faded away.

When Christian was four, he started spending more time with his father. As soon as his father came home from work, Christian followed him and learned to help with all the chores. While they worked, his father would ask what he learned that day and what he had been reading. "It's not how fast you read that's important," he used to say. "It's understanding what you are reading." When Christian was five years old, his father taught him how to use a dictionary and insisted he look up words he didn't understand. Encouraged by his mother and father, Christian could read just about anything before he started school.

There was a one-room schoolhouse nearby where Christian started when he was seven. The teacher, Miss Gracious, seemed pleased when she found that he already knew how to read. "Let's see," she said. Reaching into her bookshelf, she pulled out a copy of *Robinson Crusoe* and opened it to the first chapter. "Can you read this?"

Christian's parents had taught him to read aloud at home and were always including him in the things they talked about, so he wasn't a bit bashful. In a strong voice and with expression, he easily read a whole page. "I'm very impressed," Miss Gracious said. "You do read very well." As a result, Christian was placed in a reading group with much older kids. Christian liked the school because he could hear all grade levels reciting their lessons, and this helped him when he got to where they were. Miss Gracious taught some things like geography to all the students at the same time. Christian was at the beginning level in arithmetic. Between the drill at school and his mother helping, he quickly learned his addition and subtraction math facts. To Christian, school was fun.

After school, Christian went to the flour mill where his father worked. It was by the river, not too far from their house. The owner, Mr. Miller, said it was all right for Christian to be there as long as he was being useful. The miller was a big man and hardly ever smiled. Christian was a little bit afraid of him, so when he said, "A mill is no place for boys who don't work," Christian made it a point to always be helpful. He liked working with his father. Christian's job was to sew the top of each full flour sack. Then he would get the next empty sack ready while his father was grinding the wheat into flour.

Mr. Miller took note of Christian's diligence. One day, he came over to Christian and said approvingly, "You're a fine boy, and you're really useful. I'm going to increase your father's pay from $2.00 a day to $2.20." After Mr. Miller left, Christian's father said, "I'm so proud of you, son. From now on, I'm giving you 5 cents a day, because you earned it." This made Christian feel good, and he was even more alert to what he could do to help. His mother's birthday was coming up and he was going to buy her a new book, *The Silverado Squatters* by Robert Louis Stevenson, which described Stevenson's two-month honeymoon in California. Christian knew his mother would like it.

At home after work, Christian's father taught him how to use a hammer. Christian was clumsy at first. His father held his hand and they would hammer together until Christian could make long straight blows on a single spot. After he had practiced for a while, Christian was allowed to hammer a real nail into a board that was part of the work shed they were building. Nails were expensive. His father taught him not to pound hard at first, but just concentrate on pounding straight so the nail didn't bend. With the board nailed in place, his father said, "Well done, son! You're the best son a father could ever have." When business was slow at the mill, Christian's father used the finished shed as a workshop to make chairs and things which he could sell.

Next door to their house lived old Mr. Mountainman, a master storyteller who loved to yarn about what it was like to live in the western wilderness. Christian loved to go next door and listen to him recount tall tales of his days living alone trapping for fur and his endless stories of his life among the mountain Indian tribes. His descriptions of how to make a fish trap, a snare, and a dead fall later became very important.

One day, when Christian was nine years old, his father came home worried. He had heard at the mill that a smallpox epidemic was sweeping through their town. Christian was told not to go to school or come to the mill until it was over. The next morning, his father felt like he ached all over and was too weak to go to work. Two days later, his mother came down with the same symptoms.

For several weeks, Christian did his best to care for his parents. Mr. Mountainman also caught smallpox and died. Christian felt fear when he saw men put Mr. Mountainman in a wagon which carried him off. The doctor came to Christian's house and left some medicine, but it didn't seem to help. One by one, both of his parents died, first his mother and then, the next morning, his father. Christian couldn't believe they were dead until the doctor came by again. He told Christian they weren't sleeping, they were gone. Christian began to cry and tears were forming in the doctor's eyes as he left quickly.

Soon, the same men who took Mr. Mountainman away came rumbling up the road in their wagon. Christian could not bear to watch and stayed out of sight. After only a few minutes, the men left with his parents and their bedding. All the victims of the epidemic were buried south of town, and their bedding was burned.

Overcome by a cold paralyzing fear, Christian felt like he was drowning and had no strength to fight the vortex that was pulling him down. For the next couple of days, he was alone, numb with despair. Living on what food was left in the house, he couldn't even think about what to do. When he saw men coming up the road once more, he was frightened and hid under his bed. The men looked at every room, talking about what had to be cleaned out in order to rent the house again. Faced with everything in the house about to be taken away, Christian knew he had to pull himself together and decide what to do.

If he went to an orphan asylum and asked for help, he might be adopted. But there was a good chance that he would be adopted by folks more interested in the work he would do than really being parents to him. Then again, he might be adopted by people who would love him and raise him as their own. But Christian wasn't willing to take the risk.

An orphan asylum might put him on the orphan train that took orphans west. As the train traveled along, it would stop off and town people would come out to look the orphans over, adopt those they wanted, and sign a contract to educate them. Part of the contract was to teach the orphans their own trade, usually farming. Older boys were in demand because they could do more work. Older girls were second because they could help mothers with younger children. People who wanted a child to love took the little ones. As a nine-year-old boy, he had reason to be wary. As he thought about this, all the encouragement he had received from his father converged into a single resolve. Proclaiming loudly to the empty house, Christian said, "I won't ask for help, not ever, never." His decision to survive on his own was made.

He had to act quickly. Making several trips from the kitchen, he took food, an iron skillet, a pot, a knife, the flints, some dishes, and whatever he thought he would need and carried them into the nearby woods. Everything he took brought back memories of his parents, and tears silently dripped from his cheeks. Returning, he had just gathered up his clothes, his own bedding, and his mother's sewing basket when he heard the sound of a wagon. Several men jumped off and began to clear out the house, taking everything until the wagon box was full. While they were working, Christian crept into the work shed to retrieve a hatchet, some knives, a bucket, and his father's fishing gear.

Christian worked quietly, hoping no one would see him. The shed windows were dim with wood dust, and the sawdust reminded him of his father. Christian choked back a sob. He almost felt as though his father were right there, still working at making furniture and encouraging him to be strong and make his own decisions that he could stick with. Christian felt like he could hear his father saying, "You can do this. I know you can." With tears now streaming down, he said out loud, "Yes, Father. I can do this."

After wiping his face on his sleeve, Christian peered out. The men were still busy by the wagon. Quickly, he carried the bucket filled with things to the woods. While waiting for the men to leave, he was thinking about what else he might need. "The whetstone!" he said. In the shed, his father had a small slow-turning whetstone that could make everything razor sharp. *Will the men go to the shed and clear it out?* he wondered. Finally, Christian saw the wagon pull away. He ran to the house and gave a quick look inside. There was no one to be seen. Christian hurried to the shed, holding his breath. *What if everything is already gone?* But the shed was untouched. The wheelbarrow was still leaning on the wall. Christian loaded it up with the whetstone and all kinds of tools. Making several trips, he took everything—garden tools, baling wire, nails, coils of rope. If the men came back, all these things would be hidden in the woods.

Hoping the men would not return that day, Christian returned with the wheelbarrow one last time to see if there was anything left in the pantry. There were only a few potatoes, some apples, and a large hunk of cheese. He knew he would need the cheese as bait to trap rabbits and squirrels. He remembered that worms made good bait, too, so he stopped off at the compost pile, dug up worms, and carried them off in a tin cup.

Back to the woods he went, and pushing the wheelbarrow trip after trip, he transported everything to a lonely place he knew by the river, far away from any houses. By the time he finished, it was getting late in the day.

Christian and his father had often come here to go fishing. They'd even built a campfire ring on the shore, made out of stones from the river. Taking his father's fishing pole, Christian went down to the river and soon managed to catch some fish. As he cleaned the fish, gathered kindling, and lit a fire, it brought back memories that somehow cheered him. Comforted and calmed by the familiar routine, he said in his heart, *"Yes, Father, I can do this."*

After the sun went down, Christian spread out a blanket and lay down, rolling himself up like a cocoon. Watching the stars slowly coming out, he was soon asleep. At least, for a while, he was asleep! Ants began to crawl on him, and occasionally, one would bite. Getting up, he moved to a place where there were no ants. In the morning, breakfast was an apple and another fish that he caught. After splashing his face and hands clean in the river, Christian thought about what to do next. He remembered that Mr. Mountainman told him about making a bark shelter. So he took the hatchet and cut down some saplings, which he trimmed into poles. He tied the frame of a lean-to so the high end would be supported by two trees. Then he shingled the frame with pieces of bark. It took all day. The low end was facing the wind, and he was satisfied that if it rained, he would not get completely soaked.

The next day, Christian thought about how to get more food from the woods. He remembered what Mr. Mountainman had told him about traps and figured out how to make a deadfall. He found a large rock that was flat on one side and propped it up on a fragile trigger made of sticks that he whittled. If any small animal even touched where the bait was attached, the rock would fall on them. Though Christian was terribly hungry by this time, he faithfully saved the cheese for bait. That day, he also made snares out of baling wire with a loop on one end that would tighten when an animal pulled against it. He placed the snares in nearby animal trails at varying heights. Next morning, he found a rabbit caught in a snare. Christian hated the thought of killing it, but he knew he had to if he was to survive. That day, he had rabbit for dinner.

And so the early spring days passed. Christian was often hungry, but worst of all, he missed his mother and father. When night came, he sometimes cried himself to sleep. He would have given anything just to hear his mother sing again. The only relief from the grief he felt was to work hard on what he needed to survive.

But finally he was so hungry that in the middle of the night, he walked toward town and raided someone's garden. He felt bad about it and was ashamed as he thought how disappointed his parents would have been if they knew he had done such a thing. But the pangs of hunger were sometimes unbearable. After having done this twice, he decided that no matter how hungry he was, he would not do it again. "I ought to plant a garden of my own," he told himself.

The next morning, the birds sang loudly as a golden sun came up. Christian walked around till he found a flat piece of ground with good soil. Then he spent the whole day working on poles to make a fence to keep the deer out of his garden site. He also collected stones to place around the fence to keep rabbits from digging under it. He dug holes and put up posts. Then he wove branches between them till he had a deer-proof fence. He worked from sunrise to sunset, driven by his determination never ever to steal food again, plus a fear of the future and what might happen. Once the fence was built, he worked hard at making the soil loose and soft.

While working, Christian dug up many roots. At first, this made him frustrated, but then he remembered Mr. Mountainman telling him about fish traps made of roots. After that, any roots that were long and not too thick he set aside, then tied them in bundles. Using rocks, he sank the bundles in the river to keep the roots pliable.

He formed the soil into furrows and planted precious seeds he'd saved from the shed. He was very careful with the tiny carrot seeds and also planted onions and beets. He made hills and put bean and corn seeds together so the corn would act as a beanpole. He carefully made a few more hills and planted squash. He saved one potato that he cut into pieces, each with an eye, and planted those too. He would have planted an apple seed in hopes of growing a tree, but he didn't want to attract bears since they love apples. After watering the garden using water from the river, he placed the stones he had collected around the outside of the fence.

With his garden finished, he turned his attention to making a fish trap by weaving the roots together. Through trial and error, he eventually made a trap that looked like it might work. Eager to see what would happen, he baited it with cheese and rabbit guts.

Christian anchored the trap in the river with rocks and waited. And waited. And waited. Not one fish went into the trap. *I could catch more fish with my father's fishing pole*, he thought. Then Christian remembered something else that Mr. Mountainman had told him. "Every day, throw animal and fish guts into the water by the fish trap. This gets the fish used to the trap as a place where they might find food. After that, they swarm after the bait inside the trap. Hey," Mr. Mountainman emphasized, "fish talk to one another, you know. They spread the word until they all know where the food is and crowd into the trap." A few days later, Christian put fresh bait inside the trap and found that Mr. Mountainman was not exaggerating very much.

With a steady supply of fish, Christian started to think about how to preserve them. Building a smoker would be the easiest. So Christian made a teepee out of sticks. Inside, he attached short sticks to hang things on and covered the teepee with bark. On the ground inside, he used rocks to make a fire ring. There were cottonwoods growing nearby. Cottonwood branches with the bark removed are good for smoking. He knew that eating things smoked using the wrong kind of wood might make him sick. He also remembered Mr. Mountainman had told him that the fire needed to smolder and not burn too hot. If the anything were to cook while being smoked, it would spoil sooner.

Summer arrived. Christian's garden was growing well, and Christian spent many days building a little one-room cabin. He was glad of his father's whetstone. Chopping down many small trees, his axe and hatchet grew dull.

One warm day, he was checking his fish trap when a boy he knew from school walked out of the woods carrying a fishing pole. Christian was amazed at the feelings that swept over him. He realized how horribly lonely he had been. Trying to keep his voice steady, he called out a greeting. "Hello, Thoughtful. Let me get my pole and I'll show you the best fishing holes." He and Thoughtful fished and talked all afternoon.

Before he left, Thoughtful said, "You know, there's people who need somebody to do jobs for them. Why don't you go wait outside Mr. Helpful's store? He wouldn't mind, and everybody would see you." So the following day, Christian walked to town and sat on the bench in front of Mr. Helpful's general store. He greeted people who walked by and asked if they had any work that needed to be done. "Sure," said one man, "I've got a barn that needs mucking out." Christian was thrilled. The man paid him a whole fifteen cents. Christian took five cents and bought himself a loaf of bread as a special treat.

A year went by, then another year. Christian was getting older and stronger. Mr. Helpful didn't object to Christian being on his bench, and when there were no customers he would come out to talk. Folks in town got to know that they might find Christian in front of the store when they had a job for him to do. But the pain he felt because he missed his mother and father was still with him. Now that he was often in town working, he sometimes heard angry shouting coming from the houses and wondered why many of the families didn't always get along. He felt so alone in the world that he thought everyone should appreciate their family. He so wished his mother and father had not died. They loved each other and never yelled. He tried not to think about them, but occasionally a tear would silently run down his cheek. The hardest part was at night when he had to close his eyes.

# 2 CHRISTIAN FINDS CHRIST

One night in particular, Christian was feeling so alone, and it grieved him that his life seemed empty and had no purpose. *There has to be more to living than just surviving,* he thought to himself. For the first time in a long time, he started to pray. "God, is this all there is? If I can know You, I want to know You." Looking up at the sky, Christian spent some time venting his frustration to God before going to bed. As the darkness of the night closed around him, Christian fell asleep and began to dream.

He dreamed there was a Family that lived up in the mountains north of the river. They were rich and had everything They could wish for. One day, the Son came down in the family carriage and stopped at Christian's little cabin. It was a covered carriage, brilliant white with gold trim, and a picture of a lamb on the doors. The Son got out, dressed in a long white robe with a brilliant red sash. around His waist.

One look at the kindness and genuine concern that seemed to shine from His eyes told Christian that he had nothing to fear. Using his father's tools, Christian had made chairs that stood in front of his cabin, so the Son sat down and visited for a while. He seemed to know everything about Christian and was genuinely concerned. Finally, the Son said, "The Family has been watching you for a long time. We know how hard it has been for you. We have decided to ask if you would like to come up the hill and live with Us." In his dream, Christian couldn't say "Yes!" fast enough. Into the big carriage he climbed, and off they went across the bridge and up the mountain.

Servants came to welcome and attend him; Christian was soon clean and dressed in what he thought were wonderful clothes. Christian's favorite color was green and the servants had given him a shirt that was green with gold edging. Then they took him to a beautiful room with a view across the whole valley and told him, "This is yours now." Christian was amazed and awed. The servants then led him downstairs to a bright, elegant hall. The ceiling was high and two walls had ceiling-to-floor windows. Long golden draperies were tied back to frame the view of the valley below.

There Christian was introduced to the Father, who exclaimed, "If you are willing, I would like to adopt you as my own son." Christian was amazed and the Son was delighted. He gave Christian a hug and said, "Now we are brothers."

Then yet another member of the Family, whose name was Spirit, took Christian by the hand and said, "We are so glad to have you in our Family! Welcome." Christian did feel welcome, and he felt loved.

They all sat down on yellow overstuffed chairs embroidered with purple clusters of grapes. While the servants brought delicious things to eat and drink, Christian ate and listened as the Family talked about many of the things they were doing. From what Christian could understand, they were interested in influencing people to make good decisions—decisions that would change their lives. The Father said to Christian, "Deciding to do what is best for others no matter what the cost to yourself has a good effect on you forever. That's why We're always trying to help people choose to live that way."

As the conversation continued, Christian began to notice how kindly each Member of the Family talked to the others. When the Son addressed the Father, the word Father as it was spoken seemed to be carried on a wave of affection. And it was so as the Father addressed the Son or Spirit. How differently this Family lived! There was no tension, no pettiness, no selfishness.

After a while, the Father and Son excused themselves, but Spirit stayed and said to Christian, "Let's go for a walk." As they went through the glass door into the garden, Christian asked about the kindness that characterized the Family. "We're an ancient family," Spirit said. "The kindness you noticed, what We call grace, comes from our love for one another. And we always follow certain principles that make it natural and easy to be kind to everyone. Following these principles is called righteousness."

*Oh!* Christian thought, *I wish I knew how to live that way.* Then he blurted out, "Please tell me about righteousness!"

Spirit said, "Righteousness is the courtesies we practice. You could call it, Our etiquette of love. The first rule is that We never exert our power to force each other to do what We want. Actually, We never force anyone to obey us. And the second rule is that We trust each other to live by the principle of doing what is best for others." Spirit paused and looked intently at Christian. "That means We will also trust you. Trust is very important to Us. We call it faith.

If We didn't trust each other, We wouldn't be able to love each other in a full way. We always want to live in a life of love for each other, with nothing to hinder it."

Spirit paused. He could see that Christian was thinking. Finally, Christian said, "I hope I never fail to do what is best for others. It would cause You so much pain. What would You do?"

Spirit replied, "We would never stop loving you and watching over you. We saw what was in your heart, and we invited you to be part of our Family because of your desire to love Us and live righteously. But if you fail to do what is best for others, We're very patient. Eventually, you would recognize that you've failed. But our love for you might have to become tough love that encourages you to come back to a place where We can trust you. And We might have to let you experience the natural consequences of your wrong decision."

Even more than before, Christian saw the pain it would cause the Family if he failed to do what was best for others. He was impressed that the Family would love him anyway. "So we trust each other. Is that how it works?" he asked.

"Yes," said Spirit. "Though the Father, the Son, and Myself are one with each other, We also express love, righteousness, and faith toward one another. Our faith working by love is an important part of our belonging to one another. So Christian, it's Our intent to also express faith toward you. Love, righteousness, and faith are part of your new relationship with Us."

Christian thought about some of the bitter, angry people he'd worked for down in the valley and said, "I know people who probably won't ever want to live the way you do or do what's best for others. What happens to people who will never change their minds?"

Spirit responded, "We offer them trust by giving them more time to change their minds. We also try to persuade them by letting them experience the consequences of their choices. But if they continue to refuse, We accept their decision and do what is best for them, which is that their madness be stopped and the righteous be protected. In the end, the wicked will be put in a place where no one will force them to be righteous."

Just then, the Son came by and suggested, "Christian, there are others who also live here. If you like, you can wander about, meet some of them, and explore your new home. If you get lost, just call my name and I'll be there by your side."

"I'd like that," said Christian. The Son and Spirit quietly left, and Christian began to explore. He walked all over the garden, marveling at its beauty, and then returned to the enormous house. Then he found Ezriel, a servant who had met him when he got out of the carriage.

"Hello, Christian," said Ezriel. "How are you getting along?" After they talked for a while, Christian asked curiously, "I used to live down in the valley. Where did you live before you came here?"

"Long ago," said Ezriel, "before any of us were here, the Family lived alone. What was important to them was their love for one another. There was never any competition for control. Rather, each Person limited Themselves. That allowed and encouraged love and faith in one another. And it gave Them unrestrained freedom to think of new ways to express love. Their desire to do what was best for each other was unconditional. You could say, 'the Family is love.'"

"I lived alone too," Christian said, "and sometimes I felt lonely."

"The Family was alone," said Ezriel. "But They were never lonely. They always were very creative and powerful, so the love they expressed to each other was magnificent, giving them great joy. The very act of expressing new ways of love to one another gave Them pleasure."

"What a wonderful way to live!" Christian marveled. "And the Family would never change. I think I'm just beginning to understand the love They've shown me."

"The Family," Ezriel continued, "living in love, didn't need anyone else. Then the Son spoke some words, and out of nowhere, we servants were all created, billions of us, to serve the Family. The Father, Son, and Spirit told us to always remember one rule: that the greatest among us are those who are the best at humbly serving."

Christian was amazed. "It sure doesn't work that way where I come from!" he marveled. "People who are leaders get there by being bossy, not by humbly serving!"

"Well," said Ezriel, "I will say this. It's been my observation that the Family is better at humbly serving than any of us. They're always doing good things for us. They are always humble and kind."

Then Ezriel frowned and looked very sad. "You would think that we servants would be grateful. You'd think that we would never want anyone but the Family to rule over us. But a terrible thing happened.

"One of the servants, named Lucifer, whom we all looked up to because he was beautiful, talented, and smart, decided that being humble was not for him. He wanted to rule over all of us, like he was the master of the house. He recruited lots of us servants and started his own government, based on pride and power."

Christian was horrified. "Did many join him?" he gasped.

"Yes, enough to wage war with the rest of us."

Amazed, Christian exclaimed, "Lucifer must have been a great persuader! What did he say to get so many on his side?"

"Being able to rule others because you are stronger seemed exciting to many of us. Lucifer pointed out that strength to rule over others could even come in the form of being clever and tricking others to follow. He appealed to our pride. 'The weak should serve the strong,' he said, and he made that idea look so good that many joined him."

Now it was Christian's turn to frown. "But what could the Family do?" he asked. "From what you've said, it looks like they have a thing about humility. How could they be humble and still stop Lucifer?"

"Oh, the Family made a fiery prison," said Ezriel. Christian looked horrified, so Ezriel quickly went on, "but They didn't put anyone in it yet. Just the fact that it was there discouraged any more of the servants from joining Lucifer. It was not the kind of thing the Family likes to do, but when They saw that further patience would only make matters worse, They took action. Because of their decisiveness, many of us were spared from what would have been a horrible fate."

"I know I certainly wouldn't want to end up in a fiery prison!" Christian exclaimed. "Why aren't Lucifer and those who joined him in that prison now?"

"The Family allowed Lucifer to continue what he was doing in order to demonstrate what his idea leads to. And Their plan worked. It wasn't long before we could all see clearly that Lucifer's way was very wrong, and following principles which encourage expressions of kindness, what the Family calls righteousness, is the only way to live.

"If Lucifer had been put in the prison right away, we servants would not have seen how foolish and wrong it is to abandon righteousness. In fact, if the Family had simply grabbed him and stuck him in the prison by a show of raw power, we might have thought the Family was acting according to the way Lucifer does things. We might have even thought Lucifer was right, that ruling because you're stronger is the only practical way to rule. Lucifer is being allowed to try and prove that the Family cannot rule without acting as he does. He still thinks it's impossible to rule by humbly serving, and he's still out to prove his point by trying to force the Family to act in prideful strength. He's tried and tried, but every time, he's only proved himself wrong yet again. The Family never acts in arrogant strength. They only use Their power in humility, love, and righteousness. They always do what's best for us. Eventually, what is best for us will be a judgment where those who want to obey the Family will be kept with Them forever, separated from those who do not. The servants who have joined Lucifer along with all of the valley people who reject the Family will be cast with him into the Lake of Fire where the Family is not there to interfere with anything they do."

Christian hesitated. "I've been unrighteous, just like those servants that rebelled. But the Family has forgiven me. Can't They just forgive Lucifer's followers if they change their minds, like They did for me?"

Ezriel shook his head. "No. You valley people are very different from us. You were created after us, and even before you were created, the Family promised you a special relationship with Them which we don't have. You were created in Their image and can actually be adopted into the Family. We can't. You can change your mind about doing wrong. Once we decide to reject righteousness, our decision changes us so much that we can't change back to what we were. But you can be born again, a new creation in the Son, so He is able to change you and make you into someone the Family wants to live with forever. That possibility isn't open to us. So there's no way for the Family to forgive the servants who have rebelled."

Christian was uneasy. He said, "I feel bad for anyone who will be in such a terrible prison. It almost seems unfair that the servants have no way to change their minds."

"I know it's painful," Ezriel replied. "The whole situation was a dilemma for the Family. They knew you valley people could change your minds and They wanted to forgive those that do, but They had already set up the penalty for rebellion. You're concerned about fairness? Well, it would be unfair to arbitrarily offer forgiveness to valley people who rebelled and not to us servants. The Family are always fair. Being unfair is the kind of thing Lucifer would do."

"I think I understand," said Christian. "If the Family was not fair, They might have to use force to keep everyone's loyalty. As it is, the Family is loved and are obeyed because They are righteous and fair."

"Yes," said Ezriel. "And keeping our loyalty through love is for our benefit. It's for us that they would make any sacrifice in order to only do what is best for each one of us. They are truly worthy to rule with all power and authority.

"To solve Their dilemma in a way that was consistent with the love and fairness that is in the Family's character, the Son was punished in your place. It was horrendous." Ezriel bowed his head and was silent for a moment. "It was a horrible thing. He was tortured beyond belief. We servants finally began to shout to the Father, 'It's enough!' And the Son...He died."

Christian hardly knew what to say. *He died for me!* was all he could think. Ezriel continued, "But the Father raised Him from the dead! Because of the price the Son paid on your behalf, you've been ransomed from that fiery prison."

Just then, a bell rang a few rooms away, and Ezriel stood up. "Looks like I'm needed. I have to go," he said kindly. Christian was hardly able to whisper, "Thank you" as Ezriel hurried away.

Feeling very grieved yet very thankful for what the Son had done for him, Christian went back outside and lay on the soft green grass. The sun felt so good. Thinking about what the servant said and looking up at the clear blue sky, Christian closed his eyes and fell asleep.

Finally, from a distance, Christian began to hear the sound of rain on a roof, like he heard when he was in his little cabin. It seemed to get louder and louder. Opening his eyes, he saw rough shingles above him and realized he was back home. *What a dream,* he thought to himself. *It seemed so real.* Then he remembered how discouraged he had been the night before and how he'd pleaded with God. *Could the dream be God's answer to me? Maybe God is really there and He does love me.* Christian bowed his head. "Please, God," he whispered. "If You're there, please show Yourself to me in a way that I will understand. I need to know You and I don't know how to find You."

Nothing happened, so Christian got up and was eating breakfast when he heard the church bell ringing in the distance. He always felt like he didn't belong with church people because he was so ragged and they were so well dressed. But today was different. Something inside him was resolved to go to church no matter what people might think. Hurriedly, he put on his rabbit skin coat and ran through the rain thinking to himself, *I'll go to church, and someone there can tell me how to find God.*

Arriving out of breath, he was greeted by a smiling Mr. Friendly who said, "Welcome, son. You're just in time for Sunday school. Could you tell me how old you're getting to be?" Christian had been keeping track. "I'm eleven, sir."

Christian was directed to a class with kids he remembered from when he went to school. Mr. Knowsalittle, the teacher, was a short plump man with grey hair and glasses that occasionally slipped down his nose so he had to push them back up. He owned something he called a variety store and sold handkerchiefs, buttons, ribbons, thread, toys, and things like that. He was saying, "Today we're going to talk about Omniscience. That's a big word, and it means God knows everything."

While Mr. Knowsalittle explained that everything means everything, Christian was thinking about his dream. He raised his hand and asked, "Does that mean God knows every thought He will ever think?"

"Yes," said Mr. Knowsalittle.

Christian found this hard to believe, so he asked, "Does that mean God can't think a new thought ever again?"

"Yes," said Mr. Knowsalittle, though he wasn't quite sure. He knew he was only repeating what he had been taught and had a feeling he was about to get into something that was over his head.

"Why would God change from someone who thought of everything into someone who will never think again?"

"If God didn't know everything, it would mean there would be free will apart from Him," said Mr. Knowsalittle.

Pursuing the lack of logic that bothered him, Christian asked, "So who planned everything that God knows?"

"God, of course," said Mr. Knowsalittle. "There wasn't anyone else. And circumstances cannot force God to do anything He has not planned. So everything that takes place is what God planned. Everything we see around us, even the movement of every leaf, it had to be God who planned it!"

"When was that plan planned?" Christian asked, fighting against what this all meant to him personally.

"I don't know," said Mr. Knowsalittle, who now knew for sure that he was in over his head.

Almost crying, Christian blurted out, "I don't believe any of this.

God didn't plan for my parents to die. He doesn't do things like that. I know He didn't. He loves me. I know it!"

Everyone in the class sat there, staring at Christian. Finally, Mr. Knowsalittle, looking confused and embarrassed, said, "I don't know how to answer you. Just wait a minute." He hurried out, and moments later, he was back with Mr. Knowsalot from the adult class. Christian noticed Mr. Knowsalot's heavily calloused hands and guessed that he was a farmer. "Let's sit outside," suggested Mr. Knowsalot, and he led Christian to some chairs in the church foyer where they could sit and talk. "You seem to have some questions," he said gently. Quickly trying to organize what bothered him into a question about God having already planned everything, Christian asked, "Did God have a beginning when He planned everything?"

Mr. Knowsalot said, "No, He always existed. He's three Persons, yet He is One." Mr. Knowsalot knew he wasn't really answering the question being asked. He thought, *This boy has a tough question. Yes, having a plan requires that there was a beginning. I haven't a clue how that could be.* It had always bothered him that there were so many things in his theology for which he had no answer. He hated it when he was cornered and had to say, "It's a mystery," or "It's a paradox," so he just avoided saying it.

Meanwhile, Christian was trying to digest what he was hearing. It just didn't make sense. Looking earnestly at Mr. Knowsalot, Christian asked, "So if God is three Persons, doesn't that mean They each have Their own thoughts and Their own will? If each of the three Persons knows the same everything, how are They three and not one person?"

"Certainly, the three Persons of the Trinity don't become just one person," Mr. Knowsalot assured him. "The love God has within Himself is not self-love, but love between Persons."

Christian was still bothered by the idea that God planned for his parents to die. He remembered how his mother used to put notes in his father's lunch box. And his father put notes in the sugar bowl. They called them love notes, and the notes made them very happy. Christian imagined the Father, Son, and Holy Spirit doing things for one another like that. So he asked, "Don't They want to do things that are special for one another?"

Mr. Knowsalot responded, "They can only do what They already know They will do."

"But God is God," Christian said. "He can do anything He wants with Himself and everything around Him. Why wouldn't He do everything He could to make the love He had within Himself as wonderful as possible?"

"I'll have to think about that," said Mr. Knowsalot, thinking, *Yes, What would it be like if God arranged everything that could be arranged to encourage the love that He is? I really do have to think about this.*

Christian felt a great sadness and thought, *I know God does everything He can to be as loving as possible.* So he said, "God can do anything. The three Persons of the Trinity can create anything necessary to have the best possible love for one another."

"I suppose God can," said Mr. Knowsalot. "The Father is Almighty. The Son is Almighty. The Spirit is Almighty. Yet there is only one Almighty. God is Almighty. There's nothing He cannot do." Then he thought, *I really like this boy. He's a thinker.*

Christian thought about his dream. It gave him a framework that helped him ask questions about what he was hearing. *Maybe God did show Himself to me in my dream. But what I'm hearing is so different. They're telling me His love isn't much, and He planned awful things, and even the love God has within Himself is like last year's newspaper.* Then he said, "I want to understand, but I just don't understand."

Mr. Knowsalot looked at Christian and was thinking, *This boy's hard life has made him mature quickly, and he asks good questions. In time he'll find answers, and the church needs men with seeking minds like what he will grow up to be.* Silently, he prayed, "Lord, how can I help him?" Then he asked, "Christian, do you have a Bible at home?"

"No, sir."

Impulsively, Mr. Knowsalot handed Christian his own personal Bible. "Here, take this Bible home and read it for yourself. Our time is up and church is about to start." People were already walking past them into the church, so Christian and Mr. Knowsalot filed in behind them.

Sitting as far back as he could, Christian read the Bible verses that were painted on the wall spaces between the windows:

> "Christ died for our sins according to the Scriptures, and that He was buried, and that He rose again the third day according to the Scriptures." (1 Corinthians 15:3–4)

*Christ died for my sins,* Christian thought, *and I know He loves me!*

"As many as received Him, to them He gave the right to become children of God, to those who believe in His name." (John 1:12)

*That's what I want. I want to receive Jesus,* thought Christian. Then he read the next verse:

"Believe on the Lord Jesus Christ, and you will be saved." (Acts 16:31)

*What is this? What does it mean to believe?* wondered Christian. Just then, everybody started singing:

Holy, holy, holy! Lord God Almighty!

Early in the morning our song shall rise to Thee;

Holy, holy, holy, merciful and mighty!

God in three Persons, blessed Trinity!

As the last verse was sung, Christian began to think about the Bible verse, "Believe on the Lord Jesus Christ, and you will be saved." *Maybe this is how to find God! But I don't know what it means to believe, and how do I do it?* he asked himself. *I know what I'll do! To be sure I've done it, I'll go as far as I can in the direction of believing.*

Quietly, Christian began to pray, "Lord Jesus, I believe You're really there to hear me. I believe you died for my sins. I'm sorry for the wrong things I've done. I give my life to you. Please take me. Please come into my heart. I want to know You. You are my Lord and I will always obey You. Amen." Then he thought, *I did all the believing I know how to do. I did what the Bible told me to do, so I must be saved.* At this thought, a warm joy that made him feel thoroughly clean filled his heart, like he just took a swim in the river; only the feeling of being clean was on the inside. Slowly, he became aware of his surroundings again. The congregation was singing another hymn. Finding it in the hymnal, Christian joined in with a joy and gusto arising from new life in his heart. Christian was born again, a new creation in Christ, and he knew it.

Pastor Caring, in a dark suit, mounted the pulpit. He had a round friendly face. In spite of his bass voice, which gave him an air of authority, he had a disarming way about him which projected his genuine love for the people he was talking to. The sermon that morning was on faith. Christian listened and he thought, *Faith takes things God would do for us or to us and changes them into things we do together. This makes sense. God created us so he could love us. To do things with us, together, is what He created us for.* For a few minutes, Christian closed his eyes and let his imagination soar. *Faith, prayer, and obedience are things I can do with Jesus. I can live a life that brings joy to God. And He shares His joy with me. Right here, where I am, I'm as happy as anyone in heaven. I have the joy of the Lord.*

After the service, the people were friendly. They couldn't help but notice the change in Christian. The look of sadness that had only increased since his parents died two years before was replaced with a joyful smile that occupied his whole face. And inside, he was rejoicing even more. He could hardly contain himself. The rain had stopped and all the way home, he ran and leaped and praised God.

Christian wanted to start reading the Bible, but there were things he had to do first. Putting the Bible in a safe place, he went and checked on his snares, which yielded a rabbit for dinner. Then he went down to the river and checked on his fish trap. There were two good-sized fish. Walking along the fence he had built for his garden, he made sure nothing had gotten in. The rocks he'd put next to the fence discouraged animals from digging to get in, but he liked to make sure.

The garden reminded him of when he was desperately hungry and had gone sneaking into someone else's garden to steal vegetables. Christian felt bad about the wrong things he had done. *But now I'm forgiven,* he thought. *God has already changed me. I used to just think about how harshly life had treated me. Now I feel fortunate.*

Counting his blessings, Christian also thought about how much bigger and stronger he had grown. People often hired him to do anything they didn't want to do. *I mucked out a lot of horse stables, but it doesn't matter anymore,* he thought. *I have Jesus with me everywhere I go, and we'll do everything together.* Then he laughed as he thought, *And Jesus doesn't mind mucking out stables. He was born in a stable.*

Then he wondered, *What would happen if I lost my trust that God loves me? I would have nothing to put my faith in. I wouldn't have the faith that brings joy to both God and myself.* This thought filled him with resolve. *I will never doubt the love of God. I don't care what anyone says to me. God never fails to do the most loving thing possible, not ever!* Then he thought a frightening thought, *But what will I do if no one in the church agrees with me?* Then he had a more frightening thought, *What if the Bible says that what Mr. Knowsalittle said is true? Then I would have to believe horrible things about God.*

---

[1]Hebrews 2:11-12
[2]Psalms 33:4-5, 100:4-5; 1 Corinthians 1:9, 10:13; 2 Timothy 2:13; Lamentations 3:22-23

John 7:16-17; Matthew 7:21-23; Isaiah 44:22
Psalms 81:11-12, 119:67; Hebrews 12:5-11
Galatians 5:6
2 Peter 3:9; Romans 2:4
2 Peter 2:4-9
Matthew 10:17, 17:5; Acts 20:35
Matthew 18:4, 20:26-28
John 13:14-15, 14:7-11; Matthew 11:28-31; Psalms 8:3-4
Isaiah 14:12-15
Revelation 12:7-9
Psalms 138:6; Luke 1:51-53
Matthew 25:41
Ephesians 3:10-11; 1 Peter 1:12
Titus 1:2
Hebrews 2:16
Hebrews 3:1; 1 Peter 2:9-10, 2:24-25; Titus 2:14; Philippians 1:6
Romans 2:6, 11; Colossians 3:25
Deuteronomy 10:17-18
Mark 15:44
Revelation 5:11-12, 1 Timothy 2:5-6
Isaiah 43:10, 44:6
1 Chronicles 29:17, Psalms 147:11

# 3 CHRISTIAN DEVOURS THE BIBLE

After dinner, Christian carefully washed and dried his hands before opening the Bible. He noticed the cross references and quickly learned how to use them. There were notes at the bottom of the pages that explained the meanings of some Greek and Hebrew words. In the back was a concordance. *This is a wonderful Bible,* he thought and began reading the New Testament with the excitement of someone reading it for the first time.

As he read Matthew, his fear that God planned horrible things melted away. The loving character of God that shone through Jesus gave him the assurance that God would never do anything not motivated by love. That week, he read the whole New Testament. He was thankful that his mother had him practice reading until he could read rapidly and with comprehension. Thinking about her insistence on that made him ashamed as he remembered how he'd sometimes resisted. *But she kept after me until I learned to enjoy reading. Then she had to start telling me, "Put the book down and do your chores!"*

Often, Christian stopped at Old Testament quotes and followed the cross references to read them in their Old Testament context. He noticed that Adam and Eve were mentioned several times in the New Testament. So out of curiosity, he also read the first ten chapters of Genesis. The joy he felt in studying the Bible knew no bounds, and he read it at every opportunity.

Christian remembered what the servant in his dream said about Lucifer and decided to find a verse about him from the concordance and follow cross references from there. This led him to read in Ezekiel that Lucifer was created perfect on a certain day.

Using the cross references, Christian found that Lucifer, who was also called Satan, was puffed with pride and wanted to be leader of the angels. Christian remembered that God doesn't like pride. *Satan's pride is the opposite of God's humility,* he thought. *It may have taken some time for Satan to change from the perfection in which he was created till he became someone who was prideful. And it would have taken even more time to get other angels to join him.*

*Pride destroys people's ability to be close, to love and appreciate one another. It must have been painful for God to watch as more and more angels joined the rebellion. I guess God had no alternative but to create the Lake of Fire. And if the Lake of Fire was created for the devil and his angels,* he reasoned, *it seems that God never planned to put people there. Our universe may not have even been created yet. It would take a long time for all those things to happen. Surely the angels were created long before us. I wonder what it's like in heaven. Do they have angel houses? Did God have to change heaven before He created angels? It would have to be different than what was perfect for Him when He was alone.* Christian tried to imagine what an angel house looked like, but he couldn't think of anything. Then he remembered what it said in Hebrews 12:22, about angels in the heavenly Jerusalem. He laughed to himself. "Living in the New Jerusalem is like living in angel houses, something that's perfect for angels. Then he thought about Abel, the first person to die. *There he was all by himself in the heavenly Jerusalem with all those angels. And God was there with him. What a great adventure. He was so lucky! And there's a river too. I wonder if he went swimming. And there must have been fish in the river.*

It was dark now. Christian sat in front of the fire and his thoughts turned to the things Mr. Knowsalittle said about God never thinking a new thought. *That would mean God could never have a chain of events,* he considered. *How awful! He couldn't have faith or enjoy planning new things to do or make or create. He couldn't just drop everything and go fishing with friends who come to visit. Why would He want to do that to Himself?*

It was Saturday night. Christian went to bed wondering about God and heaven. *God created everything in six days and rested on the seventh. Did He do all of creation in that way just to show us how to live? It makes more sense that He was simply doing what He was already used to doing.* He imagined Abel and all the angels going to a special meeting every seven days. *I wonder if God does do that?* he thought. *What would be a day in heaven?* He thought about Mr. Knowsalittle's class. *I have to agree with Mr. Knowsalittle about one thing. Time began with our creation, and before that, there was no time. But this doesn't mean there was no such thing as a chain of events. Besides, there's a tree in heaven that yields fruit every month, forever. Changing fruit and different months mean there will be a chain of events forever.*

Christian punched up his pillow and lay staring at the dark underside of the roof overhead. *God lives in heaven,* he thought. *I live in my cabin. I wonder what His home looks like. Before He created the angels, God must have made heaven exactly what He wanted. Maybe what we call time that He created for us is like a shadow of what happens there in His home, like the temple was a shadow of what's in heaven?*

*There's one thing I'm certain of, God is love. Whether or not there always were new thoughts in heaven would depend on what worked best to support the things God cares about, like love within Himself. At least, that's the kind of power I think God has. God can change heaven to be anything He wants. Come to think of it, the Bible says He's going to change a lot of things to make a home for angels, for us, and for Himself forever.*

Christian knew that all this was mostly conjecture. *But,* he thought, *why would God want things way different now, just because He created us? If there is such a thing as the best possible conditions for showing love, He would want us to fit into that and Himself as well!* What Mr. Knowsalittle said really bothered him. *What can I do?* he thought. *Perhaps those places in the Bible that talk about God having new events might help settle the question.*

Ignoring the cold, Christian got out of bed, lit the lantern, and turned to a verse he remembered, John 10:17. There he read again Jesus's words, "Therefore My Father loves Me, because I lay down My life that I may take it again." Christian began to think, *This was an event of love! It really touched the Father's heart. And it had an event chain in it! The first event was before Jesus came to earth. The second was when Jesus came. The third event was Jesus died for our sins. According to this verse, Jesus's willingness to lay down His life added something new to the Father's love. So for this to happen, God chose to live in some kind of sequence of events. In fact, the event took place both in heaven and in our time. It would be something new that the Father could think about. Why would anybody say differently? I don't understand. What were Mr. Knowsalittle and Mr. Knowsalot talking about?* Puzzled, Christian turned off the lantern and went back to bed. Before he dozed off, he thought, *I need to understand what they're telling me.*

Sunday morning, Christian rose early and made sure he was clean for church. Walking briskly, he bounded up the church steps, greeted Mr. Friendly, and slipped into class. Mr. Knowsalittle began by summarizing last week's discussion. "Last week we talked about how God, by living in eternity, knows everything, not just for the present, but for all eternity, all at once." Christian couldn't help but ask, "Is everything God knows in His mind right now, or is some of it in His memory?"

Some of the other kids snickered while Mr. Knowsalittle, with a worried look, said, "God knows everything, just like we know some things."

So Christian said, "When I want to bring something into my mind, I point my mind at it, and there it is, ready to think about. My senses are also part of what I know. If I want to know what's behind me, I can turn around and there it is in my mind. And since my Bible is in my hand, the same is true for every verse in it. To me, what I know is everything I can quickly bring into my mind. So if God is like me, He can choose what He wants to think about."

Mr. Knowsalittle stared blankly with his mouth open. Finally, he said, "Why wouldn't God want to know everything all at once?"

Christian responded, "Because by choosing not to know everything all at once He could have faith, and faith is something He seems to enjoy. I think having faith, at least among the three Persons of the Trinity, is part of the love They have for one another. Being able to have faith means not having all knowledge of the future."

Puzzled, Mr. Knowsalittle asked, "Why can't God know everything and still have faith?"

Christian answered, "Faith is trusting someone, not knowing for sure what they're going to do. If the outcome is certain, there's no faith involved."

Hesitantly, Mr. Knowsalittle said, "For God to choose not to know everything in the future would give us a free will. He doesn't do that." He tried to think of a Scripture that says we don't have a free will, but couldn't remember one.

Christian knew he had said enough and ought to stop, but he couldn't help himself. "Before the Flood, people chose to be really bad. God said He was sorry that He had made man on the earth. He wouldn't be sorry that He created people unless things didn't turn out as intended."

Mr. Knowsalittle was quiet for a moment, and a worried look crossed his face. He knew he had no answer. Wishing he understood more about the things he had been taught, he said, "Thank you, Christian, for pointing that out to us. Today we're going to talk about Omnipresence. God is everywhere. He knows what happens everywhere and He is everywhere. So what does Omnipresence mean to us when we pray?"

Convicted in his conscience for upsetting Mr. Knowsalittle, Christian thought, *The Holy Spirit is telling me to shut up and love Mr. Knowsalittle. I better do it.* Although he wanted to say a lot of things, he quietly listened until Sunday school was over. Then they all filed into church.

The sermon was about mercy, and Pastor Caring said that because

God is merciful, we need to be merciful. "God really wants to be part of our lives," he said, "and we should live in such a way that He can." Christian started feeling bad about how he had behaved in the Sunday school. He had not been very merciful to Mr. Knowsalittle. He was glad that God had reminded him to be quiet instead of asking more questions. Then Christian thought, *I need to apologize to him.* The sacrifice Mr. Knowsalittle made to faithfully teach the class every week flooded into his mind. He prayed, "Lord, help me be as faithful. Thank you for helping me to appreciate this man who loves You."

After church, Christian found Mr. Knowsalittle and apologized. Graciously, Mr. Knowsalittle also apologized to Christian, "I'm sorry. I just don't know enough to answer your questions. I wish I did, but I'm really a simple person trying to serve the Lord as best that I can." Christian thanked him for his patience and looked for Mr. Knowsalot. He wanted to thank him again for the Bible and make sure it was all right to keep it. Mr. Knowsalot had just gotten some coffee when he saw Christian coming his way with a different happy look about him. *Something's happened between this boy and Jesus,* he thought. When Christian told him how much he'd read and how he enjoyed the cross references, Mr. Knowsalot's face just lit up. He said how happy that made him and how glad he was that he had given his Bible to Christian. In that moment, it was like they made a special connection, and Christian knew they were going to be good friends.

Then Mr. and Mrs. Friendly came up and invited Christian home for Sunday dinner. The thought of a home-cooked meal was overwhelming. Now it was Christian's turn to have his face light up.

A short walk took them to the Friendly's house. On the way, their son Steady and Christian got to know one another. Steady was really interested in how Christian set snares and made a trap that would catch fish. Christian invited him to come over sometime and see for himself. Coming near the house, Christian could smell the roast that was in the oven. Mrs. Friendly had expertly banked the fire in the stove so the roast would cook slowly while they were at church. Sunday dinner was roast beef, mashed potatoes, gravy, bread and butter, peas, and all kinds of pickles followed by a large slice of apple pie. As Christian ate, he was beaming. In the warm congenial atmosphere of the Friendly house, he felt accepted and loved.

Mr. Friendly wanted to be sure Christian knew Jesus as his Savior, so after dinner, he pushed back his chair and looked intently, but kindly at him and asked, "You really like asking questions, so here's one I'd like to ask you. If you died, do you know for sure where that journey would take you?"

Christian said, "Two weeks ago I didn't know, but last week. I gave my life to Jesus, and now I'm sure I will be in heaven with Him."

"So what has it been like this last week?" asked Mr. Friendly.

"I read the whole New Testament. And I've learned that saved doesn't just mean going to heaven. God is teaching me how to love and care about other people. I can see from the way the people at the church have treated me that God has been teaching them too. If somebody really is saved, it will show up in how they act."

Mr. Friendly then asked how Christian was getting along, living alone in his cabin. "I'm fine now," he said. "But when my parents died, I was scared a lot. In the beginning, it was hard. Now I have a big garden and enough to eat. I have plenty of smoked fish and meat in a shed I built. I even built a clay oven to bake sourdough bread. The days when I went hungry are over.

"As for being alone, I've made it a point to go to town and meet people. Now everybody seems to know me. I get enough jobs to bring in some cash. When boys come down to the river to fish, I sometimes join them. Thank you for asking. You needn't worry about me. Now that I have Jesus, I'll never be alone again."

Mr. Friendly said, "If anything does come up and you need help, I want you to know that I want to help." While thanking Mr. Friendly, Christian was thinking, *I'm looking at what the love of God does to Christians.* Silently, he prayed, "Lord, make me a loving person, just like this man."

On his way home, he made a decision. Having gotten over the shock of learning that the people at the church believed things that didn't seem to make sense, Christian decided that he was going to first think about the most loving thing he could say before he opened his mouth to say anything. He also decided to let the Holy Spirit and God's Word be his teacher. He decided to study the Bible for himself and believe it. *This puts a huge responsibility on me,* he thought. *I have to thoroughly study everything I think is important to believe. I have to be sure I believe what the Bible really says. What people tell me it says may not be what it really says. If I study hard, someday I'll know for myself what the Bible is saying!*

When evening came, Christian lit a small campfire and relaxed in one of his chairs. After it was dark, there wasn't much Christian could do, so he had learned to enjoy sitting by his fire and listening to the evening sounds in the woods around him. Occasionally, he would hear a coyote howl or an owl asking, "Whoo?" This became his time to think about what he had been reading in the Bible. And on Sunday, he also thought about and prayed about all the things he had heard and the people he had met at church. Today, he prayed for Mr. and Mrs. Friendly and Steady. As he prayed for them, he could almost taste and smell again that wonderful home-cooked meal. Then he thought about the things in the Bible they'd talked about.

Christian looked into the darkness of the woods around him. The trees looked like great dark shadows against the sky, but stars still twinkled through their branches. As he glanced down toward the ground, he saw a number of little beads of light. Eyes! The firelight was reflecting on little eyes watching him out of the darkness. Christian was reminded that he had mice for neighbors. *It would be a disaster if one of them chewed on my Bible*, he thought. *And I also have to protect the Bible from getting wet. I'll have to figure out what to do.*

---

[1] Job 34:12; 1 John 4:8-10
[2] Ezekiel 28:12-17
[3] Isaiah 14:12-15
[4] James 4:6; Luke 1:51-52
[5] Matthew 11:29, 20:28; John 14:7-11; Psalms 8:4
[6] Ezekiel 28:17
[7] Matthew 25:41
[8] Hebrews 1:7; Job 38:4-7
[9] Revelation 2:7, 22:1-2
[10] Exodus 20:11, 31:17
[11] Revelation 22:2
[12] Hebrews 8:5
[13] 1 John 4:16
[14] Revelation 21:1-3
[15] Galatians 5:6
[16] Genesis 6:5-7
[17] 1 Thessalonians 4:9

# 4 SPRING

The next morning, Christian walked into town and bought a half yard of green oil cloth from Mr. Knowsalittle. Starting on his way home, Christian walked past the general store and spotted a metal breadbox in the window. *Perfect,* he thought to himself, *I can keep my Bible in there and it will be safe from hungry mice.* So he went into the store and bought the breadbox too. At home, he had some cotton string and a block of beeswax. Running the string through the beeswax made it twice as strong and waterproof. In a glass bottle, he kept a big needle soaking in oil to keep the needle from rusting. After cleaning the oil off, he sewed the oilcloth with the string and made a waterproof pouch for his Bible. As he worked, he thought about what he had to do now that spring had arrived. Some of the ladies at church who saved their own seeds had offered to share with him, so there would be little need for him to buy seeds this year. Christian was very grateful.

Boys from the church and other boys from town had started coming to see him, and Christian would go fishing with them using a hook and line, just for the fun of it. Somehow, he always got around to talking about what he was reading in the Bible. The boys said they liked how he talked because it was so different from what they heard at church. With only himself to rely on, Christian was in the habit of thinking about everything. Before he was saved, he used to mostly think about how to avoid going hungry. Now that his world had expanded, he found himself thinking more and more about God, the Bible, the church, and the people he met there. He enjoyed talking to the other boys about things in the Bible he had been studying.

However, as the spring weeks passed, there was something Christian was considering that started to bother him. He noticed the New Testament talked about Christ in us and we in Him and being members of Christ's body. *This sounds like a lot more than just friends,* he puzzled. *This sounds like being really, really close to God.* But then he said to himself, *The problem is we are so selfish. If God wants to have us as His close friends, we can't keep on like we are. God is holy. He would have to make us holy enough that we can truly be friends. But how can that be? I could never be anywhere near good enough.*

Then one morning, Christian was reading Ephesians 5 and the very first verse said, "Therefore be imitators of God as dear children." He thought about what this could possibly mean. Then he read the next verse. "And walk in love, as Christ also has loved us and given Himself for us." Trying to understand, he prayed. "Lord, this commandment sets a standard that's too high for me. I could never be as good as Jesus. What does this mean?"

*Calm down, Christian,* he thought to himself. *What exactly is the love of Christ? Look at how He lived. He lived like He considered us more important than Himself! He said of Himself that He came to serve us. Servants are not very important people. And Jesus even gave up His life for us. That really shows His attitude that we're more important.* Christian shook his head sadly. *So what this means to me is that I should consider everyone else more important than myself and act that way, no matter what the cost or sacrifice. This is too hard. It's impossible! But it is a commandment. What am I going to do?*

As Christian was thinking, he remembered Pastor Caring's visit to his family. Christian just knew it was something he should remember. *It was so long ago,* he thought. *Pastor Caring said something about God that I thought was important at the time. What was it he said to my parents? "God would find pleasure in changing your life, to make you the kind of person He wants to live with forever." But how? What should I do? The commandment in Ephesians isn't talking about the future. It's something I should do right now!*

Then somehow, Christian knew deep inside that Ephesians 5:1–2 was telling him to lay aside the feeling that made him think he was too selfish to consider others more important. *Trust God* came the thought, clear and kind. *It's like Pastor Caring said. It's a change God finds pleasure in making. Trust in His willingness to change you.* Christian hesitated, and then on an impulse, wondering what would happen, he did what he now knew the verse was asking him to do. Spreading his arms wide with his eyes toward heaven, Christian prayed, "Heavenly Father, I love you and I trust you. I promise that with your help, I will consider everyone else more important than I am. And I trust you to make me able to keep this impossible promise with You. Amen."

Christian was not at all sure what to expect, but in the days that followed, the decision he had made never left the back of his mind, especially when he was talking with other people. God was holding him to his promise. And best of all, almost every day God was showing him more and more about Himself. Christian was starting to understand God in a way that was wonderful. He no longer felt puzzled and wondering about being in a close relationship with God.

Christian concluded, *God sure is changing me, and He's doing it with me. I guess He's really good at making the impossible become possible.* Every day, Christian felt himself growing closer to God. His faith that God was with him, watching over him for good, became unshakable.

One day, when the boys from town had come down to the river to fish, a grumpy-looking boy named Resist, who never went to church, scowled at Christian and asked, "If God is so loving, why did He kill everyone in the Flood and order Israel's army to slaughter everyone in Canaan?"

Christian said, "So you think it's okay for children to be born in a place where everybody is evil and violent and the kids are taught from very young to be cruel and heartless to others."

Resist looked a bit uneasy and said, "Uh…no."

Christian continued, "So you think it's all right for future generations of children to be born into a place where they might be sacrificed to an idol?"

Resist just said, "Oh!"

Christian persisted, "So the answer is, God wanted some really bad people to be taken away because they influenced their whole world as well as their children toward being really bad. So wouldn't it be better if children were born into families of good people who taught them to love and respect others?"

Resist knew he had no answer, so he said, "Okay, I guess so."

Christian then asked, "So you admit that God did the most loving thing possible?"

Resist was feeling a little bit cornered, but he had to admit that Christian was right. "Yes, I see your point."

Noting Resist's evasive answer, Christian asked, "Why wouldn't you want to share your life with God, who never fails to love?"

"I have to think about it," said Resist.

Christian responded, "What specifically do you need to think about?"

Resist knew exactly what he was thinking. He said, "I might have some things I want to do that God wouldn't want me to do. I want to live the way I want to live first. After I'm old, then maybe I'll accept

Jesus." Christian didn't say anything more. He quietly prayed that God would put pressure on Resist and help him change his mind.

Christian prayed for Resist every day. Finally one Sunday, when it was almost summertime, Resist did show up at church. One by one, the other boys who had talked to Christian began coming to church, and one by one, they accepted Christ as their Savior.

Righteous, one of the boys who had become a believer in Christ, confided that he was often crushed by thoughts of his past. "I've done so many wrong things," he said. "And the devil keeps reminding me of them."

Christian said, "Christ died for your sins and God has forgiven you. Don't you believe that?"

"Of course I do!" said Righteous. "I just occasionally feel jumped on by a load of guilty feelings. The devil is really messing with me. What do you think I can do?"

Christian silently prayed for wisdom and finally said, "All I know is this: God wants a close friendship with us. I think God wants you to solve this problem together with Him. So what you have to do is figure out how to work together with Him in dealing with the problem. If you expect Him to do it all, nothing happens."

"That's for sure," said Righteous. "I asked God to help me a hundred times, and nothing has changed. But you better tell me how God and I can work on this together."

For a minute, both boys sat and looked at each other. Then Christian said, "You could honestly pray this prayer: 'Dear God, I promise I will believe I'm forgiven. I promise I will forgive others in the same way that You have forgiven me. And I trust You to make me able to keep these promises with You.'"

Righteous was very interested, but he asked, "How do you know this will work?"

Christian answered, "Because saying that prayer is like telling God a decision you have honestly made in your heart. If you say, 'Yes, I can pray that prayer,' I figure that you want to see forgiveness the way God sees it. Praying this way, you invite God into solving the problem together with you, because you're agreeing to think about forgiveness the way He does. Then it really is a together thing—you and God. And that's something

God really enjoys! It's like He wants you to take His Word seriously, so He takes your words seriously when you pray to Him. He will then gladly occupy the forgiveness section of your life and keep the devil out."

Righteous began to realize what Christian was saying and what it meant to him personally. But it sounded like a big step to take. He had never before promised God to forgive other people. *This might mean a big change in my life,* he thought. *But to forgive others the way God forgave me is a change I think I would want. Okay, I'll go for it.* And he prayed in the way Christian had suggested.

A week later, Christian met him by the river and asked how he was doing. Righteousness rejoiced, "I'm free! And I'm sure God loves me—really sure! When I listened to you before, I didn't quite get it. Now I understand. God really loves me! He really is pleased when I give Him a chance to be with me in one more part of my life. Learning to do things with God is an adventure. I get it. I'm happy that I learned this, and I'm happy to be free! I'm doing great!"

One day, Steady came over to Christian's cabin with a boy from town, whose name was Careful. Steady had told Careful, "I have a friend who really knows God. He can tell you how to meet Him. Do you want to come and see?" Careful was curious, so he came along. Christian didn't waste much time. He looked at Careful and said, "Jesus died on the cross for the wrong you have done, and He rose from the dead. Now He offers to come into your life to change the attitude of your heart to become the kind of person God wants to live with forever. Does that sound like a good offer to you?"

Smiling, Careful replied, "Absolutely."

Christian explained some more. "The change He will make is that you will consider other people more important than yourself.

This doesn't happen all at once, but a little at a time as God changes you more and more and you learn to live His way. Besides that, if someone does to you what they did to Jesus, instead of getting angry or wanting to hurt them, you'll think from your heart, 'What do they need? How can I help them?' Knowing that's the kind of change He would make in your heart, is that what you want?"

"I'd have to think about it."

Christian asked, "What is it you need to think about?"

"Bad things happen, like what happened to you. Your parents died. How could there be a God?"

Christian said, "Good question. Here's the explanation. The first man, Adam, did the one thing that he knew would wreck his friendship with God. He did it so he could live on his own. Every generation since has also wanted to live independently from God. So God stepped back and let us see what living independently from Him looks like. You know what it looks like. Bad things happen. That should encourage you to come to God and take the forgiveness He offers."

"That makes sense."

"So is there any reason not to receive Christ right now?"

"Yes, I still want to think about it some more."

"What else is there to think about?"

"How could a loving God put people in a terrible place like hell?"

"Without God's influence, men and fallen angels would fill with violence any place God put them. That in itself would be hell. In His love, God provided a place where the environment is sufficiently unpleasant to be a distraction from the violence they would otherwise be doing to one another."

"Good point. I never thought of that."

"Besides, God has no other place to put them. He can't put them in heaven where they would be forced to live by God's ways. That would be slavery. There's no reason to doubt that hell is the most loving place God could put them. The creation of hell is not a reason to abandon the idea that God is love."

"That also makes sense."

"So you don't have to think about it anymore."

"Yes, but I still want to think some more."

"What else is there to think about?"

"I need to think about whatever I may need to think about."

"That's okay. You can come over any time. Hey, would you like to go fishing with us?"

Christian did his best to make friends with Careful. The next day, Careful came back and his face was shining. Christian took one look at him and thought, *Looks like Careful finished thinking!* And sure enough, it turned out that Careful had prayed the night before to receive the Lord. Christian asked, "What changed your mind?"

"You and Steady," Careful answered. "Besides everything you said, I saw how happy you were. I wanted to be part of that. Besides, I knew you were right." When Sunday came, Steady and

Christian went over to Careful's house, and together, they walked to the Sunday school class.

In the days that followed, Christian found he had a new friend as Careful often came to his cabin, eager to understand everything Christian had to say about the love of God. One day, Christian asked what Careful liked best about school. "Arithmetic!" Careful answered. This surprised Christian, and he said, "I know how to add and subtract, but I don't remember much else." Careful responded, "Well, there's multiplying and dividing. Multiplying is harder, but you have to learn to multiply first, before you learn to divide. You want me to make you a list of the math facts? I'll bring you a list if you'd like to learn." Wondering if he could still remember any of them, Christian said, "Oh, yes, I do. Before, I was so busy trying to survive, I simply forgot about school. Now I think I have time to learn things."

Besides church, Christian went to a Wednesday evening Bible study and prayer meeting at Mr. Friendly's house. Careful began to attend as well. Most churches didn't have meetings like this, but Pastor Caring really believed in it. He pushed it until almost everyone in the church who could attended a Wednesday night meeting. The wonderful thing was that once people discovered how helpful it was getting to know and pray with a small group of believers, Pastor Caring didn't have to keep reminding everyone. They went because they really wanted to.

Almost every Sunday after church, someone would invite Christian home for Sunday dinner. The subject of conversation was always the sermon or something in the Bible. He was a popular guest because he was fun to talk to, clearheaded, knew his Bible, and seemed to overflow with the joy of the Lord.

There was one theme Christian seemed to talk about almost all the time: the love of God. He was careful not to push it if people resisted. The discussions helped him to learn how to explain things he felt passionate about. He also learned to listen carefully so he could respond in a way that was helpful to the other person.

As people brought up the places in Scripture which they thought were proof that God limits His love, Christian went home and researched the verses. He was surprised to find that every verse he was given, when researched, turned out to have a very different meaning that didn't say anything that would limit God's love. Usually, all he had to do was read the context and it would be obvious.

One Sunday, Mr. Confident invited Christian over for Sunday dinner. After dinner, Mr. Confident said, "Because of Adam's sin, we're all equally spiritually dead. Dead means dead. We can't even want to reach out to God unless God gives us the desire to seek Him. And since a lot of people aren't interested in God, it's obvious that God puts the desire to know Him in just a few people whom He chooses." Then, knowing Christian believed everyone is given a desire to seek God and has the ability to choose, he asked, "So what do you do with Ephesians 2:5 where it says we were dead in sins?"

Mrs. Confident had already thought their discussions were getting a little too animated. Looking a bit horrified, she said, "Please, dear, Christian is our guest." Mr. Confident and Christian had to assure her that there was no problem and that they really did enjoy lively theological debates. Christian was relieved when, still a little dubious, Mrs. Confident let them carry on. He'd been really looking forward to answering Mr. Confident's question.

Christian leaned forward and looked earnestly at Mr. Confident. Romans 7 and other places in Scripture came to his mind and he said, "How Ephesians 2:5 is interpreted depends on how you define 'dead.' Why not let Scripture define what dead means?"

"It seems to me that Scripture defines dead as dead," said Mr. Confident.

Christian turned in his Bible to 1 Timothy 5:6. "Look at this," he replied. "It says a young Christian widow living in pleasure is dead while she is still alive. Notice she is a Christian! I hardly think a Christian is spiritually dead in the sense of being unable to repent or reach out to God. But here it says, a true Christian can turn their back on God and seek their own pleasure, and at that point, the Bible calls them dead." Mr. Confident frowned. Christian went on, "The parable of the prodigal son is another example in Scripture where the term 'dead' is used to describe a very much loved son turning his back on the Father in order to seek his own pleasure. In the parable, when the son contritely returned, the father spoke tenderly to his older son, 'It was right that we should make merry and be glad, for your brother was dead and is alive again, and was lost and is found.' Even though he was 'dead,' the younger son was able to repent and return to his father.

In the same manner, the Christian widow living in pleasure, though dead, could also repent. And in the same manner, everyone who is lost can repent. According to what I see in these verses, dead means any rebellious departure from God's perfect righteousness. Death is the natural result of excluding God from how we live."

Mr. Confident quickly pounced on what he thought was a weak point in what Christian had said. "Oh, but in the parable, Jesus is talking about a son. Not everyone is a son. So not everyone can repent."

"You're forgetting something," Christian kindly replied. "This parable is third in a series of three similar parables. The parables of the lost sheep and the lost coin are about a sinner, any sinner, who repents. If the third parable of the lost son did not mean the same thing, then the first two parables would be pointless.

Christian continued, "But I agree that you're partly right! We don't have any way to choose to seek God without His direct influence."

"Ho-ho," Mr. Confident said cheerfully, "so you see the light!"

"I only said partly," said Christian. "I just see that dead or not dead is not relevant to our discussion. For instance, how did you receive sufficient influence from God to seek Him?"

Mr. Confident said, "I received His influence because He gave me the faith to believe. He did this because I was chosen to be saved before I was born."

Christian responded, "But the Bible tells us God influences everyone in the same way that He has influenced you. John 1:9 and Acts 17:26–27 say God's influence is not restricted, but is for all mankind. Everyone has the ability to choose, the same as you did. So I can agree that we do need God to reveal Himself sufficiently to make such a choice possible."

After looking up and reading these verses, Mr. Confident asked, "So what are you saying?"

"I'm saying God first reveals Himself liberally to everyone. To those who choose to respond to the Holy Spirit and seek God based on what they now know of Him, he reveals Himself even more. God looks at their desire to seek Him and grants saving faith based on what He sees."

"I see," said Mr. Confident. "You believe dead doesn't matter because God sufficiently influences everyone to seek Him! You actually believe that everyone could seek God! That's outrageous! Indeed, I do disagree."

Christian and Mr. Confident continued in a lively discussion for quite a while till it was time for Mr. Confident to go milk his cows. "This was fun," he told Christian. Then he confided, "And I appreciate your skill in handling God's Word. You've given me some things to think about."

As the weeks went by, more and more people began to consider what Christian was saying. They began to think there might be another way to understand God than what they'd been taught. This became a matter of concern to some of the elders, particularly Mr. Stubborn and Mr. Tradition. They thought someone needed to put this young upstart in his place.

---

[1] Matthew 20:28
[2] John 15:7; Colossians 1:27; 1 Peter 1:16, 2:9; 2 Peter 1:2-4
[3] Colossians 1:10-13, 2:9-10; Romans 6:22
[4] John 17:20-23; Romans 8:9, 15-16
[5] Matthew 5:22; 7:7-8; 12:37; 1 John 5:14-15
[6] Matthew 6:12-15; Ephesians 4:32; 1 John 5:14-16
[7] 1 Timothy 3:7; 2 Timothy 2:25-26
[8] Luke 15:24, 32
[9] Luke 15:1-10
[10] Matthew 7:21, 13:3-9, 12; John 7:16-17; Exodus 20:6; James 1:12

# 5 ELDERS

The first Sunday afternoon of every month, there was an elders meeting at Mr. Hospitality's house. He had an enormous dining room table where they could all sit around with room to spare. And Mrs. Hospitality would keep the coffee coming with platter after platter of fresh from the oven cookies. She alternated between sugar cookies and oatmeal cookies and was always amazed at how quickly they disappeared.

Mr. Knowsalittle mentioned how his Sunday school students were doubting what he had to teach. "That young man Christian is very respectful while he's in my class," said Mr. Knowsalittle. "But outside class, he's persuading the boys to believe God's love is unlimited, and He would like to see all humanity repent and believe in Jesus, without exception!" Pastor Caring had heard similar things on his visits. No one complained. They enjoyed Christian's enthusiasm and love for the Lord. Still, Pastor Caring was concerned. He said, "I think we need to talk with Christian. Perhaps we can help him get his theology straight." Mr. Knowsalot smiled. He knew from his conversations with Christian that it would probably be Pastor Caring who got his theology adjusted. He laughed inwardly at the thought.

Mr. Knowsalot remembered when he was first convinced that Christian was on to something. Christian had challenged him to choose between God being able to think something brand new and God knowing everything, including every thought He would ever think. Mr. Knowsalot knew others would dismiss the challenge by saying, "It's a mystery." But he had thought, *If I say I'm convinced of something about which I claim to know nothing, I would be talking nonsense.* So he'd allowed himself to think about the choice he was being challenged to make.

The result was profound, and the implication of what he previously believed hit him like a ton of bricks. Mr. Knowsalot was shaken to the core and finally chose to believe, *Of course God can continue to think and be creative.* This opened to him a further possibility: *God can respond to us, and our relationship with Him is a real relationship in which we respond to one another.* Mr. Knowsalot had believed this before, but it was tied down and caged within the confines of the idea that God planned and controlled everything. Now he felt a new awareness of the precious relationship He had with his Savior. His faith that he truly was in Christ had taken a giant leap forward.

Mr. Hospitality suggested that the elders meet at his house next Sunday afternoon. "I know it means another Sunday afternoon doing church business, but this is something we have to do. It'll give us the whole rest of the day to talk if need be."

Mr. Knowsalittle cocked his head to one side and reminded the other elders, "Christian has a thing about the meaning of 'know,' as in God knows everything. He's very sharp and he knows the Bible. We need to come prepared, particularly about the meaning of omniscience."

Pastor Caring responded, "I have some notes I'll bring. I just hope he won't be frightened with all of us sitting there."

"I don't think that will be a problem," suggested Mr. Knowsalot. "He's unusually precocious."

Christian was carving wooden spoons to be sold in Mr. Helpful's store when Pastor Caring rode up on his horse. As he approached, Pastor Caring noted Christian's Bible attached to a stand in a way that he could read it while working and commented, "It warms my heart to see how you love God's Word."

"Thank you, sir," Christian beamed. "There's no greater pleasure than to read the Bible. Having it here, I can read some and think about it while I'm working." Pastor Caring got right to the point. "The elders and I were thinking you may need some input from us. We'd like you to come over to Mr. Hospitality's house for dinner next Sunday. We have some things to talk about, and that will give us plenty of time."

"I'd like that," Christian said.

Pastor Caring replied, "Then we'll see you there right after church."

As Pastor Caring rode away, Christian was thinking, *I don't know what they want to talk to me about, but I have a suspicion. No worries! God will be with me. And if He's not, and I'm wrong about something, then I welcome being set straight. But for sure, God will be there and I have nothing to fear.* Christian bowed his head and prayed, "Father, I know you will be with me. Please help me be faithful to Your Word and communicate the love I know You are."

Sunday, after the church service, Christian headed for Mr. Hospitality's house. When he got there, he noticed that no one else had arrived, so he sat under a tree where he could see the house and read the Bible. Once the Hospitality family arrived, he wandered over and joined them.

Before dinner was ready, Pastor Caring and Mr. Evangelist also arrived. While the food was being prepared, they talked about a work day to clean up the church, and especially the stable.

The rest of the elders showed up as the dishes were being cleared after dinner. Pastor Caring got out his notebook and opened by praying for God's guidance. Making his voice sound as gracious as possible, he said, "I have some items to discuss, beginning with the concept of omniscience. So, Christian, what are your thoughts on omniscience?"

Christian began, "This raises some hard questions. Did God create Satan, knowing all the bad things he was going to do? Did God create us, knowing we would also rebel against Him? Does God create people whom He already knows will spend forever in hell? Would God purposefully create a world of wicked people so He could destroy all but eight and take the rest to hell where they would be tortured forever? This doesn't sound like 'God is love.' So it isn't unreasonable to ask if there are other possibilities.

"There are two things I keep in mind when thinking about really hard questions like these. The first is that God is love. The second is how big His love is. So as I answer your questions, everything I say will relate to these two things. The way I see it, without God's love, nothing in the Bible makes sense. But when you always remember God's love, everything makes sense.

"Okay, you want to know what I think about omniscience. Well, one time, when I was thinking about it, I took a piece of paper and drew a line down the middle. On the left side, I wrote reasons why God would want to limit what He knows—things like 'then He could think new thoughts,' which He could not do if He knew every thought He would ever think. I also wrote down 'Then God could have real unplanned events of love,' like what caused the Father to say He was well pleased with His Son. The third thing on the list was 'God really thinks faith is important.' He has faith both within Himself and toward us, like the faith He had in Job. To experience faith like that, God would have to limit what

He knows. Last of all, I put down that 'if God chose to know our moral choices ahead of time, before we even make them, the love and friendship He wants to have with us would end up losing a lot of what makes relationships special.'

"On the right side of the paper, I tried to list reasons why God would want to consciously know everything. But that side was blank. I couldn't think of any reason why God would want to know everything. Maybe you can help me with this."

"Surely, God would not want to be surprised by something bad the devil might come up with," Mr. Stubborn suggested.

Christian answered, "It's true nothing could be worse than the devil causing a rebellion in heaven and here on earth. But the real reason I didn't put that on my list is I see God as courageous. Perfect love casts out fear. God is love. And since God is both loving and courageous, He would always do the most loving thing possible without being limited by fear that something might surprise Him."

"But wouldn't God need to know everything in order to know what He doesn't need to know?" Mr. Stubborn persisted.

Christian shook his head. "No matter what happens, God is always faithful. We can put our trust in Him to do the most loving, righteous thing. No knowledge of the future would ever change that. So knowing the future would make no difference in how God acts." Christian paused and said softly, "Remember what happened to Mr. Faithful and his wife? They were engaged when she was diagnosed with cancer." All the elders nodded sadly. Christian continued, "Mr. Faithful knew there would be difficult times ahead, and she would soon die slowly and painfully. But in spite of what he knew about the future, he made his decision to go through with the marriage based on what he thought would be best for her. And it was hard. Within a year, she died in his arms, in horrible agony. He knew ahead of time that would happen. His knowledge of the future didn't stop him from doing what he felt was the right thing—loving and marrying his wife." For a moment, there was silence around the table before Christian continued, "Mr. Faithful is a righteous man. For someone like him who does what is right no matter what, even knowledge of the future will not cause them to change their mind and turn away from righteous behavior. If a mere man can live this way, surely God can too. So to answer your question, 'Wouldn't God need to know everything in order to know what He doesn't need to know?'

the answer is no. He doesn't need to know the future in order to be loving and righteous."

Pastor Caring said, "Well, does anyone else want to add to this? If not, we'll move on. So, Christian, do you have any more ideas on omniscience?"

"Yes, I do. When we read the Bible, it sure looks like God mostly focuses on our present time. If you look at what it says, what you see is God choosing not to know everything in the future. He asked Jeremiah the prophet to write down what He was going to do to Judah. God said:

It may be that the house of Judah will hear all the evil which I purpose to do unto them; that they may return every man from his evil way; that I may forgive their iniquity and their sin. (Jeremiah 36:3)

"If there was no chance of that happening, the words, 'It may be' certainly weren't true. If God said it wasn't for sure, we should believe Him."

"I still think God knows everything for all eternity," said Mr. Stubborn.

"Well," said Christian. "Think about this: everywhere in Scripture we see God doing His best to put our sins behind him. He said, 'I, even I, am He who blots out your transgressions for My own sake; And I will not remember your sins' (Isaiah 43:25).

"If God chooses to not remember sins and even blots out every record of them, doesn't that subtract from what God knows?" Nobody said anything so Christian continued, "Mr. Stubborn, do you agree that Scripture says God chooses not to look at our past sins since we trusted in Christ?" Mr. Stubborn nodded. "Then He could also choose not to look at every one of our future choices, and let us choose as we please. This is something He could do."

Mr. Tradition spoke up loudly, "But the Bible says God guides history and makes things happen. He would have to know the future in order to do that!"

Christian agreed, "Yes, obviously He did have to look into the future in order to set things up for Jesus when He was on the earth. And don't forget, God has other options for knowing what will happen. The Bible says one way is God can simply make His plans happen. Another option is that God can look at our present behavior and figure out really well what we will likely do, even generations into the future. And there may be other reasonable ways God can see the future which the Bible hasn't told us. But

God does tell us that He can choose what He looks at, whether it's our past sin or future actions."

"Hah!" said Mr. Tradition. "Then you agree God knows the future!"

"Wait a minute!" urged Christian. "Can or cannot is not the issue. The issue is whether or not God chose from the beginning to allow free will within Himself, in heaven, and on the earth. And you're forgetting something. The Scripture also talks about us being Christ's bride. To have love between Himself and us that is anything like the love He has within Himself, He wouldn't want to know all our future choices. At least, not if God wanted real conversations with us like He had with Moses. He would want His faithfulness to us in the present where we're living to be more than something He's faking. And what we see in the Bible is people responding to God and God responding to them. We shouldn't be making things up that change the obvious facts of Scripture."

Mr. Tradition said, "But God can see all our future choices and then respond to us as we make them."

Christian replied. "I don't think so. When we look at the Bible—the whole Bible—it sure doesn't sound that way. If God looked into the future, He might have started with Noah, Daniel, or Job instead of Adam!" Mr. Tradition frowned, and Mr. Knowsalot suppressed a smile. Christian continued, "Anyway, He could have done something to avoid the mess we're in. Before the Flood and later on after He made Saul king, God said He was sorry because of things He had done. Yes, He did have to destroy the world in a Flood. But He wasn't happy about it and promised first to Himself, then to Noah, that He wouldn't ever do it again."

"But the world we now see is what God wanted. He's using our fallen world to reach out and save people to be with him in heaven," Mr. Tradition sputtered.

Christian looked straight at Mr. Tradition and responded, "Scripture says, 'If we are faithless, He remains faithful; He cannot deny Himself' (2 Timothy 2:13). The 'self' that He cannot deny is who He is: He is love. He won't do anything contrary to who He is. And look at the Scripture that says, 'But You, O Lord, are a God full of compassion, and gracious, longsuffering and abundant in mercy and truth' (Psalms 86:15). He would never deny who He is by planning the sin we see around us."

Pastor Caring said, "I have to agree with Christian on this. Scripture is clear that God never does anything unrighteous. He doesn't plan unrighteousness. We sinned and brought its consequences upon ourselves. The decisions we make are our own, and it would be out of character for God to deliberately plan that we would sin."

Christian cheerfully agreed, "Exactly! Of the possibilities, the least likely is that God planned for a fallen world. So I believe that the other possibility is true: God would not want to know our future choices. I think there is much more evidence for that idea."

Mr. Tradition frowned, "What evidence? I don't see any!"

Christian answered patiently, "I guess it all comes down to whether you believe God really is love. God doesn't lie. He didn't pretend to be love while at the same time carrying out a plan for sin and pain and death to come into our world. John 3:16 is not talking about a scripted make believe act. When the Bible talks about the church being a bride whom Christ loves, the Bible is telling the truth about that as well. God wants a love relationship with us that is a real give and take relationship, not some script we are both acting out. God's real desire is that from the depths of our heart we love and adore Him, which Christians do. It's a real us who loves Him, not something imposed upon us. Like the lover He is, He wooed us with love, and we responded to His love. In order to have that relationship with Him forever, God extends to us the courtesies that allow it to happen. He would not destroy the relationship He desires by looking at our future choices. I look at that and am amazed, and say 'Wow! Loving like that takes courage! Yes, God's love isn't an act. With courage, He takes every chance He can get to love us. And His love isn't constrained by the cost."

"I still don't see it! Why couldn't God love and still know everything in the future?" Mr. Tradition persisted.

Christian was quiet for a moment and finally said, "Well, I guess I should go back to the basics: the Father, Son, and Holy Spirit have faith in one another." Christian looked earnestly at Mr. Tradition. "There are examples of this in the Bible, like Jesus's temptation in the wilderness, and His prayer at Gethsemane. Faith is part of the love within the Trinity, a relationship God wants us to be part of, too."

Mr. Tradition crossed his arms and leaned back in his chair, looking very dubious. But Christian continued, "So what does faith look like when it's part of love? It looks like this: You live in a way that you always expect the best from the other person." Christian smiled. "If God does this within Himself, He's not going to change when it comes to us. He has faith in us. When we fail, why does He give us another chance? It's because that's who God is. He chooses to live as though He expects the best from us all the time."

Mr. Tradition laughed cynically. "Well, considering our track record as sinners, He should know we will always fail to do what's right."

Christian quickly disagreed. "No—look at what God does! When we fail to do what is right, He waits for us to admit our failure and confess it. Then He gives us another chance by living as though He expects us to do what's right in the future. Perhaps we will fail in the same way again. But in the meantime, with faith that works by love, God treats us as though we will not fail. He acts as though our future choices haven't happened yet. In faith, God does the most loving thing possible without looking at all our future choices.

"The Bible says that faith, working by love, is a major thing that should matter to us. I think God wants faith to matter to us because it matters to Him. God has even made faith the means by which we are saved. He's not going to work against His goal of love between Himself and us that includes mutual faith. If He wanted to look into all our future choices, He could have made sure that He knew in advance every detail of our lives. But I believe the love relationship He wants with us is at a higher level than that."

Pastor Caring interrupted, "This is interesting. I was wondering if you were making an issue over whether or not God practices faith. That would be a rabbit trail. But then you pointed out that it is part of love, and God is love. Thank you. I hadn't thought of this before."

Mr. Tradition wasn't satisfied. "God can still know everything while He requires us to have faith."

Mr. Evangelist said, "I understand what Christian is saying, and it does make sense. When we as Christ's bride accept Him as our Husband, faith is part of the package. Of course, faith is part of the relationship He wants with us."

Christian silently prayed, *Lord, what more can I say to help Mr. Tradition to see your love?* Then he continued, "God wants to trust us because faith is part of the fellowship that He created us for. We ourselves wouldn't want to be married to a wife we couldn't trust. Surely, God wants a relationship with us, His bride, where we really trust each other. Even in the Old Testament, look at what it said when He talked about Israel." Finding the place in the Bible, Christian read:

I will betroth you to Me forever; Yes, I will betroth you to Me in righteousness and justice, in loving kindness and mercy; I will betroth you to Me in faithfulness, and you shall know the Lord. (Hosea 2:19–20)

"Nowadays, we say, 'trust has to be earned.' That's not how God does things. Every day, in faith, God gives the unrepentant another day to repent. He doesn't look at their future choices, and He lives as though He expects that they will repent. Look at how patient He is! Why would He bother being as patient if we had no free will and He knew the future? Rather than seeing our relationship with God as if it were a play where we and God are just reading a script where all the lines are known, we should look at how He actually treats us. Everything God does is pointed in one direction, and that is to draw us into a real love relationship with Himself where we truly respond to one another. It's a special relationship where Christ is in us, and we are in Him, sharing a relationship where faith in one another is part of the love we have for each other." Then Christian quoted 1 Corinthians 1:9:

God is faithful, by whom you were called into the fellowship of His Son, Jesus Christ our Lord.

Pastor Caring said, "I had not thought of this before: God's patience is an example of His faith in us. That is a different way to look at it, and I have to admit I'm finding myself agreeing with you. Interesting, very interesting."

Mr. Stubborn and Mr. Tradition were dismayed. They thought for sure that Pastor Caring would pin Christian's ears back. Mr. Stubborn whispered, "Just wait until we get to Jacob and Esau."

Pastor Caring considered the Scriptures Christian mentioned. Finally he said, "I can't make the Bible say anything other than what it does say. If I did, I wouldn't have any way to believe anything."

Christian said, "So if God is always faithful, always doing the most loving thing possible, He doesn't have a great need to look into the future. And Scripture clearly indicates God doesn't always look into the future. He only selectively looks at our future choices."

Mr. Stubborn said, "Surely God lives in eternity outside of any kind of time, and all past, present, and future are the same to Him. There's nothing outside of what He knows."

"Yes," said Pastor Caring. "What are your thoughts about that?"

Christian remembered the cold, dark night when he had been

lying in bed thinking about this very question. He remembered getting up in the middle of the night to light a lantern and look at what the Bible said. So he responded thoughtfully, "To me, eternity means a very long time. I just don't think we should define eternity as 'past, present, and future happening all at once.' But if you assume that God knows every thought He will ever think for all eternity, then you're forced to take that definition. When I read Genesis 1:1–2:3 and Exodus 20:8–11, the part about creation and the Sabbath, it just seems that when God gave us what we call a day, it was something He was already familiar with. If the passing of events is something that happens in heaven, He would also create something similar for us because He loves us and wants a close relationship."

"Look at what The Bible says about Satan." Christian opened his Bible to Ezekiel. "'You were the seal of perfection, full of wisdom and perfect in beauty…The workmanship of your timbrels and pipes was prepared for you on the day you were created. You were the anointed cherub who covers; I established you; you were on the holy mountain of God…You were perfect in your ways from the day you were created, till iniquity was found in you. By the abundance of your trading you became filled with violence within, and you sinned; therefore I cast you as a profane thing out of the mountain of God…Your heart was lifted up because of your beauty' (Ezekiel 28:12–17).

"This is talking about real events that took place in heaven, events that are now part of the past. Though time as we know it in our universe had not been created yet, there did exist a sequence of events. There was an event when Satan was created as a beautiful angel. Then there were more events when Satan was actively employed as a cherub, attending the throne of God. Finally came the terrible event when Satan changed his mind and rebelled against God. So it seems likely that some kind of chain of events is something that characterizes heaven. Perhaps it's different from our created time, but still it is there. But one thing is clear: when God created our time, with past, present, and future events, it was something the angels were familiar with."

"Oh yes," joked Mr. Knowsalot. "The Bible also says that Satan knows his *time* is short. That is one angel with a grim future."

"I don't understand," said Mr. Stubborn. "I was always taught that God lives in eternity, completely outside time and events and any kind of timeline. Now you're saying He does have events. Where's your proof for that?"

Christian paused to think for a moment. He remembered the verse he'd read by lamplight. Then he said, "Look at John 10:17. It's sort of like a window into where God lives." Christian quickly turned to it and said, "'Therefore my Father loves Me, because I lay down My life, that I may take it again.' Jesus going to the cross at a point in time had an effect on God the Father. It was an event which added a new richness to God's love. You asked for proof. This is one."

Mr. Knowsalot thought it was time to take Christian's side. He said, "We all take Scripture seriously. And we have to admit that there are places in Scripture where it says God repented. Since talking to Christian, I started studying that for myself." Mr. Knowsalot pulled a piece of paper out of his Bible. "Here's my list. The most glaring example is when God was sorry He made man just before the Flood (Genesis 6:5–11). In Jeremiah 15:6, God said he was 'weary with repenting' concerning the destruction of Judah. In Jeremiah 18:8, God said if a nation repents, He will repent of bringing destruction on them. And in Jeremiah 26:1–3, God says if Judah will repent, then He will also! And there's 1 Chronicles 21:15, Psalms 106:45, Amos 7:1–6, Joel 2:12–14, and many other examples." Mr. Knowsalot tucked the paper back in his Bible.

"In the past, we said these places in Scripture were anthropomorphisms and ignored them. I was always uncomfortable doing that. I knew in my heart that it was just a sly way to ignore Scripture that didn't agree with my theology. I'm not going to do it anymore. I agree with the point Christian made. Scripture does teach that God lives in a sequence of events. I cannot deny that Scripture teaches there is such a thing as the past and there is such a thing as an unknown future. It's not a future God can't control. He continually frustrates the plans of the wicked. Scripture is very clear that God responds to the wicked, and He responds to the righteous. This is how God chooses to do things, and I'm no longer refusing to accept it.

"Instead, I'm excited about and challenged by what Christian is saying because it opens up an understanding of God's love I didn't have before. It hadn't occurred to me that I was being anthropomorphic in limiting the extreme depth of God's love. Now that I know how much He loves me, I can't do that anymore."

Pastor Caring said, "Well done, Christian! It seems you have a convert. But unlike Mr. Knowsalot, I don't fully agree with you."

Mr. Stubborn interjected, "God can do as He pleases. He's the

Creator and has the right to do what we may perceive as mean. He's the standard for righteousness. So if His meanness is righteousness, we shouldn't question that."

Pastor Caring said, "The Bible does say God is righteous, loving, and merciful. This is how God describes Himself. Christian has made some good points, and we've not been able to answer him from Scripture. But we're not finished yet. So, Christian, in regard to the subject of time, what do you do with Titus 1:2?" Pastor Caring read aloud:

In hope of eternal life which God, who cannot lie, promised before time began.

This was one of Christian's favorite verses to think about. He said, "This verse does show God outside of our created time. For us, there was a beginning. However, it does not say He can't have some kind of changing events outside of our created time. It's interesting that in the verse, God has two 'befores.' One is before the promise, and the other before our time. The making of a promise took place in the present at the time the promise was made. And by definition, a promise is about a future event. So there is a chain of events with a *before* the promise, a *present* when the promise was made, and an *after* the promise. But it's a chain of events that took place before our time ever even began."

Christian pointed to the verse in his Bible. "But the whole point of what it's saying here is to help us see the hope of eternal life in Christ that has come to us through the Gospel. *Paul is making the point that the promise was made before sin came into the world.* It's an unconditional promise, and God will stand by His Word. Our sin will not cause Him to go back on His Word. This verse is not written to make a doctrine about God living in an eternity that does not have time." Christian paused and looked straight at Mr. Stubborn. "And look at this," he said. "We were not there when the promise was made. It's a promise made within the Trinity."

Mr. Stubborn frowned and Pastor Caring was debating how to respond, when Mrs. Hospitality brought in a platter of cookies and lemonade. She said she was trying something new called the hermit cookie, made with cold coffee and lots of cinnamon. There was temporary silence while Christian was eating a cookie and the lemonade was being passed around. Christian decided it was the most delicious cookie he ever ate.

Suddenly, there was a knock at the back door. A few seconds later, Mrs. Hospitality came in with Mr. Dairyman, who was carrying a rope. He said, "I'm sorry to bother you. I'm by myself today and the cows broke through the fence again. I would appreciate some help rounding them up." All the elders pushed back their chairs, left their half-eaten cookies, and followed Mr. Dairyman. Sure enough, there were cows in Mr. Hospitality's front yard. Mr. Dairyman pointed out the lead cow, Bluebell. He said, "If you fellers can corner Bluebell so I can put a rope on her, I'll be able to lead her back to my pasture. The rest of the cows will follow."

As everyone converged on Bluebell, she knew something was up and was determined not to be caught. Seeing an opening, she took off with all the other cows following. Mr. Dairyman put his hands to the top of his head and shouted a pathetic, "Oh no!" He watched helplessly as the men charged off chasing after Bluebell. But cows can run fast and soon left the elders far behind.

Steady showed up to join the fun. Christian motioned Steady to follow him as he climbed over the split rail fence. Once in the pasture, the boys ran as fast as they could along the fence row. When Bluebell thought she had safely escaped, she stopped to eat some grass. This allowed the boys to quietly run past her without her seeing them. They climbed back over the fence and started toward her. When Bluebell saw them coming, she gave them a disgusted look, then turned around and ran back the way she came. All the other cows followed her. Pastor Caring and the elders saw the herd running right at them and thought they were going to be trampled. They ran for the fence and climbed over it, but Mr. Dairyman fearlessly ran straight at Bluebell. She slowed down enough for him to slip a noose over her head and hang on.

Bluebell could have easily dragged Mr. Dairyman wherever she wanted to go, but when she felt the rope, she apparently gave up and thought, *Okay, it's over.* She meekly let him lead her back into her own home pasture and over to the barn where Mr. Dairyman tied her to a post. All the other cows followed Bluebell. With the cows back in, Mr. Dairyman went out to thank his neighbors and survey the broken fence.

He said, "Thank you so much for your help. Who knows what mischief and damage they might have done before milking time!" Christian, who had never owned a cow, asked, "Why? What happens at milking time?"

"Oh," said Mr. Dairyman, "The cows would have returned to the barn if they could find their way back." Pastor Caring asked if he needed any help with the broken fence. Mr. Dairyman said, "No, I'm getting used to fixing that fence after Bluebell breaks it down. She found out she can lean on it and push her way through. What I need is some of that newfangled barbed wire fencing. But thank you for your offer to help."

Mr. Stubborn rushed back into the house and had a look at Pastor Caring's notes. *Ah yes. What can we contribute to our salvation? Let's see him answer that. How can God have a standard as to who is saved? Let's see him dance around that. Then the coup de grace, Jacob and Esau. Perfect.*

---

[1] 2 Chronicles 33:1-13; 1 Timothy 2:4-6; 2 Peter 3:9
[2] Genesis 6:13-14, 7:23
[3] Job 1:7-12, 2:3-6; Hebrews 2:18
[4] Revelation 21:8
[5] 1 John 4:18
[6] 2 Chronicles 16:9
[7] Isaiah 44:22, 55:7; Jeremiah 31:34; Micah 7:19
[8] Hebrews 10:16-23; Romans 6:14; 1 John 1:9
[9] 2 Chronicles 32:31; Luke 7:9
[10] Isaiah 46:10
[11] Deuteronomy 31:21
[12] Exodus 33:11
[13] Ezekiel 14:14
[14] Genesis 6:6; 1 Samuel 15:10-11
[15] Genesis 8:21, 9:11
[16] 2 Chronicles 19:7; James 1:13-17
[17] Exodus 32:10-14, 33:5; Amos 7:1-6
[18] Psalms 145:9, 17
[19] Matthew 26:39, 42, 44
[20] Jeremiah 26:2-3, 36:2-3; John 17:20-23
[21] Galatians 5:6; Hebrews 11:6
[22] Jeremiah 3:12-14
[24] 2 Peter 3:9; Romans 2:4
[25] Job 38:6-7; Ezekiel 28:13-15
[26] Revelation 12:7-12
[27] Exodus 32:14, 33 (God repents of His plan to destroy Israel)
Exodus 33:5 (God says He is trying to decide what to do with disobedient Israel.)
Isaiah 38:1-8 (God changes His mind and adds 15 years to Hezekiah's life)
Joel 2:13 (Israel encouraged to repent because then God will change His plans)
[31] Exodus 34:6-7

# 6 JACOB AND ESAU

They all went back to finish off the hermit cookies and lemonade. As the last cookie was consumed, Pastor Caring said, "Let's go on. Christian, what are your thoughts about man's ability to contribute anything toward his salvation?"

Mr. Tradition's eyes narrowed as he said, "We've always believed that before we're saved, we have no ability and no desire to seek after God. Our salvation is all from God, even the desire to be saved."

What Mr. Tradition said reminded Christian of his conversation with Mr. Confident. Since then, he had given it a lot more thought. Christian said, "When I look at the Scripture, what I see is God showing Himself to everyone, no exceptions! And everything I read also says everyone is able to choose to keep or reject what God shows them."

Mr. Tradition interjected, "So you're saying God speaks to everyone's conscience?"

"Not their conscience," said Christian. "It's different from our conscience, but just like we can ignore our conscience, we can ignore Him." Christian opened his Bible to Romans. "In Romans 1:18–32, Paul talks about selfish, sinful people who were given the ability to believe in and obey God, but they rejected His help and wouldn't even admit that He is God. Paul wrote, 'For the wrath of God is revealed from heaven against all ungodliness and unrighteousness of men, who suppress the truth in unrighteousness, because what may be known of God is manifest in them, for God has shown it to them.'" Christian made a wide sweep with his arm. "What God revealed of Himself was big enough that even selfish, bad people were able to recognize it and know what they were doing when they chose to reject it." Christian turned back to his Bible and read all the things God protected them from before He slowly removed His protection.

Christian shook his head in amazement. "Wow," he said. "God sure was protecting them before, by holding back bad stuff from happening and even holding them back from being worse than they were. And He protected their minds, too! He did this even though they were bad people! God was doing everything He could to help them choose to obey Him, and He was making it as easy as He could for them to turn to Him. But in the end, if they refused, He respected their choice. Why would God go to so much trouble and bother to try to persuade them if they were not able to respond? Paul's whole point is that they could have repented and turned to God, but they didn't. They just kept on disobeying.

"There's something else we can see from what Paul wrote. God doesn't easily give up on bad people, withdrawing His influence all at once. He lets them see the consequences of rejecting His protection, but He does it only a little at a time, so they have time to see what they are doing to themselves and repent. In Paul's example, even after God has stepped back three times He is still trying to influence them! The last verse, verse 32, says, 'Who, knowing the righteous judgment of God, that those who practice such things are deserving of death, not only do the same but also approve of those who practice them.' So you see, God did not withdraw from them completely. For their sake, in the hope that they would repent, God kept before them the awareness that there would be serious consequences if they continued in rebellion. I don't think we would be so patient with people like that. But we should not expect anything less from our God who is love."

Mr. Friendly spoke up, "The idea that God limited His love only to a few and in an arbitrary way always bothered me. For the lost to not even have a chance to be saved made God look bad. I appreciate Christian's answer. I believe it's Scriptural and it's right."

Christian continued, "There's another verse we can look at." He turned in his Bible to the gospel of John. "John 1:9 says, 'The true Light which gives light to every man.' Every person who has ever lived has received 'light' enough to trust and seek God."

Mr. Knowsalot said, "Christian showed me John 1:9 before, and I really thought about it. The way I see it, this verse is saying that God shows enough of His righteous character to even a child that they can choose to seek after Him, and want to be like Him. This verse shows that they might be judged by what they do with the light given to them. I had always wondered how God could judge a little child or someone who had never heard of Christ. I believe Christian has answered that difficult question. What Christian is saying makes a lot of sense."

Christian added, "There's one more verse I want you to consider.

You all know Romans 3:23, 'For all have sinned and fall short of the glory of God,' I don't think there is any doubt but that this applies to everyone. Shouldn't the next verse also apply to everyone? 'And all are justified freely by his grace through the redemption that came by Christ Jesus.' Christ would not die for people who are unable to accept the sacrifice that He made for them."

Mr. Knowsalittle whispered something to Pastor Caring who asked, "Then how does God choose who will be saved? Surely, He has some sort of standard to judge them by!"

Christian responded, "I wondered about that, too, and I found the answer in something Jesus said: 'My doctrine is not Mine, but His who sent Me. If anyone wills to do His will, he shall know concerning the doctrine, whether it is from God or whether I speak on My own authority.' (John 7:16–17).

"Wanting to do God's will—this is God's standard. If anyone wants to do God's will, that person will be given understanding and faith that Jesus and His doctrine are from God the Father. This is believing in Him, which John 3:16 says leads to eternal life."

Mr. Stubborn was about to say something about man being unable to choose to do God's will when he realized Christian had already answered that objection. He was beginning to think Christian might be right and he fought against it. Silently, he made up his mind that he was not going to give up.

Christian continued, "Another Scripture is Matthew 7:21– 23." Christian turned to it and read, "'Not everyone who says to Me, "Lord, Lord," shall enter the kingdom of heaven, but he who does the will of My Father in heaven. Many will say to Me in that day, "Lord, Lord, have we not prophesied in Your name, cast out demons in Your name, and done many wonders in Your name?" And then I will declare to them, "I never knew you; depart from Me, you who practice lawlessness!"'

"Jesus said the reason they were not saved was that they were not willing to do God's will. Willingness to do God's will is repentance and it is God's standard. It's like God is asking the question, 'Do you want me?' and people judge themselves, just as Paul said in Acts 13:46." Christian turned to Acts and read,

Then Paul and Barnabas grew bold and said, "It was necessary that the word of God should be spoken to you first; but since you reject it, and judge yourselves unworthy of everlasting life, behold, we turn to the Gentiles."

Christian pulled out a piece of paper from his Bible and said, "I've written down a few verses that are about people who belonged to Jesus before they even heard of Him. How can this be? Well, it's because of what I've been saying—God gives faith to people who had a repentant heart and were already wanting to do things His way. So these people Peter and Paul met were already looking for God the best they knew how. They met God's standard." Then Christian read off the verse references, "Acts 10:4, 13:48, 16:14, and 18:10. When these people heard the gospel, God immediately gave them faith to believe."

Mr. Stubborn was horrified. These were the very verses which he thought proved that God chose whom to save, even before they were born. For Christian to use the same verses to prove that people made the choice to do God's will after they were born, that was almost too much to bear. And the idea that God had a standard for deciding who would be saved, that was the biggest shock of all.

Beginning with John 1:9, the elders looked up and discussed the verses Christian had brought up. Even Mr. Stubborn couldn't deny that what Christian said made sense. Finally, Pastor Caring glanced at his notes, "Hmmm. You already covered Acts 13:48 and John 6:44 when we talked about God's standard for giving saving faith. So give us your thoughts on what Romans 9 says about Jacob and Esau."

Mr. Stubborn and Mr. Tradition smugly sat back in their chairs, smiling to themselves.

Christian began, "The main point of Romans 9 is how God was being perfectly fair when He rejected the nation of Israel. It's all there in the first nine verses—very clear! After that, in chapter 10, he finally talks about how individuals are saved."

Pastor Caring nodded. "Right," he agreed.

Christian looked at Mr. Stubborn and said, "I suppose what you're looking at is Romans 9:10–13:

And not only this, but when Rebecca conceived by one man, even by our father Isaac (for the children not yet being born, nor having done any good or evil, that the purpose of God according to election might stand, not of works but of Him who calls), it was said to her, "The older shall serve the younger." As it is written, "Jacob I have loved, but Esau I have hated."

Mr. Stubborn and Mr. Tradition looked triumphant, and Mr. Stubborn said, "See! It says 'the purpose of God according to election.' God determined what would happen to them even before they were born!"

Christian leaned forward. "Absolutely not!" he said emphatically. "Romans 9 has nothing to do with Jacob and Esau as individual people. It's talking about the nations which would be descendants of Jacob and Esau, both of whom are descendants of Abraham. The quote in this verse is God talking to Rebecca. She is the 'her' these verses are talking about. So we should go back to the Old Testament and read what God actually said to her." Christian flipped back to Genesis and read,

Now Isaac pleaded with the Lord for his wife, because she was barren; and the Lord granted his plea, and Rebecca his wife conceived. But the children struggled together within her; and she said, 'If all is well, why am I like this?' So she went to inquire of the Lord. And the Lord said to her: 'Two nations are in your womb, two peoples shall be separated from your body; one people shall be stronger than the other, and the older shall serve the younger.' (Genesis 25:21–23)

"But during their lifetimes as individuals, Esau never served Jacob, and Jacob was afraid of Esau, even bowing to him and giving him gifts. And as for prosperity, Esau inherited all that their father Isaac had. So obviously in Genesis 25 when God spoke to Rebecca, He was speaking of nations, not individuals, and that is what Paul quoted. But that's not all," Christian said. "Romans 9:10–13 also quotes from Malachi.

The burden of the word of the Lord to Israel by Malachi. "I have loved you," says the Lord. Yet you say, "In what way have you loved us?" "Was not Esau Jacob's brother?" says the Lord. "Yet Jacob I have loved; but Esau I have hated, and laid waste his mountains and his heritage for the jackals of the wilderness" (Malachi 1:1–3).

"Esau's land was the area around Mt. Seir, which was a good place when Esau lived there. In fact, Esau moved to Mt. Seir because at that time it was fertile, fertile enough for all his herds, fertile enough to support sufficient servants that Esau could muster an army of 400 men. Even Abraham never had that many.

"Four hundred years later, when Israel was in the wilderness under Moses, God commanded that Israel should 'not meddle with them (Edom), for I will not give you any of their land, no, not so much as one footstep, because I have given Mount Seir to Esau as a possession.' This does not sound like Esau was hated! But hundreds of years later, when Israel was being punished for their sin, the Edomites (Esau's descendants) joined in with great cruelty. God responded by punishing the Edomites for this offense against Israel and brought about their eventual destruction and the desolation of their land. This was as prophesied before it took place, by Obadiah and in Ezekiel 35. In Obadiah's prophesy it says,

"Will I not in that day," says the Lord, "Even destroy the wise men from Edom, and understanding from the mountains of Esau? Then your mighty men, O Teman, shall be dismayed, to the end that everyone from the mountains of Esau may be cut off by slaughter. For violence against your brother Jacob, shame shall cover you, and you shall be cut off forever." (Obadiah 1:8–10)

Christian continued, "Then after Edom's destruction, Malachi wrote what is quoted in Romans 9.God loved Esau enough to allow his descendants to become a nation. It was the later behavior of the Edomites that brought upon themselves the punishment which they suffered both to their nation and to their land. This only proves that God guides nations, and we all agree on that."

(At this point, the elders had even more questions for Christian, some similar to those found in Appendix A.)

Having reached the end of his notes, Pastor Caring commented, "Christian, I am impressed. You did such thorough research." He paused and looked at Christian for a moment before saying very kindly, "Why is this so important to you?"

Christian sat up very straight and said earnestly, "When I lost my mother and father, it really hurt. I felt so alone. But when I could see how much God loves me, it made a huge difference. If I didn't believe how loving God is, I would have a hard time trusting that He's always with me. But more importantly, if I didn't know what He's really like, I wouldn't know what to be doing in order to be a person who lives God's way. I wouldn't know what to trust Him to change."

"Doesn't He make changes in your life without your knowing it?" Mr. Knowsalittle asked. "I know God has done that in my own life. How about you?"

Christian smiled broadly. "Yes, He sure has changed me, too! When I was first saved, He quickly changed a lot of things I was thinking and doing. I was amazed at the time. I knew a miracle was happening inside me. But I'm not supposed to camp there. It's just the first step. Now He's teaching me how we live together. I don't just pray by myself, God and I pray together. When I trust Him for something, we do this together. He's teaching me to pray and have faith together with Him in order that even my obedience is something I do with Him. Living with Him in me is something beyond God just doing things to me or for me. He's not training me to be a puppet. He wants me to really understand what His love is like and that I willingly become like Him. Becoming like Jesus is a growing process that we work on together.

"I really like what Paul prayed in Ephesians 3:16-19. It has helped me see how 'growing up in Christ' is something we do together with God." Christian turned to Ephesians and read aloud,

That He would grant you, according to the riches of His glory, to be strengthened with might through His Spirit in the inner man, that Christ may dwell in your hearts through faith; that you, being rooted and grounded in love, may be able to comprehend with all the saints what is the width and length and depth and height—to know the love of Christ which passes knowledge; that you may be filled with all the fullness of God.

"I finally saw that there is a real me on the inside who is strengthened by His Spirit, a real me who exercises faith, a real me who is rooted and grounded in love, and a real me who comprehends and knows the love of Christ which is beyond what I can know apart from His Spirit. And there's a promise given in this verse to all Christians who comprehend the love of God, that we will be 'filled with all the fullness of God.' Surely, this is what we all want. But if we carry in our hearts a theology that diminishes God's love, how will we ever experience being filled with His fullness?"

Christian seemed to be filled with new energy. Caught up in his zeal, with a mixture of severity and fiery conviction, Christian left no doubt in anyone's mind that he was speaking from his heart.

"As Paul wrote, there's something special about being able to 'comprehend the width and length and depth and height' and believing God's love. It makes us able to tell people the gospel so much better. In my heart, I want to reach people for Christ. I know that when I talk about the love of God, people respond. It's what they want. All Christians should also be talking about the love of God to those who are lost. If we all did, we would be reaping a great harvest!" Christian paused and said even more strongly, "And if we didn't just talk about it, but we lived it, we would reap an even greater harvest!

"Is there anything about who God is that He does not want to see in us too? Of course not! God wants us to be like Jesus, in our whole attitude and actions and everything. God wants us to trust Him for this. That's why it's so important to me to believe that God loves everyone, no matter what, because then I can know for sure that with His help, I'll be able to love everybody too. And what I found out is that the more I learn to love people as God does, the more God can change in my own life, and the more I become like Jesus.

"I do feel strongly about this. I believe Christ's love has no limit. He is faithful and will always respond to everyone with love. I believe this is also what He wants to see in our lives. We're growing in our fellowship with Christ where we love without limit. So you see, I will not believe anything that limits His love. My conscience will not let me say anything that would minimize His love. I cannot believe anything about God that would destroy my faith to love like He really loves!" Christian paused. He was thinking, *Oh no. Now I did it. I hope they don't kick me out of the church.*

Looking at the circle of men sitting around the table, Christian finished by saying, "Understanding God's love and trusting Him to love others with me has been the most exciting adventure of my life. I can't say it with just words. Being with God is such a joy to me."

For a long minute, everyone was silent. Finally, Pastor Caring said, "Our theology does allow us to camp in one place and not grow or change much. We've seen the change in your life. I'm convinced now that as a church, we have some growing left to do. I also have seen how many new members have come to church because of your evangelistic efforts. I can't deny that whatever you're doing, it works." After looking at his watch, he said, "I believe supper is ready. Earlier, I spotted Mrs. Hospitality carrying chickens. I think we're going to have chicken. We're going to be well fed today."

After a few minutes of prayer, Mrs. Hospitality brought in hot platters of fried chicken. Some of the elders helped, and soon the table was loaded. Supper is usually a light meal, but Mrs. Hospitality loved to cook. Though feeling emotionally drained, Christian was revived by the sight of so much good food. As always, he was ready to eat!

They talked about other things during supper. Afterward, Pastor Caring said the elders had some things to discuss and Christian went home, wondering what was going to happen. He was honest and faithful to what he knew God wanted him to say. He decided to spend the rest of the evening fishing, praying, and thanking God for helping him say what was in his heart.

Meeting together, the elders were also praying and reflecting. Finally, somebody said, "I think the boy is right." Even Mr. Stubborn and Mr. Tradition admitted Christian had answered every verse they previously trusted in. Then they both sheepishly confided that they had a feeling of relief when they realized that Christian was speaking the truth. There followed a general agreement. Pastor Caring said, "What impressed me is the gentle spirit with which the boy spoke. He is right. With our theology, we've been degrading and minimizing the love of God. I know I personally have some repenting to do."

Looking thoughtful, Mr. Friendly said, "What convinced me is the realization that God would never put Himself in the position where He can't think new thoughts or express His love by responding to us. I realized that I always did pray and expect Him to respond to me with love. I lived this way in spite of my theology, not because of it. Suddenly, all the places in Scripture that tell us to repent, a choice we have to make, are starting to make sense. Christian had talked to me about this before and I didn't get it. I finally understand what he was saying."

Mr. Evangelist said, "What I heard was absolutely wonderful. When non-Christians accuse God of things, like purposely creating a world of people so He could kill them in a flood and send them to hell, I now have a way to answer them. And I can steer my answer into a discussion of God's love. I can see a lot of potential for evangelism here."

Mr. Knowsalot commented, "What impressed me is that he made sure he knew the context and did some research before coming to a conclusion as to what any verse in the Bible says." Pastor Caring began to chuckle before he added, "Yes, and I cringed inside every time he explained a verse I had previously taken out of context." Then he opened his Bible and said, "1 Corinthians 13 isn't just instruction for us, it's also how God loves." He began to read. When he had finished, he prayed, and they all went home.

That week, Pastor Caring went over his notes on what Christian had to say. Making good use of his many study helps, he spent a lot of time in his library. What he planned for his next sermon was greatly revised. He knew he had to go slowly and carefully. Still, he wondered how people would react.

[1] Proverbs 4:16; Titus 1:15; 1 Corinthians 8:7
[2] Acts 17:26-27; Romans 1:18-20, 32
[3] John 5:24; 6:29, 40
[4] Luke 24:47; Acts 26:20
[5] Genesis 27:41-43, 28:20-22, 32:3-21, 33:1-11
[6] Genesis 14:14
[7] Deuteronomy 2:1-6
[8] Matthew 25:29

# 7 SUNDAY'S SERMON

News travels fast in a small community. By the time the Sunday service started, everyone in the congregation knew all the details of what happened the previous Sunday afternoon. Standing in the pulpit, Pastor Caring announced that he had learned more about the love of God just last week than in all his previous forty-plus years as a Christian. "I can't contain myself," he said, with his voice full of both joy and seriousness. "This morning, I'm going to preach on the love of God. In a way, I'm also preaching to myself. Thinking about the love of God, I've become more aware of my own need to understand and surrender to His love.

"When we truly understand the heart of God, our eyes are opened to see our own unloving, unkind, worldly thoughts and habits for what they are. By understanding God's heart, we can intelligently agree with Him and trust Him to free us of those things that anchor us to this fallen world. God Himself said in Jeremiah 9:24

"'Let him who glories glory in this,
That he understands and knows Me,
That I am the Lord, exercising lovingkindness, judgment, and righteousness in the earth.
For in these I delight,' Says the Lord."

"God is being very specific here. He mentions three things: lovingkindness, judgment, and righteousness. If we understand these three things and delight in them as He does, we will understand and know God in a way that He wants to be known. He can then walk with us, knowing we're going in the same direction.

"These three qualities are more than just describing what God is like. They're things that God is constantly doing. He doesn't want to miss even one opportunity to exercise them all. When we choose to also do them, consciously wanting His help, God is overjoyed, because then He has the opportunity to do them with us, engaging in the relationship that He desires as we do them together."

Mr. Helpful was listening carefully. He'd heard what happened last Sunday and was wondering what could be so different that it would create such a fuss. So the idea that God wants us to know Him caught his attention. *God is unknowable,* he thought. *What's this in the Bible that says we should know Him? That's impossible.* He frowned a bit and listened even more intently as Pastor Caring continued.

Pastor Caring continued, "So let's examine lovingkindness, justice, and righteousness, beginning with lovingkindness. The Hebrew word translated lovingkindness conveys complete devotion. And it's more than a word. It's the story of God's loving devotion to us. The closest New Testament word is agape, unconditional love that does what is best for others, not considering personal cost. It's what we should expect from God, who is love, and delights in exercising lovingkindness on the earth.

"God's character is to give, to do what is best for us. He has no limitation as to the sacrifice He is willing to make for us. God gives what's best for us at every opportunity, giving grace upon grace upon grace. God will never fail to act on an opportunity to love.

"His unconditional love for us does not depend on us. But we do have a part to play in God's lovingkindness. The Holy Spirit in us wants to express Himself in our lives. By following the Spirit, we will find ourselves willing to serve others, expressing God's lovingkindness in the way we live."

Mr. Helpful shifted a bit in his seat. He knew he personally had limits to how far he would go in helping people. *So God wants me to do what is best for others no matter what the cost,* he thought. *I don't think I can do that.* For a moment, he struggled with the idea and overcame the temptation to put it out of his mind. *What would I do if I knew for sure that God would help me live that way?* he asked himself. *I've got to think about this.*

"The next word in Jeremiah 9:24 is 'judgment,'" Pastor Caring continued. "It sounds like a harsh word. How can we say God is loving and exercises lovingkindness, then in the same breath talk about Him judging people? We need to look at God's definition of justice, which takes every opportunity to be kind, merciful, and forgiving, treating others with compassion. I'm reading from Zechariah 7:9–10 where God is telling His people how to behave.

Thus says the Lord of hosts:

"Execute true justice, show mercy and compassion everyone to his brother. Do not oppress the widow or the fatherless, the alien or the poor. Let none of you plan evil in his heart against his brother."

"Justice heads this list, followed by mercy and compassion. In a strict kind of justice, there is no mercy or compassion. But like God, we are to be compassionate, looking for opportunity to be forgiving and merciful, helping the weak who cannot help themselves.

"Although God is sometimes forced to deal harshly with the wicked, when you look at God's kind of justice, you can clearly see His love. This love in justice can be seen in 1 John 1:9:

If we confess our sins, He is faithful and just to forgive us our sins and to cleanse us from all unrighteousness.

"The Greek word translated 'confess' means to agree with deep conviction that what is being confessed is true. In context of 1 John 1:9, 'confess' means to agree with God.

"The world sees judgment as punishment that fits the crime. But God's kind of judgment is different."

Mr. Knowsalittle thought this was crazy. He remembered when he was robbed in his store, looking at the barrel of the man's gun. It looked as big as a cannon. He was never so scared in his life. *Bad people have to be punished,* he thought. *They only get what they deserve, and it makes it safe for the rest of us. What is Pastor Caring saying?*

"According to 1 John 1:9," continued the pastor, "when we confess what we have done, then God's judgment is that we are forgiven. But to be fair, it's not that simple. Confession is what naturally comes from a repentant heart. Where there is repentance, God's judgment is not to punish, but to forgive. He forgives and it's over. Well, according to 1 John 1:9, it's not quite over. He washes our soul, then it's over. Is there anything more that He could do for us? If there were, He would do it. That's God's kind of judgment, and it comes out of who He is. He is love.

"And the idea of forgiving instead of punishing isn't limited to God. He asks us to do it too. God asks us to forgive because it's His kind of judgment."

Pastor Caring turned to the gospel of Matthew and read, "Peter came to Jesus and said, 'Lord, how often shall my brother sin against me, and I forgive him. Up to seven times?' Jesus said to him, 'I do not say to you, up to seven times, but up to seventy times seven.'" (Matthew 18:21–22)

Pastor Caring paused and looked at the congregation. Seated in the back were several soldiers. "I see there are some soldiers here this morning," he said. "This doesn't mean we should not defend our nation, or the weak and oppressed, our families, or even ourselves. In the Bible, God even commands that for some crimes, there should be capital punishment. And it is in the best interest for ourselves, our society, and the criminals who prey on others, that their madness be stopped, and that they should be punished. This is why we have laws and trials. But even while we are defending our country or our society, we can still look at those who threaten us and mourn for them in our hearts because of what their pursuit of sin does to destroy them on the inside.

"And Jesus asks us to go beyond just a bit of forgiveness every now and then. He says 'seventy times seven.' We are to make forgiving others a part of our life. But He doesn't stop there. He said,

"'Love your enemies, bless those who curse you, do good to those who hate you, and pray for those who spitefully use you and persecute you, that you may be sons of your Father in heaven… Be perfect as your Father in heaven is perfect.' (Matthew 5:44–48) God sees our selfishness that separates us from Him and He mourns over what we are doing to ourselves.

"If we are willing to join Him in His ways of selfless lovingkindness and judgment that comes from love, then He wants us to mourn with Him, even for those who sin against us. He longs to see our hearts broken by the separation that breaks His heart.

"And so Jesus asks us to even love our enemies! Enemies are individual people we know who have hurt us and want to continue to hurt us. They have not come to us in repentance asking for forgiveness and have no intention to do so. In saying to forgive even these people, Jesus is not asking us to do something beyond what He Himself does. He loved us and offered us forgiveness while we were sinners in rebellion against Him. The Bible says:

God demonstrates His own love toward us, in that while we were still sinners, Christ died for us. (Romans 5:8)

When we were enemies we were reconciled to God through the death of His Son. (Romans 5:10)

"Romans 5 puts us in awe of God's love and the value He places on us. His desire to forgive, His willing sacrifice of His Son on our behalf, and the offer of forgiveness, all speak volumes about how much He values and loves us, particularly since these things predated our repentance. This is God's kind of justice."

Sitting in the middle of the congregation, Mrs. Bitter was feeling a great deal of pain. Memories flooded into her mind of the anger she'd felt when her husband left her. As years passed, the difficulties of raising five children all by herself fed her resentment. "God can do what He likes, I will never forgive that man," she had resolved. Even so, she had been tortured by the thought that God might not forgive her unless she forgave her husband from her heart. Now she faced this again. Closing her eyes and lowering her head, she struggled to regain her composure. *I certainly don't mourn for what he did to himself,* she thought. *I hope he suffers in hell.* She couldn't help but be horrified by the hardness of her own heart. Then the thought came to her, *God is mourning for my sin as much as my husband's. How can I do this to my Lord?* Silently, she prayed for God to forgive her. The cold hardness of her heart began to thaw.

"The concept of a strong desire to forgive is foreign to our normal way of thinking," Pastor Caring continued. "To be willing to make an extreme sacrifice in order to establish a possibility of forgiveness toward those who abuse us personally seems unnatural. In this fallen world, our natural way of thinking is to require the person who did the offence to make the first move, and it had better be with sufficient groveling. We have difficulty understanding the love that motivates God's kind of justice. Yet we're not only called to understand, we're called to practice it from a sincere heart.

"James writes, 'Mercy triumphs over judgment.' In God's justice, there is mercy, there is forgiveness, there is love.

"Of course, at some point, God must act for the sake of those who are being influenced by or otherwise harmed by the wicked. When He does act, He's often misunderstood. People are tempted to question His steadfast love.

"As an example, just before Christ returns, God will make a final attempt to convince unrepentant people that they should repent, because nothing could be worse than to be separated from God forever. Revelation says He will send a series of horrendous plagues. His goal is to help even those wicked people to give up their rebellion and surrender to Him. But even in the last days, in spite of the plagues God will send upon them, the Bible says that the wicked will still choose to harden themselves. Though there may be a minority of exceptions, the majority will not repent and will see God as cruel and unloving. But God is never cruel or unloving. The most unloving thing for Him to do would be to suddenly close to door to salvation."

Pointing down at his Bible, Pastor Caring continued, "The final word in Jeremiah 9:24 is righteousness. God delights in exercising righteousness on the earth. We know from the Sermon on the Mount that the righteous sometimes suffer for their righteousness. It's the nature of our living in this fallen world that we will suffer for righteousness, and that can't be helped. When we're saved, we're not immediately transported to heaven. We're here on earth where God wants us, so we can be salt and light, living righteous lives so the lost can see Christ in how we live. Our righteous living gives hope to the lost, opening for them a window into heaven as they see our loving and righteous behavior. Where our words offer some proof of God's love for us, our lives present irrefutable evidence.

"God's patience has given the wicked time to repent and be forgiven. Now that we have repented, it's our turn to be patient, to give others time to repent. By being patient, we enter into God's righteous patience in the hope that the wicked repent.

"I define righteousness as the manners or etiquette God uses to facilitate His love. God has made these rules of etiquette very clear in the Bible. He also makes it clear that being righteous isn't just outwardly keeping the rules, but also having an inner heart's desire to benefit the lives of those around us. Christ in us has given us that desire. It is there for us to walk in.

"I was talking to a man recently who said to me, 'I'm going through some hard times. I don't want to be a phony who cries out to God when things are tough. I want to wait until my life is okay, then I'll ask Him to save me.' I said to him, 'You're just being selfish. God created you because He wants fellowship with you. He wants to change your heart so you can be the kind of person He can have fellowship with. And you selfishly don't want to give Him what He wants until you're good and ready. You're breaking His heart because you won't let Him have the fellowship that He created you for. Not for yourself, but for Him, won't you let Him into your life?' To my surprise, his face lit up with a beautiful smile. He understood. In that instant, he decided to give his life to Christ. With faith in God's love for him, he prayed, not for a selfish reason, but that God's love would not be frustrated. But the matter doesn't stop there. We're to always live, not for ourselves, but to give to God what He wants, a people with whom He can have fellowship. And yes, He wants us to understand Him and His ways, so we, together with Him, can be those people of God."

By now, Mr. Helpful's eyes were as big as saucers. He realized, *My natural enjoyment of being helpful to others is just me.* Finally, he made a decision, *I want Christ. I want Him to be helpful together with me.* Without thinking about where he was, he quietly started to pray out loud. "Oh, God, I've been living without you. It was just me being selfish." Then he began to cry. People began to turn around and look at him. But he didn't care, and he continued to pray. "I want to understand You so I can live with You. Please help me give You the close fellowship that You want with me." Mr. Helpful wasn't normally emotional, and he was a little shocked by what he had done. Choking back tears, he sat quietly for a moment, wondering what had come over him. Then he thought, *I believe I've been touched by the Holy Spirit!*

Pastor Caring stopped and looked over at Mr. Helpful, who said somewhat brokenly, "Go on, Pastor, go on!" So Pastor Caring continued, "When God Himself says He delights in righteousness, I think He includes delight in what we do that is righteous. There are things we do that He delights in doing with us, like being kind to others. Our faith that He is with us, our continuing to pray about opportunities to live righteously toward others keeps us aware of the fellowship we have with Him.

"By being aware of our partnership with God, we can live righteously, with loving kindness and God's kind of justice. Then we participate in the joy of our God, who delights in exercising these things, and finds pleasure in us. Yes, our living in a way that gives God reason to bless us is an act of love for Him. It allows Him to do in us those things He delights in. God enjoys being God, and He enjoys being God in us. Let's pray."

Pastor Caring hadn't been able to hear Mr. Helpful's prayer, but everyone else had. They too were convicted that they had not included God in how they lived. The little groups that always socialized together after the service were talking about the usual things, but the sermon was percolating in the back of everyone's mind. The sermon became a topic at the Tuesday morning ladies' Bible study and several of the Wednesday evening home Bible studies. Everyone always believed the selfless way God lives, but many found it hard to believe Christ would help them live that way too. And there were some who just plain didn't want to. "I'm good enough!" they said.

So the idea that being a Christian means living a miraculous life was a little controversial. And it seemed there was always someone who would say, "Whatever happens is what God predestined to happen. We don't have to worry about it."

After the service, Pastor Caring sought Christian out and said, "I want to thank you for your courage last Sunday. You said the truth. I studied over and over again all the verses we talked about. Finally, I understood that I had been deceived into believing a false doctrine that hinders people from growing in Christ. I have my work cut out for me to do my best to convince everyone in the congregation in a way that won't split the church. We need to pray. I will be coming to visit from time to time."

"I'll look forward to that," Christian replied. They shook hands, and Pastor Caring went off to greet others in the congregation.

That night, Christian had a visitor, and it was not Pastor Caring—it was a raccoon. The fuzzy raider was climbing the fence to get into the garden when it caught a whiff of the smell of food in the lean-to next to the cabin. Christian awoke to the sound of the coon trying to get in and scared it away. Knowing it would be back, Christian wasn't sure what to do.

---

[1] Psalms 84:11; 1 Timothy 6:17
[2] John 1:16; James 1:17
[3] Psalms 33:4-5
[4] Luke 17:3-4; Psalms 103:12; Ezekiel 33:14-16
[5] Romans 13:1-8
[6] Matthew 5:4; Proverbs 24:17-18, 25:21-22; Luke 19:41--44
[7] James 2:13
[8] Deuteronomy 7:2-5; Revelation 19:2
[9] Revelation 16
[10] Matthew 5:11-12; 2 Timothy 3:12; 1 Peter 4:12-13
[11] Galatians 5:24-25, 6:10
[12] Psalms 149:4; Proverbs 11:20

# 8 ASKING FOR ADVICE

The next day, Christian went to the general store to get advice. Mr. Helpful said that raccoons, like bears, have an excellent sense of smell, and they don't like strong smells like ammonia. Raccoons also don't like plants with thorns. So Christian bought a gallon of ammonia. *Perhaps later*, he thought, *I can plant something nasty and thorny outside the fence.* He half buried old tin cans among the rocks around his garden and food lean-to. Into each can, he poured an inch of ammonia.

Using his hoe, he scraped down to dirt around the lean-to and garden. The next morning, Christian looked for tracks in the dirt. There were a few raccoon tracks all right, but they didn't come near the food lean-to. There were only a few tracks near the garden. It certainly looked as if the raccoon came up to the rocks around the fence but then left. Even though the raccoon could see what a great source of food was in the garden, the smell of ammonia drove him away. Christian spent part of the morning weeding and spreading compost. Then he went swimming and read the Bible for a while until it was almost noon and time to walk over to Mr. Friendly's house. Mr. Friendly had invited Careful and Christian over for dinner.

After a wonderful meal, which Christian thoroughly enjoyed, Steady and the other two boys headed out to go fishing by Christian's cabin. There was a dairy farm between the Friendly's house and the river, and Steady suggested taking a shortcut through the pasture. But he warned, "Goldilocks, the boss cow, will chase us if she sees us." Steady showed them a place where it was easy to climb the fence, and there was a similar place on the other side. They were about halfway across the pasture when Goldilocks spotted them and came on the run. Now the boys were also running, fishing stuff in hand. Across the field they flew. Zoom, zoom, zoom, over the fence they scrambled just in time. The cow snorted, but looked as though she enjoyed the pleasure of having someone to chase. Laughing and whooping all the way, the boys ran down to Christian's cabin. Christian got worms and his fishing pole and they settled into the serious business of fishing.

There's something special about sitting by the river, fishing. The plants give off a pleasant smell that blends with a still silence occasionally broken by insects and birds. The river flows quietly by, carrying an occasional leaf or stick. All the cares of this world seem to just float away, far, far away, somewhere downstream, out of sight and mind. Fishing has its reward that goes beyond catching fish.

Careful, who liked to get all his facts straight, invaded the tranquility with a weighty question, "What does it mean that God knows everything?" Steady, totally in tune with the peacefulness of the river, said quietly, "God knows every best way to love us right now in this very instant. Everything He could know beyond that isn't much fun to think about, even for God. So there isn't any reason for Him to want to know more."

Careful and Christian both felt they had just heard something incredibly profound, but Careful wasn't sure what it all meant. So he asked Steady. "Could you explain that?"

"Sure," smiled Steady. "God wants to love us in the way that would be best for us. And of course He wants the best possible love to happen within Himself. So more than anything, He wants to know how to make that happen. The way I figure it, the Trinity wouldn't want to know so much that it would interfere with their enjoyment of one another, or God's enjoyment of responding to our uniquenesses. He wants love and real discussion both with us and within Himself." Careful was amazed by what Steady had said, but finally decided he still wanted a more elaborate answer. So he turned and asked Christian, "What do you think?"

"I think Steady's right," Christian said. "God doesn't want to know everything...take our sins for example. He says He blots them out and forgets them. He doesn't want to know them anymore. So what Steady said makes sense to me."

But Careful persisted, "Come on, Christian! I know you've thought about this. Tell me what you've come up with."

Christian paused a second before answering Careful. "Well, since my talk with the elders, yes, I have put a lot of time on thinking about it! What Steady was saying had to do with omniscience—you know, that big word Mr. Knowsalittle likes to talk about in Sunday school. And there are three ways to think about what God knows. I'll tell you what they are so you can ask God which is right. I don't want to just tell you what I think.

Careful sighed before softly saying, "Okay."

So Christian continued. "The first way of thinking is that God knows everything for all eternity, and it's all on His mind all the time. That means God knows our prayers ahead of time, and exactly what He will do. So He can't respond to us or our prayers in any way that is different from what He had planned. And He cannot think a new thought, because He already knows every thought He will ever think. If He did think a new thought, that would mean He didn't know everything, and in this first view, that would be impossible."

"Not sure I like the sound of that," Careful said dubiously. "It doesn't make sense that God would change from thinking of everything to never having another thought. Why would anyone believe that?"

Christian thought, *Mr. Confident does,* but decided not to mention it. "The second way of thinking is this: God knows everything that can actually be known. In this view, God created us able to make totally free and independent choices, and there's no way to know ahead of time what people will freely choose."

"I see," said Careful. "That's saying there are some things that can't be known, even by God. So if this is right, then God can think new thoughts, and 'cause He can think new thoughts, He can think of the best ways to respond to our prayers and what's happening to us!"

"Right!" Christian replied. "And if God plans to make something specific happen, even far into the future, He can prophesy about it, no problem."

"Makes sense to me," said Careful.

"Hold on!" Christian said. "There's the third way of thinking, and it's sort of like the second. In this way, God can see anything in the future that He chooses to see, which isn't everything, because He doesn't want to look at everything. He simply has no desire to know all our future choices, or even His own. And of course, God plans ahead. He directs history toward what He intends to achieve. But this way, He can think new thoughts and respond to us. And like the second way, He can have His heart broken by the bad things we do. But if something is important to Him, He does look into the future, like knowing Judas was the best choice for what He wanted him to do. And by knowing Peter would deny Him three times, Jesus was able to help Peter get over his pride. So in this way of thinking, God chooses to look into the future enough to know how to enable us to see where we need to change, or know the best way to direct His love for us."

Careful asked, "But why wouldn't God look at everything?"

"Because He wants real people loving Him," Christian replied, "with a real give-and-take love. So instead of looking at all our future choices, He has faith in us. And faith is important to Him. The Bible says faith works through love, and God is love. He even made faith in His Son the way we are saved. It's like we have faith in Him, and He has faith in us. To do this, He can't be snooping and looking ahead at everything, especially our choices about what's right or wrong."

"Besides," Steady chuckled, "there's the contradiction of knowing for sure the finite number of thoughts He will think for an infinite eternity."

Christian laughed and said, "Instead, we view God as having created angels and people in a way that He can see just enough of our future choices to know how to best love us and be responsible in the way He rules over us."

"Oh yeah!" said Steady. "And there are things we know He could know, but simply chooses not to know. Like you said, Christian, He doesn't know any of the sins we have repented of. He's told us that much. He said, 'I, even I, am He who blots out your transgressions for My own sake; And I will not remember your sins.' (Isaiah 43:25) Blotted out means no record of our sins is left."

The three boys began to chuckle at where their logic had taken them. But Careful, trying to be serious and make sense out of what he was hearing, added, "And probably, if God wants to put our sins behind Him for His own sake, He doesn't want to be looking at our future sins either. He just wants to love us the most as He can."

Then Careful thought, *this would explain Lucifer and all the evil that's in the world. It's so out of character for God to deliberately create an evil enemy. The devil was created perfect. He got prideful ideas only afterward. Maybe God just didn't know. Could it be that God only looks ahead at the good that He can do for us?*

Careful thought for another moment about himself. Then he said, "I'm trying to work this out. Here I am, I don't even know half the sins I do. Every once in a while, the Holy Spirit tells me about another one of the stupid ways I treat people. If I ignore Him, I feel awful, because I'm pushing Him away. So I decide not to do that sin anymore. And at that moment, I know God forgives me."

Christian commented, "See? And from that moment He treats you as though you will never sin again… until you do. He really has faith in you."

Slowly, Careful nodded in agreement. "I guess Steady's right. It's a lot more fun for God to not look ahead at me sinning again. I guess He just wants to enjoy loving me right now." Then, looking right at Christian, Careful asked, "Okay! But three ideas about what God knows? How am I supposed to choose?"

"You're supposed to ask God," Christian answered. "But let me give you a hint. Whatever choice God made as to how much He knows, He most likely decided on it before He created angels, when He, the Triune God, was all by Himself."

"You mean He had to start with Himself," Careful commented. "Okay, I know God said He had discussions within the Trinity. There's Jesus's prayer in Gethsemane. So when God was alone, He limited what He knew to the point where He could have relationship and real discussions within Himself. And He made us in a way that we could be part of that."

Thinking out loud, Careful continued. "God loves, and He is love. God wouldn't review sins I repented of or look ahead at my future sins before He loves me. I think I'm ready to ask God what He knows." Careful quietly prayed for a minute. Then he said, "All we know about God is what He tells us. And He tells us that He is love. The most loving thing possible, that's what He would do."

"Yes," said Christian. "That's a good way to figure what God knows. And it will be in total agreement with the Bible."

"Oh yeah!" said Steady. "God is awesome love."

Turning to Steady, Careful asked, "So Steady, how did you figure this out?"

"It's glaringly obvious that God likes to think new thoughts," Steady began. "Every time He responds to us, He gets to think new thoughts, and I think He really likes doing that. But if He already knew what He was responding to, it wouldn't be a response, it would be like the script of a play." Again, Christian and Careful thought they just heard something profound. About that time, Careful felt a nibble. Jerking his pole up, he hooked another fish.

Awhile later, Timid came and joined them. The boys were talking about how much they enjoyed chores that made them work hard and sweat. "Working up a good sweat makes me tired," said Careful, "but it's a good kind of tired. And it helps me to enjoy my time off to go fishing." The other boys agreed that working up a sweat made them feel good and helped them to enjoy other things.

Then Christian said, "I enjoy reading the Bible. That's one of the things that helps me rest."

Timid chimed in, "Rest? You're kidding, right? Reading the Bible is hard! I can't seem to get going with it. Every time I try, I start thinking of something else. So I give up and start doing whatever I was thinking of. So tell me, how do you get started?"

Steady chimed in, "Oh yeah. I remember when I first started reading the Bible. Every time, for the first 15 minutes, I would feel tired, or sick, or I'd remember things I needed to do. My mind just started racing. But I kept at it, and finally that tricky ol' 'getting started' time became shorter and shorter until it was gone. Now I feel like God is with me every time I pick up my Bible to read it." Steady looked serious for a minute. "I think having a hard time reading the Bible is what Pastor Caring calls spiritual warfare!"

Careful said, "Yeah, the same thing happened with me. I thought I was the only one who was having a hard time. But I did what Steady did. I didn't quit. There's probably a lot of people who struggle to study the Bible and just can't get started, without even knowing that there are other Christians going through the same thing. But if you keep at it, you can do it. Don't give up too soon."

"Or," said Christian, "in the little bit you did read, you may have skipped over something you should have paid attention to and obeyed it and done it. The Bible says if you don't put what you read into action, you won't understand much of what you read. That makes it hard to read! So do you know what to do if you get to an impossible commandment, like love your enemy?"

"Yeah," Timid responded. "I just try to get something read before my mind starts wandering, and skip over what I can't do. But I want to know. What can I do?"

"What I do," Christian answered, "is pray and think about what the commandment means to me personally, promise God that I will obey, and tell God that I trust Him to make me able to keep my impossible promise. And I do trust Him. And it's okay to stop reading while you do those things."

"Okay," said Timid. "I'll try again and I won't quit. And I'll stop, talk to God, and think about what every commandment means to me, and promise God to do it. It sounds scary, but I'll do it. And I'll tell God I'm trusting Him, and I won't give up again…It must be working. I think I just promised to promise God I'll read the Bible."

On his way home carrying a string of fish, Careful was still considering what Christian said about omniscience. He prayed,

"Lord, I think it is true. You do love me and I know You really like thinking of new ways to love me. And You do respond to my love for You. Teach me to respond to Your love as You do to mine."

Careful was not the only one who would be headed home that day thinking about the things Christian had said. That same afternoon, while the boys were fishing, Pastor Caring had been out visiting people. He'd decided to talk privately to every member of the church so he could find out how attached they were to the concept of "God is in control of everything that happens." He was thankful that Christian had a number of them suspecting there might be something wrong with such a concept of God. But in his visits, he'd also been discovering that even though people agreed Christian's ideas made sense and made a much more satisfying picture of God, there was one huge problem. Old Mrs. Homebody said it best: "Pastor, when things are hard, I just tell myself, 'Don't worry, God is in control.' And that gives me peace. I just can't bear to think of God not planning and being in control of everything."

Gently, Pastor Caring explained that believing in a God who has control over not just the good but also all the evil in the world should be a cause for insecurity, not for peace. "Think of it this way," he told Mrs. Homebody. "Our security is in knowing God loves us and is always with us even when we go through hard times. There's comfort in knowing that He listens to our prayers and responds to us creatively. There should be no comfort in thinking He causes evil." Mrs. Homebody was still doubtful, however.

Country folk go to bed around 8:30 p.m., so Pastor Caring finished his visiting for the day before eight o'clock. His horse knew the way home so he could concentrate on praying for the people he had visited. *They need to understand the real relationship God wants us to have with Him. It's beyond trusting God is in control. God wants to respond to each one of us in a true loving relationship. God wants fellowship with us.*

The next morning was Wednesday, and Christian was up at first light. After reading a Psalm, he was off to Mr. Helpful's barn, shoveling furiously till the stable was clean. It didn't take long, and it brought in a little bit of cash. But coming home, along the path to his cabin, he saw bear scat and tracks. "Oh no!" Christian said to himself. He ran all the way home and breathed a sigh of relief when he found his food lean-to untouched. *I've got to do something to keep bears out!* he thought. *Not just raccoons.* He stood and looked hard at the cabin and lean-to until he thought of a plan. Then he set to work. First, he cut a whole bunch of stout poles and sharpened them on one end with his hatchet. Then he lashed the poles to the cabin roof rafters using rawhide strips to tie them on so that they extended well beyond the roof eaves. On the lean-to side, the poles came out from the cabin eaves all the way over the lean-to. Onto the lean-to itself, he fastened even more of the sharpened poles. *This setup might not totally stop a bear, but it sure will discourage him,* Christian thought.

Christian finished building his bear defenses that afternoon and had started a fire under his tea kettle when he saw Pastor Caring riding toward him on the trail through the woods to the cabin. "Hello, Pastor!" he shouted cheerfully. "I was just starting to make tea—sit right here and it'll be ready in a jiffy!" Pastor Caring swung off his horse, sat down on one of the chairs Christian had made, and sighed. Christian waited to see what he would say. Finally, after Christian handed him a mug of tea, Pastor Caring began to talk. He explained how folks felt insecure at the thought that God had truly given them free will and did not control everything. "Turns out they really depend on thinking 'God is in control.'" Then Pastor Caring looked at Christian and asked, "How do you think I can help them?"

Christian took a deep breath. Here he was, a skinny eleven-year-old, having known Christ only a few months, giving advice to the pastor. What flashed through his mind was what a humble, godly man Pastor Caring was. Not quite sure what to say, he just started talking. "Either God is in control, or God respects our choices. Both can't be right! But let me see if I understand what the people are saying. They think God doesn't respect the free will He has given us, but is in control of even bad things. And they think God does this so He can bring something good out of everything that is bad. Is that what they think?"

"Yes," said Pastor Caring. "That seems to be it." Christian thought for a minute while Pastor Caring waited patiently. "Hmmm," said Christian. "There's a lot of unrighteousness in the world, but I can't agree that God plans and controls unrighteousness in order to make something good."

"Yes," said Pastor Caring, "but people still cling to Romans 8:28 as a proof text, although they use it out of context. 'And we know that all things work together for good to those who love God, to those who are the called according to His purpose.'"

"Oh yes," said Christian. "People have mentioned that verse to me, too. It just means the bad things that happen now will end, and we will have good things after we die. Verse 28 is in the middle of Paul's discussion of our hope. Verse 18 says something very different from what they're thinking." Christian grabbed his Bible and flipped to Romans 8. "Verse 18 says, 'For I consider that the sufferings of this present time are not worthy to be compared with the glory which shall be revealed in us.' But I usually point out that the verse after verse 28 begins with the word 'for' and have them read verses 29 and 30."

Pastor Caring leaned forward. "Those verses talk about our destiny," he said. "At least, that's how I see it."

"Yes," Christian replied. "Exactly. Those next two verses show that 'His purpose' that is 'good' refers to our being with Him in heaven after we die."

"What worries me," Pastor Caring continued, "is that in other religions, their god controls everything from way up on high. But the true God we worship offers fellowship. That's completely different! Our God is faithful and loving, not far away and manipulative. In good times and tough times, He's right there with us. But I hear people speaking of God as though He were far away and blaming Him for what the devil is doing. I'm not sure what I can say to them."

Christian whistled. "That's pretty serious," he said.

"Yes," said Pastor Caring. "But I can sympathize. I didn't know I was doing that until you pointed it out to me."

Christian responded, "God really does respect our choices and lets us act on them, too. Then we get to have the consequences of pushing Him away. For some people, when they go through this, it helps them repent. So that's another really good reason God has for not controlling everything."

Christian paused for a moment before continuing, as though he were thinking about what he had just said. "Besides, when things are hard, how can we trust God if we think that all along He's been in control over the source of our distress? That's crazy! It's when things are difficult that we need to know for sure what God is really like and how much He loves us. Besides, if people just keep on thinking 'God is in control,' they won't be prepared if something really bad happens."

"Don't be too hard on them." Pastor Caring said sadly. "These are good people, and they do try to trust God to do what is right when things are difficult…but you're right—when something really horrendous happens, many times they don't handle it very well."

"Yes," said Christian. "Really, it comes down to this: they don't see how great God's love is. They don't understand how awfully much God wants to walk with them in their difficulties. He wants to love them, not be up high controlling everything. It isn't 'God is in control.' It's 'Christ loves His bride.' How could we possibly be thinking of God in control of wickedness when we are living in fellowship with Christ and thinking, 'Christ loves His bride'?

"Okay," said Christian, leaping to his feet. "There's only one answer! We've got to help people to really know God's love! I mean really truly know—not just know about." Christian sat down slowly, wondering if Pastor Caring understood what he was trying to say. Pastor Caring said nothing. Finally Christian said, "I'm trying to figure out how people might react to somebody telling them that they don't really know God's love. The problem is that for people to be really close to God—the way God wants it—they will have to be willing to put Him first in everything they do, even in what they think about and what they pray for. Some people might find that a little scary. Even though they are good people and they already show the love of Christ in their lives…I think that once they understand there's so much more to God's love, they'll be as excited to be part of it as we are."

Pastor Caring thought about this. Then he said, "You talk about understanding God's love. What is your understanding of God's love?"

Christian scratched a line on the ground with the stick he was holding. "I'll tell you the path I took to figure it out. I noticed that we have all these songs about how Christ died for our sins. We sing them at church every Sunday." Pastor Caring nodded. Christian went on, "From our point of view, looking up at God, this is only natural. We're thankful, and we sing about what God has done for us. But we don't have any songs from God's point of view. We don't think that way. So one day I tried to imagine what it would be like to look down from His point of view, and here's what I figured out.

"God wouldn't want a relationship with machines or puppets. Jesus wants us to be His bride. I remember how my mother and father loved each other. It was more than just being in the same house. They really shared their lives with each other. I know I had my struggles with choosing to let God really share His life with me. I had to let go of just thinking about what was best for myself and make what was best for others the most important thing in my life. Sometimes that was hard. When old Mr. Grumpy called me 'orphan trash,' it wasn't easy to answer with kindness. I had to stand there while I prayed first, before I said anything. Then God helped me. I could hardly believe what I was saying. I told him, 'Even orphan trash can know God who loves him, and Jesus also loves you. He wants to be part of your life.' Then I asked him how his life would be different if he let Jesus be his Lord. I really felt the love of God for him."

"Yes," said Pastor Caring. "Even as a believer in Christ, you could have reacted in anger and spoken out in an equally rude way. But God wants us to be sure that He's right with us in our ordinary daily life, to be with us when we talk to one another, when we plow our fields and milk our cows. You don't have to be full time working for the Lord or in a monastery. God being with us is made up of every little thing we do every day."

Christian agreed and commented, "Yes, and if we're not careful, we just think we're doing ordinary things, and we forget how much God wants to be part of them." Christian got up, paced around, and sat down again. "You know, those people who just want to feel secure may sincerely think they're trusting God, but in reality, they're thinking of God as up in heaven, pulling strings for reasons they don't understand, while they live their lives in what they think is faith. The weird thing is, this gives them peace. I guess it's because then they don't have to bother finding out what God really thinks. They don't really have to walk in or even trust His love." Christian hesitated. "I hope I'm not being too hard on them. It's just that when I thought about loving God the way He wants, that's what I came to."

Pastor Caring was very quiet. Finally, he said, "You're right. But that's a very hard message to give, telling good people, who really have trusted Christ as their Lord and Savior, that they're living like they're trying to be religious without God. I don't think anyone wants to hear it. Perhaps there's a way to get the word across without getting people on the defensive. I'll have to think about this."

Christian continued, "Let me tell you about something else that helped me to avoid falling into the trap of saying 'God is in control,' instead of trusting in God's love. I was thinking about what it was like for God before creation, when He was living alone in eternity. I thought about how each Person of the Trinity used their almighty power and creativity to do what was best for the Others and what would give Them joy. And not only that, but I realized each Person of the Trinity did this totally unselfishly, without thinking about the cost to Themselves of what They did for Others." Christian stopped and said very slowly and softly, "Then I realized that God's love for me was the same as the love between the Father, Son, and Holy Spirit." Pastor Caring held his breath, wondering what Christian would say next. Christian continued, "God is love and He can never be less than who He is. When I saw that He included me in His perfect love, it left me feeling foolish to be in any way selfish. The message you gave Sunday was just right. But you still have to get people to see that true freedom is to trust and yield to the love of God. It isn't just hunkering down on our own and telling ourselves, 'God is in control' while we keep on living mostly for ourselves." Christian paused and said fervently, "From God's point of view, the whole reason He sent Jesus into the world was so He could have a relationship with us. The last thing He would want is to just control things."

Pastor Caring nodded. Then he said, "Perhaps God foresaw the need to communicate what real relationship with Him is like and gave us marriage. Because of marriage, we understand that merging our lives with someone else is possible. Marriage helps us understand that we can accept the relationship with God that He offers us.

"I've noticed some married couples delight in doing things for one another. They seem very happy in their marriage. They couldn't have that happiness if they resisted one another's love. It took them time to fully realize that the love of the other could be counted on. It seems that it takes us time to come to that realization with God. He wants a relationship with us where we fully realize that the love of Christ can be counted on. He calls this faith."

Christian commented, "I had an advantage. I was someone whom nobody loved. When I came to Christ, I was ready to receive all the love He had for me. I know He will never fail to love me, and He's always looking for a chance to do things for me. Like you said in your sermon, this is a delight to Him. And because I believe it, He lets me share in His delight."

Pastor Caring responded, "Since I've been talking to people about this, I've come to see how very insecure so many people are. But now I get your point. If people understand that God will never fail to do what is best for them every single day, even when outward circumstances are difficult, insecurity would no longer be an issue. I think you're right. What you said reminds me of some verses in 1 Peter. 'The eyes of the Lord are over the righteous, and his ears are open unto their prayers.' and 'Casting all your care upon him; for he cares for you.' I think your strategy of starting by explaining the love of God is a good one. Come to think of it, it's the one I started with myself. I guess it was the Lord, and He knows what He's doing."

"There's one more thing," Christian interjected. "You also have to remember that God is fearless. Think about Genesis 6:6 where God said He repented of having created man. If this is so, what a courageous thing He did in creating us in the first place! We would even call it reckless. According to Titus 1:2, He even promised us eternal life before we were created. According to Scripture, eternal life is more than living forever. It's like it says in John 3:16, the eternal life God promised is God's own life, shared with us forever."

Pastor Caring slapped his knee and exclaimed, "Yes! And like you said at the elders' meeting, since we weren't created at the time of the promise, it must have been a promise made within the Trinity."

"Right," said Christian. "I think of it as like an engagement vow on the part of the Son. It's a commitment that He will never break.

"After the promise was made, we were created, and then things went sour. The whole earth became filled with such violence that maybe even God considered His commitment a little reckless. He said He was sorry that He had made man. But He still did not flinch. He held true to His promise. That's what unconditional love does. That's who God is.

"The more I look at it, the more I see that God's love throws caution to the wind. Like you said in your sermon, His love for us does not depend on us. The only power we have over His love is that we can reject it. The only power we have over His doing what is best for us is that we can push his love away and go our own way. And even though He applies pressure on each person to persuade them to accept His love, in the end, He honors each person's decision.

"In Revelation 21:8, God lists the people who will not be in heaven. First on the list is the 'fearful.' I think this is because 'perfect love casts out fear.' God not only loves fearlessly, but He expects us to do the same, because here on earth, we are ambassadors for heaven. Lost people can see what God's love is like by seeing it in us. Scripture says,

Let nothing be done through selfish ambition or conceit, but in lowliness of mind let each esteem others better than himself. Let each of you look out not only for his own interests, but also for the interests of others.'

"That takes fearlessness. That takes total trust in God's love to help us live that way. That takes saying to ourselves, 'Christ loves His bride.' And oh, how faith in His love helps us become Christ centered. In this life, we're not promised an easy time, we're promised persecution. That would be hard to face without knowing His love. With God's love in my heart, I can go through anything this life can throw at me." Suddenly, Christian noticed the coals under his teakettle had gone out and said, "Would you like more tea before it gets completely cold?"

"Thank you, I would," said Pastor Caring. "And I don't mind if it's cold." Christian poured the tea and brought out two tin plates, forks, and some smoked fish. Pastor Caring smiled and said, "And let's take some time to pray about this. I agree with your conclusions, but I have no idea how to tell it to anyone!"

Tea and smoked fish were an odd combination, but Pastor Caring found it was actually tasty. After the snack, Christian and the pastor prayed together, then Pastor Caring began to think about what to tell his flock. "I remember when I was a younger believer," he said. "I looked at the needs of others and was also tempted to avoid getting involved because it made me feel insecure in myself. I didn't have much confidence in the love of God. Even though I was saved and born again, there was still a part of me that wanted to live independently from Him. I remember even saying one time, 'I know the Lord is going to return, but I hope it doesn't happen anytime soon. I've got some things I want to do first.' But God kept working on me till I changed my mind. Actually, He changed my heart so much that I laid aside my big ambitions and became a poor country pastor."

"You've answered the question I came here with, 'How can I help people who depend on thinking "God is in control"?' I will talk about the way God constantly cares for us. He watches over us in order to take advantage of every opportunity to do what is best for us. We have faith that this is true to a degree. But God wants more from us. That's the challenge, to make people see themselves loved by God, living their lives with Him."

Suddenly, Pastor Caring realized that even though he'd only stated the obvious, it sounded completely impossible and unrealistic. He commented, "Where people seem satisfied with the bit of God's love that they know and find themselves clinging to shreds of independence from Him, I will trust the Holy Spirit to answer every objection. It's not up to me. It's up to Him." Overcome with emotion, he prayed, "Oh, Lord Jesus, I do offer myself to you to answer all their objections that have to be answered." After a moment of silence, Pastor Caring stood up and said, "Thank you, Christian. You've been a great help."

Climbing back on to his patient horse, Pastor Caring rode to the church, stabled the horse, and went straight to his library. After closing the door, he fell to his knees. He felt an urgent need to be right with God so he would be able to help the people of his congregation. The sun was setting before he had finished praying.

It was only a short walk to his home, but Pastor Caring arrived late for supper. Mrs. Caring was worried about him and asked where he was. He said he had been praying. "I had to stop by the throne of God and ask for help in time of need." Then he added, "I asked God to help me understand His total commitment to love us. Then I had to give myself to Him anew, asking Him to help me totally commit myself to love others, holding nothing back. I felt so inadequate to the task of leading others to the understanding of the immensity of God's love. I prayed for His help to explain it, even though I barely understand it myself. When I got up from praying, I just knew the Holy Spirit would give me the grace to share with the others a full understanding of God's love, and that this was the very thing He desired them to have."

That night, lying on his bed, Pastor Caring prayed for individuals he had recently visited. He remembered a conversation with a widow who lost her husband in the smallpox epidemic. She said, "Part of me is still angry with God for allowing it to happen." Pastor Caring thought about what he had said in response, *We're all part of humanity, which pushed God away. God was patient with us before we opened our hearts to Him and were saved. Now it's our turn to be patient. Yes, it is hard. The world we live in where people want to live independently from God is a hard world to live in. Even good people suffer and die. But unless people see what it is like to live independently from God, no one would want to turn to Him. The pain you feel is only part of the pain God feels. In the meantime, we have to let the world see the pain and suffering that being independent from Him leads to.*

But even when the widow understood that God needed to let all humanity see the consequences of their rebellion, in order to help them repent, that didn't change her mind. She said that God should have made an exception for her husband. But when Pastor Caring gently pointed out that the ability to love her husband was something He created in her, she began to weep uncontrollably.

*What did she say later? I remember. She said, "I suddenly realized that when my husband died, God's heart was broken too. I felt His pain. As I cried, I felt like God and I were crying together. And I was also crying because I was so sorry I'd stopped loving Him, which then caused Him more pain, and yet He kept loving me anyway."* Pastor Caring lay there a while longer, then he thought, *It seems that God wants more than I do that His children open their hearts to His love. It was the Holy Spirit who changed her heart. Knowing God's heart is broken because of what we have done to ourselves is what I have to talk about next Sunday.* Pastor Caring prayed for the widow and finally fell asleep.

Christian also lay on his bed that night praying. He prayed for Pastor Caring and the church. When he was finished, he closed his eyes and was soon asleep. Hours later, in the middle of the night, he was awakened by the sound of scratching coming from the food lean-to. When he got up to investigate, he discovered a bear cub trying to get in. The cub was small enough to go under the long sharpened poles. Christian looked around and didn't see anything but dark woods. Then he stepped sideways between the poles, grabbed the cub by the scruff, backed out with him, and gave that cub a good toss. It landed on its feet and was off like a shot into the darkness.

Christian took a few steps toward the cabin door when he saw a large dark shape rushing at him like a freight train with a full head of steam. Mama bear! There was no time to either reach the cabin door or to roll under the sharpened poles. Christian braced himself, determined to fight for his life.

[1] Psalms 147:11, 149:4
[2] Genesis 1:26, 3:22; 18:17-33: Exodus 32:7-14; Titus 1:2;
[3] 1 Corinthians 13:5; Acts 3:19
[4] Matthew 9:36; Mark 1:41; Luke 7:13
[5] Revelation 21
[6] Ezekiel 6:9; Psalms 78:40; Isaiah 63:10
[7] Galatians 5:6; 1 John 4:8
[8] Hebrews 11:6; Ephesians 2:8
[9] Genesis 4:7
[10] 101 Corinthians 13:5
[11] Hebrews 2:14; Matthew 13:36-39
[12] Ezekiel 28:15; Isaiah 14:12-14
[13] Exodus 33:5
[14] Habakkuk 1:13
[15] John 15:15, 16:23-24
[16] Genesis 1:26, 3:22; Titus 1:2
[17] Jeremiah 9:24; Deuteronomy 29:20; Psalms 147:11, 149:4
[18] Mark 4:13-25
[19] 1 Corinthians 1:9
[20] Job 32:6-9
[21] Psalms 7:9-17, 145:17; Romans 3:5-8, 6:1-2
[22] Romans 8:9, 16, 35-39, John 17:23, 1 John 1:3
[23] Psalms 119:67-72
[24] 1 Peter 1:5-8
[25] Psalms 149:4; Colossians 3:17, 23; 1 Thessalonians 5:17-18
[26] John 17:23
[27] 1 Peter 3:12
[28] 1 Peter 5:7
[29] John 17:3; 1 John 5:11, 20
[30] Genesis 6:5-6
[31] 1 John 4:18
[32] Philippians 2:3-4; Matthew 5:42-45
[33] Psalms 5:11-12, 11:7
[34] Hebrews 4:16
[35] 1 John 5:14-15

# 9 FALL

Just before reaching him, the bear suddenly stopped. Only inches away from Christian, it barked a throaty, foul-smelling bark. Just the presence of this huge animal that could easily rip his arms off made Christian step backward and almost fall over. For a few seconds, the boy and the bear stared at each other. Then the mother and cub disappeared into the night.

Still shaking inside, Christian went back to bed. After thanking the Lord that he was still alive, he remembered what Mr. Mountainman told him about what to do if attacked by a grizzly bear. "If the bear attacks you, just roll up and play dead. If you're lucky, the bear will think you really are dead. Then he'll go about his business, unless he's hungry. But a black bear will usually just bluff charge." Then Christian thought, *I'm so glad there aren't any grizzlies around here. I don't know what I'd do if that wasn't a bluff charge. When I get to heaven, I'm going to ask Jesus if He had anything to do with my being alive right now.* Then he remembered what Mr. Helpful said about bears having sensitive noses. The ammonia had long ago evaporated from the cans around his food lean-to. There was still plenty of ammonia left in the gallon jug. So when morning came, he topped off each can.

That Sunday, Christian told Steady about the bear. Just the thought of a bear barking in his face sent shivers up Steady's spine. Wide-eyed, he said, "Weren't you scared?"

"The only time I was more scared was when my parents died," Christian admitted. Then he said, "I think the bear was also scared so maybe she won't be back. The whole thing was no fun for her either, even though she proved herself to be the alpha bear." They both laughed at that, but Steady was relieved that his friend was all right.

When Pastor Caring got up to do his sermon, Christian noticed how tired he looked. *Pastor's been really working hard,* Christian thought to himself. And he was right. Pastor Caring had been out visiting every day, putting in eighty-hour weeks. On top of that, he had spent more time in prayer than ever. Little by little, the congregation had begun to accept the idea that God really was loving them and wanting to do things with them every minute of every day. Even plowing their fields and doing their chores became something they shared with their Lord. Then slowly, their expectation of His presence with them developed into making the decision to love others as God loved them. Many of the church members also began to realize that they were representatives of heaven. And for some, their commitment to be true representatives of God's loving character grew until they were able to see that in a way, they already were in heaven. As Christian predicted, their feelings of insecurity were gone. They felt more secure in God's love than they could have imagined possible.

So many things were doing well. But Christian felt a sadness because Mr. Confident was still hanging on to the idea that God had the right to do as He pleases, and it pleased Him not to love everybody. Mr. Confident still said, "Before people are born, God predestines them to either heaven or hell." Christian was very grieved to hear this and prayed every day for Mr. Confident to believe the full measure of God's love.

Finally, Christian had an idea. Paying a visit at a time when Mr. Confident would be home, he knocked on the door. Soon, he and Mr. Confident were launched into a discussion of theology. Finally, Christian said, "Honestly, do you have even one verse of Scripture to support what you're saying? Is there even one verse that when studied supports your determinist theology?"

Mr. Confident said, "I've got hundreds of verses. But I see no profit in discussing them. You will never convince me to change my mind." Christian reached into his pocket and pulled out a ten dollar gold piece, laid it on the table, and said, "This is yours if you can show me one verse that can prove your point."

Mr. Confident knew how long it would take Christian to earn that much money. Of course, he would never actually take Christian's hard-earned dollars, but he was impressed with the sacrifice Christian was willing to make. So he named a verse, then reached out his hand as if he were going to take the coin. "Wait," Christian said laughingly. "The verse has to be studied and proven that it says what you say it says." Then Christian gave a clear, logical explanation of the verse, an explanation which showed that it was actually saying something completely different from Mr. Confident's interpretation. Mr. Confident was caught by surprise. He did not anticipate how well Christian could do. So Mr. Confident named another verse. One by one they went through verses (which are found in Appendix A of this book), and many more.

Finally, Mr. Confident ran out of verses, still unconvinced. After a few minutes of silence, Christian said, "God is always right here, loving you and instantly responding to your love for Him. He watches over you and He is waiting for the next opportunity you give Him to show His love for you." After a few more minutes of silence, Christian thanked Mr. and Mrs. Confident for their hospitality and enjoyable conversation, picked up his gold piece, and went home.

Though Christian disagreed with Mr. Confident, he thought of him as part of his church family, all of whom he had grown to love. It was with anticipation that Christian looked forward to Sundays so he could be with everyone there. And he couldn't help but notice that the church was growing spiritually in their love for God.

This spiritual growth was even becoming noticeable in the Sunday church services. In the past, there always was a short prayer and testimony time before the sermon. Most of the prayers were for the sick or injured and testimonies were about bits of "good luck" that had happened to people that week. But little by little, Sunday after Sunday, more church members were praying for people right there in the town to find Christ. Testimony time was different too. People started talking about changes God was making in their lives. Then one Sunday, an amazing thing happened during the prayer time. A man began confessing his bad attitudes and sin, asking God to change him. Others joined in. It was like the Holy Spirit took over. His presence was felt by everyone. But it didn't stop there. The next Sunday at testimony time, people stood up and told how God had delivered them from years of bondage to selfish attitudes and self-centered thinking. Pastor Caring was amazed and overjoyed. He let the testimonies continue until there was hardly any time for his sermon.

The next Sunday, testimony time went well past when church normally would end, and Pastor Caring didn't preach at all. He knew the ladies of the congregation had all their Sunday dinner preparations set for church finishing on time, so he didn't dare keep them for another half hour. But on Monday, he got an idea. The church had a fair-sized fellowship hall and a kitchen. Why not move Sunday dinner to the church? He approached the Tuesday morning ladies' Bible study with the idea and they just took it and ran. In no time at all, they divided into teams. Each team was responsible for a part of the dinner. Ladies whose houses were close to the church volunteered their kitchens. Before Pastor Caring knew what was happening, everything was organized. Pastor Caring did arrange for men to help move tables and carry things.

The following Sunday, it all came together. It took only twelve minutes from the time the service ended to when everything, including the food, was in place. The ladies had spread the word about the dinner at church, so everyone stayed.

But what astounded Pastor Caring was that at each table, people were not discussing the usual topics of farming, business, and families. They were talking about the sermon, what they had been reading in the Bible, and what God was doing in them. After dinner, no one wanted to go home. They began singing, interspersed with prayer, sharing from the Bible, and giving more testimonies. Finally, as chore time for anyone with animals drew near, they had to leave for home. Pastor Caring noticed this and realized he had to call an end to the meeting. Someone shouted, "Let's do this again next week." There was chorus of "yes" and "yeah." Pastor Caring said, "I'll make it official. We will do this again next week." As people rode away, he could hear them still singing.

The next Tuesday, Pastor Caring visited the ladies' Bible study again and was greeted by a unanimous joyful encouragement. "Let's do this every Sunday!" they told him. Pastor Caring happily agreed.

Soon, everyone in the valley noticed the change in the church. Attracted by the obvious love and joy of the Christians, they began to ask questions about what it all meant. The congregation began to grow.

Christian noticed how the people of the valley were suddenly interested in knowing Christ. He thought about his own conversion and tried to make sense out of what happened to him. In his heart was a hunger to understand how to communicate the gospel and how to best help those coming to Christ. It was a yearning that stayed with him from day to day.

Christian was up early Tuesday morning. His trap yielded a couple of fish for breakfast. The autumn chill was in the air as he quickly built a fire for his tea kettle. Last year, he had built a rock wall behind his fire ring to reflect the heat. Sitting with his feet on the fire ring rocks and enjoying the warmth as the sun slowly rose higher, he turned his thoughts to the Bible for an answer to his questions about the best way to explain the gospel. He wanted to go deeper, to understand what he was doing so he could reach more people.

*Pastor Caring is right*, he thought. *The whole Bible from beginning to end is about God's wanting to put our sins behind Him. He promised in front of Adam to send a Savior and kept right on going from there.* Christian sat quietly for a while, thinking of examples from the Bible which showed God's eagerness to forgive people. Then he thought about the times when God had to let people experience the consequences of their sin. *Look at how God treated Judah right up to the time when they were taken away to Babylon as prisoners,* he said to himself. *He kept telling the people that if they would just repent, He would forgive all they had done.* Then Christian thought about King Manasseh and turned to 2 Chronicles 33 to review this example of God's love and justice at work.

He (Manasseh) did evil in the sight of the Lord, according to the abominations of the nations whom the Lord had cast out before the children of Israel...So Manasseh seduced Judah and the inhabitants of Jerusalem to do more evil than the nations whom the Lord destroyed before the children of Israel.

*Whoa, he was one bad king,* Christian sighed. *But God still kept on trying to get him to repent.*

And the Lord spoke to Manasseh and his people, but they would not listen. Therefore the Lord brought upon them the captains of the army of the king of Assyria, who took Manasseh with hooks, bound him with bronze fetters and carried him off to Babylon.

Christian thought, *At this point in the story, I might rejoice in God's justice. But God was not rejoicing. He was doing what He had to do, but He was not rejoicing. One look at the end of the story and you know what God was really thinking.*

Now when he was in affliction, he implored the Lord his God, and humbled himself greatly before the God of his fathers, and prayed to Him. And He received his entreaty, heard his supplication, and brought him back to Jerusalem into his kingdom. Then Manasseh knew that the Lord was God.

*I believe God rejoiced at Manasseh's repentance,* Christian reasoned. *To simply forgive Manasseh was all He really needed to do, and maybe give him some comfort in his exile would be nice, too. But God went way beyond that. He restored Manasseh to his kingdom. Talk about above and beyond and way over the top! God's love and mercy is never a half way measure. Maybe God's generosity with Manasseh was because God was rejoicing at his changed heart. Like the shepherd with the lost sheep.* Christian took his kettle from the fire to let the tea steep while he fried his fish.

Sitting back in the chair while the fish were sizzling in the frying pan, he thought, *It's God's love that attracts people to Him. This is what I have to talk about when I tell people about Jesus. When people see God's heart of love, they will get lots of encouragement to want to be like Him. And wanting to do things God's way was what Manasseh wanted when he repented. This is the same as in the New Testament! God looks for people who deep down inside want to do His will, who want to be like Him. Then He saves them like He saved Manasseh. It doesn't matter that we're not very good at actually doing God's will. God looks at our hearts before He saves us.*

After transferring the fish to a tin plate and pouring himself some hot tea, Christian thought, *Yes, I want to help people know Jesus, and I have all the pieces of the puzzle on how to do it, but something seems missing. And the other problem is, I don't know how to put the pieces together. What order should they go in?* Christian finished eating the first fish, and then he thought, *Maybe the place to start is to help people want to do things God's way. Wanting to do things God's way instead of insisting on our own way is what the Bible calls repentance. Talking about the wonderful change God would make in people's lives is what I have been doing. Maybe I have been doing it right. The hope that Jesus could change them did make people want Him. And seeing the change in the Christians has been making people in town ask questions. I think people are starting to see that God could change them too. That's why they've been asking questions and coming to church. And they're getting saved, because the Holy Spirit finally has something He can work with, in their minds and in their hearts.* Christian paused. He knew he was on to something. *That's it!* he thought. *When people want to be like Jesus, then the Holy Spirit can give them faith. Yes, it's all about what the Holy Spirit does. That's the missing puzzle piece. I think I put too much trust in myself, doing it right. But without the Holy Spirit, I'm just saying words.*

Christian raised his eyes and prayed, "Heavenly Father, I believe you want to save everyone who is lost. While the Holy Spirit works in their hearts to want You, I trust that He will give me the right words to convince them of Your wonderful love, so they might be persuaded to really want You And I trust You to help me to live in a way that people will see You in me."

Christian read his Bible until the rising sun shown directly on his cabin. Then he washed his breakfast dishes and went for a morning swim. He was used to the cold water and found it a great way to start the day. As he swam, he thought, *I have to be able to put God's love into words that I can tell people.*

That afternoon, Steady came to visit. He wanted to go for a hike up Hermon's Peak, a mountain nearby. Christian agreed, because he found that he could think better when he was walking, and he still had a lot to think about. The trail the boys took climbed steadily up the steep hillside. Suddenly, Steady stopped. There on the path stood an enormous black bear, acting like it owned the trail. Steady turned to Christian and suggested they had better back off and find another way to go. But Christian knew about black bears and was in the mood to show off. He said, "Not to worry." Stamping aggressively toward the bear, Christian shouted, "I'm the alpha bear. Go on, get out of here." After an amazed look, the bear huffed and grunted, and then it took off running. For almost a minute, the boys could hear it crashing through the forest, while they stood on the trail cheering and laughing.

"Black bears are like cats," said Christian. "They're easily frightened. If they think you're more easily frightened than they are, they won't be afraid of you. But if they see you acting like an alpha bear, they always run away. That is, if they're not cornered or they're not a mama bear and you've given their cub a toss." Remembering Christian's encounter with a mama bear, Steady said, "Yeah." A verse came to Christian's mind as he thought about how quickly bears run away when people let them know who's in charge, *Submit yourselves therefore to God. Resist the devil, and he will flee from you.*

There was grass on the top of the mountain and the boys had an unobstructed view of the surrounding mountains and valley below. The trees were decked out in brilliant autumn hues, so that it almost looked as if an artist had been painting the mountainsides. Steady was very quiet on the walk back down, and that gave Christian a chance to finish considering what he was going to say to people about how to know Christ. Now that he had something figured out, he found himself longing to put his plan into action and tell someone about God's love. When the boys got back to Christian's cabin, they were both hungry and devoured some dried venison and cornbread. Then Christian said, "Let's go down to the town square."

"Why?" asked Steady. Picking up his Bible, Christian continued, "I want to talk to people about Jesus!" Steady just shook his head.

He wasn't surprised at anything Christian did, but he enjoyed the fun of seeing Christian's latest ideas in action. The boys soon arrived in town. Christian didn't hesitate. Crunching through the carpet of fallen red and yellow leaves, he walked right up a man sitting on a bench and said, "Hello. Could I talk to you for a minute?"

"Sure," the man said.

"Have you ever heard of being born again?" asked Christian.

Oh yes," he replied.

What do you think it means?" Christian asked.

"Starting over with God, or something like that," the man replied.

Suddenly, Christian was aware of a crowd gathering. Steady had started telling other people on the square that his friend was talking to someone about how to find God and they might want to listen. Christian turned back to the man on the bench and continued, "It means Christ died for your sins and offers you forgiveness. He rose from the dead and offers to come into your life and change the attitude of your heart to become the kind of person God wants to live with forever. Does that sound like a good offer?"

"Yes. It's a wonderful offer," the man said.

"If you had Christ come into your life to change you, what do you think He would change?" Christian asked.

The man hesitated. He was amazed at the boldness and yet the kindness of this gangling almost teenage boy. Finally he said, "I would be nicer to my family…and I wouldn't drink so much."

"Knowing that's what He would change, do you want to be that kind of person?" Christian asked.

"I've tried to change. No luck. I guess I am what I am," the man responded.

Christian quickly responded, "It's a change Jesus does with you. Inviting Him into your life means you have a real relationship with Him, and you change to be like Him, but you do it together with Him. Is this what you want?"

The man laughed and said, "I'll have to think about that one."

Then Christian turned to those gathered around him and said, "Every time we do something that hurts somebody, we have to first harden our heart against them. Even if it's something small like gossip or calling a person a name, it makes no difference. We still have to harden our heart. And afterward, even weeks, months, and years later, some of that hardness remains. This is true of each of us.

"If you keep on living this way, hardening your heart bit by bit, after a while, you can gossip, be easily angered, and do all kinds of things that hurt other people, and you won't feel anything. But God has a solution. Christ died for your sins and offers you forgiveness. He rose from the dead and offers to soften the hardness and put love in your heart. It's what the Bible calls being born again. It's being born into a relationship with God, a give-and-take relationship that is real. With the Holy Spirit, working as a team, you truly live a life of caring for others. It's something you do with God. Does this make sense to you?"

Someone nearby said, "Yes. Others have tried to tell me about Jesus and I didn't understand. But this does make sense." The others nodded.

"Jesus will soften your heart, you will even treat other people with love, as though they were more important than yourself, and you will have friendship with God. Is this what you want?" Christian asked.

Even the man on the bench said yes. Christian continued, "The Bible says, 'For whosoever shall call upon the name of the Lord shall be saved.' The word 'saved' is what I'm talking about, to have the selfishness taken out of your life and instead have a relationship with God where He teaches you how to do what's best for others. The hard part of this Bible verse, 'For whosoever shall call upon the name of the Lord shall be saved,' is the word 'Lord.' It means that Christ is the one you obey. It means you really do give Him permission to change you. Is this what you want?"

Some of the crowd were silent, but most of the people still said yes, so Christian continued, "If this is what you want, you can do something about it right now. I'll help you. We'll do exactly what this verse says. I'll say the words and you say them after me, but remember you're talking to God."

Christian led them in a sinner's prayer and challenged them to show that they really meant what they prayed by coming to church on Sunday. He told them when Sunday school began and where to find the new believers class. Then he asked if there were any questions.

The man on the bench said, "Aren't you the orphan kid who lives by the river?"

"That's me," Christian replied.

"I knew your parents. They would be proud of you. So help me God, I'll be there on Sunday. And if God is merciful, I'll bring my family."

Everyone in the crowd, even the ones who'd refused to participate, knew that this was a special moment. Christian didn't know what else to do, so he prayed for them and started for home. Steady told him that nine people had prayed the sinner's prayer. Christian realized that a miracle had taken place. Just the same, he wondered how many of them would be at church next Sunday. Then he realized the sun was starting to drop below the treetops.

Steady said, "It's getting late. Why don't you come to my house for supper?" Christian had come to love Mr. and Mrs. Friendly as if they were his real parents. "I'd like that," he replied. "Are you sure it's okay and you'll have enough food?"

"My mother said you have an open invitation to come anytime. She's been wanting to tell you that for a while, but didn't know how. So she asked me to tell you."

Christian felt the joy of being loved.

The next Sunday, twenty-five new people showed up for Sunday school and church. Christian need not have doubted. He recognized some of them from the group at the square. They had brought their families. The man who was sitting on the bench was also there with his wife, two girls, and a boy. *The church is going to be packed,* Christian thought. *This is going to be a church service like these new people have never seen before. And once they see what God is doing, I think they're going to bring others.*

Mr. Friendly directed the crowd to the new believer's class led by Mr. Evangelist who was amazed and delighted to see so many people. He had them write down their names and where they lived, because he wanted to visit them all. But he did think to himself, *How will I ever manage to follow up on so many people all at the same time?*

Pastor Caring took one look at the bulging new believer's class and thought to himself, *What will we do when all these people move on to be in the adult Bible study class? I'd better figure something out.*

The next morning, Pastor Caring came riding over to Christian's cabin. It was a cold day, and soon, he and Christian were sitting close to Christian's little tin stove. "Well, Christian, looks like we've got a sister problem to the big problem of how to fit everybody into the church," said Pastor Caring. And then he described how Mr. Evangelist told him that the new believer's class was getting too big, and he wanted to divide it into three parts. "Seems there are some folks who still have questions and they're taking up too much class time," said Pastor Caring. "So I decided to take those folks to a separate class, get to know their questions, visit them in their homes, and do everything I can to help them. But I've been thinking about the third group who are ready to move on."

Christian was a bit puzzled. "But what about the adult class?" he asked. "Pastor Caring paused, and looked serious. "I was thinking of Mr. Knowsalot," he said. "The problem is Mr. Knowsalot tends to go into minutia that only a seasoned Christian could relate to, and the class members he has right now really enjoy that. But..." Christian spoke up, "But what about the brand-new Christians who are moving up from the new believer's class?" Pastor Caring looked at Christian. Then he said, "That's where you come in. I think you'd be perfect for teaching a new class. Being young, you wouldn't intimidate anyone. But you've got some iron in your backbone. No one's going to push you around. You know your Bible. The opportunity is yours if you're up to it."

Christian was quietly looking down and was thinking. Finally, he said, "I don't think I can teach like other people. They seem to get into all the details that are in the Bible. I'm more interested in the main idea. I always want to know the big picture of what God is saying. How He says it is not what I'm too interested in."

"Yes," said Pastor Caring. "I knew you would be perfect. New believers don't need all that detail stuff. What you described is just what's needed."

Christian was still worried and hesitantly said, "I'll give it a try. If I get into trouble, I'll ask for some help."

"Splendid," said Pastor Caring. "I'm there for you if you need anything. What would you like to start with?"

"Well, I've been reading and thinking about Romans," Christian said. "I wrote down some notes about what Paul was trying to do. It's not about details. It's about the main ideas he was thinking."

Pastor Caring thought about the two-inch thick commentary on Romans that sat on his library shelf, but he simply said, "Yes. Romans would be good. Come Sunday, be ready to start teaching the class."

---

Hebrews 12:22-24; Philippians 3:20
Isaiah 55:7; Micah 7:19
Luke 15:4-7
Matthew 7:21; John 7:16-17; Luke 23:42-43
Luke 24:46-47; Acts 26:20
James 4:7
Romans 10:13

# 10 BURSTING AT THE SEAMS

The next Sunday, twenty-five new people showed up for Sunday school and church. Christian recognized some of them from the group at the square, and they brought their families. The man who was sitting on the bench was there with his wife, two girls, and a boy. *The church is going to be packed,* Christian thought. *This is going to be a church service like these new people have never seen before. And once they see what God is doing, I think they're going to bring others.*

Mr. Friendly directed the crowd to the new believer's class led by Mr. Evangelist who was amazed and delighted to see so many. He had them write down their names and where they lived, because he wanted to visit them all. But he did think to himself, *How will I ever manage to follow up on so many people all at the same time?*

Pastor Caring took one look at the bulging new believer's class and thought to himself, *What will we do when all these people move on to be in the adult Bible study class? I'd better figure something out.*

After the service Pastor Caring asked the elders to stay in the church for a short meeting. He asked Christian to also stay. Then he said to Christian, "As of now, I'm making you an elder. I don't care what your age is. You qualify!" Christian gulped and said softly, "Yes, sir."

Pastor Caring looked tired. "This church is bursting at the seams," he said. "We're growing so fast, it's hard to keep up with helping all these new folks. Some of them are coming with problems. I've spent hours counseling, and I'm exhausted. At the rate we're growing, we'll outgrow this building in a month. We're going to have to go to two services. This is not going to be popular, and it's not going to be easy. I have no idea what to do with the Sunday dinner and the fellowship after the service. I'm open to suggestions."

Mr. Friendly said, "Our time after church is a blessing from heaven." There was general agreement with this. But everyone knew that the Sunday dinner seating had packed out the fellowship hall. Winter was coming and moving outside was not an option. With cold and snow on the way, there was no time to build anything to expand the church, and there wasn't time to even plan what would be needed.

Everyone was silent for a minute. Going through each of their minds was the thought that the growth came about because they as a church decided to emphasize the love of God and their responsibility to conform to His love. They wanted to preserve that emphasis.

Christian had been thinking about this problem since early that morning, so he broke into the silence by saying, "There is a solution. We can do like the early church did. There were a lot of them, and they didn't have big meeting places. There are nine of us here. Eight of us have fair-sized houses. There are many others who also have fair-sized houses. Suppose we divide adults in the church into groups of 12, like the Lord had. Then we count how many groups that gives us. For example, if there were 96 adults in the church, that would give us 8 groups of 12. Then one week out of every month, one-fourth of those groups would meet as house churches. That could cut the number of people meeting in this building by a fourth and give us more time till spring comes and we can make the church building bigger." Christian smiled at himself. He knew he was showing off with the math that Careful had taught him.

Mr. Knowsalittle asked, "What about the fifth week?"

"We can work that out," Pastor Caring interrupted. "The groups could rotate the fifth week among themselves or something. Let's think about the idea itself. What do you all think?"

To Christian's amazement, Mr. Knowsalittle said, "I like the idea. I think it's the only thing that would work."

Pastor Caring said, "Okay, let's give this idea to the Lord." They all bowed their heads, and one by one, they prayed, giving Christian's idea to the Lord. It was a custom among the elders to do this and then wait awhile when they had an important decision to make.

Pastor Caring said, "I know we're all hungry, but one more thing before we have dinner…I need to talk about visiting all those new folks. 6:30 Thursday night we'll all meet at the church for some training on how to do follow-up visits to people who've started coming to church. You'll need to bring notebooks to take down the information because you may have to teach it. Bring your wives if you can, and anyone else you know who would be willing to help. I apologize for the short notice, but Mr. Evangelist and I are in over our heads and have to multiply ourselves quickly.

"I know we're all ready for dinner, so let's go now, but continue praying about Christian's idea. We'll meet back here at 6:30 tonight and discuss what the Lord has shown us." On coming into the fellowship hall, they were happy to see the ladies had saved plates of food for them. Christian, who loved these Sunday dinners, thought, *Oh yes, and I'll be back for more.*

That evening, they all came back and Mr. Hospitality brought a bag of warm cookies Mrs. Hospitality had just baked. After a round of prayer, they shared their thoughts. Everyone liked the "house church" idea, and no one liked the idea of two services. The only concern was that people might not want to go to a house church. They also decided the new people should come to the church for six months before being asked to join with a house church.

Pastor Caring said, "Every Sunday, I will announce which home Bible studies will be meeting as a church the following Sunday. I know all the Bible study leaders, and they can handle the change. You need to talk about it, beginning with those at your table for dinner today. You may need to plead with and lean on everyone to go to their house church when it's their turn. Everyone knows the squeeze we're in. When we ask them to do this sacrifice, not for themselves, but for the Lord, I think they will attend their house church. You may have to lay it on thick about how they would feel if they knew they displaced one visitor who could not fit into the building. It will be a tough sell, and it will take all of us to promote it." Then Pastor Caring gave each of them the names of a couple of home Bible study leaders to visit and explain what they planned to do.

Before leaving, Pastor Caring said to Christian, "I'd like to go with you on one of your visits if it's all right with you." Christian said, "I'll be happy to have you along."

Tuesday morning, Christian hurried to town and found Pastor Caring in his library. As they walked over to the stable, Christian was amazed to see two horses saddled and ready to go. "Do you know how to ride, son?" asked Pastor Caring. Christian stared at the horses and shook his head. "No?" said Pastor Caring. "Well, I thought that might be the case, so I've got good old Nelly here for you. She's a fine, wise animal. Here, I'll show you how to get up there on the saddle." Somewhat awkwardly, Christian stuck his foot in the stirrup and managed to pull himself up on Nelly's back. Pastor Caring chuckled, "Now you just trust Nelly. She'll know what to do.

If you want to stop, pull the reins back. If you want her to go, give a slight nudge with your heels." As it turned out, there was little for Christian to do; Nelly just followed Pastor Caring's horse.

They were soon at Mr. Courteous's house. When Mrs. Courteous saw them, she stepped out the kitchen door, put her fingers in her mouth, and out came a shrill whistle. Mr. Courteous then came bounding across the field. Christian thought, *I wish I knew how to whistle like that.* Soon, they were all sitting around the kitchen table, drinking hot tea.

Pastor Caring said, "Christian and I have something we wanted to tell you about," then he let Christian do all the talking for a while. Christian loved talking to people. He explained what was happening and which week the Courteous family would have church and Sunday dinner at their house.

Then Pastor Caring turned to Mr. Courteous and said, "When the group meets for Sunday church at your house, I'd like you to be in charge, and that can even include your group having a communion service." Mr. Courteous stared in amazement, and then he started to laugh. "This should be fun," he said. "Me, in charge of a church."

Pastor Caring, who loved being a pastor, laughed heartily and said, "I know you can handle this. You'll do fine."

Meanwhile, Christian was thinking, "Pastor Caring has the best job in the whole world. All he has to do is visit with folks. Maybe I'd like to be a pastor when I'm old enough." As they were riding away from the Courteous's farm, he mentioned this to Pastor Caring who again laughed heartily and said, "It would be my pleasure to have you join me on my visits any time you want. And I'll teach you everything I know. But I must say this: there's a lot more to being a pastor than just visiting folks."

Christian did indeed start regularly going out with Pastor Caring and soon found out something he didn't know before: people being visited usually offer something to eat. After a few days, he felt like he'd been eating mostly apple pie. Christian did not mind this—he was glad for every piece of pie he could get—but he noticed that Pastor Caring had a way to take only a small piece or none at all. When Christian pointed this out, Pastor Caring said, "I'd soon be as fat as a hog before butchering time if I ate everything people try to give me."

Next Sunday during the announcements at church, Pastor Caring told the congregation that he wanted Christian as an elder, but didn't want to wait until the annual meeting to make it official. "Since we're all here," he said, "let's vote now. All in favor say aye." There was a deafening roar of ayes. "Opposed…none… motion carried. It's now an official." There was a great cheer, and everyone around Christian either shook his hand or patted him on the shoulder. It took a few minutes before things quieted down.

Then Pastor Caring announced that he'd assigned every regular attender to a home church and posted the information on the bulletin board. Everyone was encouraged to check the bulletin board and attend their home church on those Sundays it met. Pastor Caring ended his impassioned yet tactful plea for cooperation by saying, "Hopefully, this will make it so we can all continue to fit in this building. We don't want to have to turn anyone away."

That Sunday was October 5, Christian's birthday. To his surprise, at the Sunday dinner, the ladies brought out a big cake with "Happy Birthday, Christian" written on it. It wasn't hard to blow out twelve candles. Christian thought about where he was a year ago. Then he wondered where he would be next year. He thought, *I know one thing. I'll have learned to ride a horse.*

On his way to the dessert table to get another piece of cake, Christian spotted Rider, one of the boys from the Sunday school class. He hurried over and asked him, "Could you teach me how to ride a horse?"

Rider said, "Sure, come on over tomorrow after school."

Christian was delighted. "I'll be there," he said happily.

Christian didn't know it at the time, but Rider always rode bareback. When he walked down the road to Rider's farm, Christian saw the boy sitting on the corral fence. "Hi, Rider!" he called. Rider dropped off the fence into the corral. He walked over to a big brown horse and swung himself up. Christian stood and stared for a moment, but he was game. Climbing over the fence, he went to the white horse standing near Rider, and by doing the same movements, he found himself sitting on top of the horse's back. *At least I'm facing the right direction*, he thought. Rider said, "Well, you made it up. Not bad."

Christian grabbed a handful of the horse's mane to keep his balance in case the horse moved. "Relax," said Rider. "Let your legs hang long and only grip with your thighs if you have to. It's okay to grab the mane. It won't hurt the horse." Christian tried to follow Rider's directions.

"But how do I make him go?" he asked. "Give him a little jab with your heels. That tells him to trot," Rider replied. "If you move your feet a few inches back and jab him again it will tell him to canter. If you lean forward with a quick little grip with your thighs and gently jab him there again, it will tell him to gallop. But don't forget—when you're riding, you want to sit upright, heels down, toes up. Sort of rock with his movements, and shift your weight forward. After a while, you'll get it. You'll feel like you're one with the horse."

Christian tried to follow Rider's directions, and to his amazement, the horse started walking around the corral. Rider headed over to open the gate. "Wait!" cried Christian. "I don't know how to steer him. How do I tell him which way to go?" Rider pointed to the reins. "The horse feels the reins on its neck. That tells him which way to turn. Turn your body very slightly as you turn your head before doing anything with the reins. The horse will know you want to turn that way. If he gets stubborn, you may have to pull some." Rider leaned over and opened the gate. "Oh yeah, one more thing," he said. "How to stop. If you want the horse to stop, just sit back instead of sitting upright, and say 'whoa.' You may not have to pull back on the reins. Trust the horse to obey you, and he will. Let's go."

Christian was amazed. Rider's brown horse didn't even have a bridle, but it seemed to do whatever Rider wanted it to do. Opening the corral gate, Rider was off and running. Christian didn't have to jab his horse hardly at all. It wanted to run too and thundered out of the corral in hot pursuit. Christian felt like he was being jerked in every direction. Then he remembered, *Sit upright, shift your weight forward until you become one with the horse's movements.* Christian watched what Rider was doing and copied him. It wasn't long before he got the hang of it. He thought it was much more fun than riding with a saddle.

After a while, as the horses ambled along side by side, Rider explained that there were more things Christian could learn about horseback riding. "You're doing well for a beginner. I thought you would have fallen off at least once by now. After a while, you can really start to have fun." That day, Rider and Christian became good friends. Every so often, Christian would go over to Rider's house, they'd jump on the horses, and off they would go on some sort of adventure.

Wednesday came and it was announced that Christian's Bible study group was scheduled to meet for home church the very next Sunday. The ladies worked out the food details with their usual efficiency. Everyone was looking forward to the new experience of church in a house.

During the prayer time that was normally part of the Wednesday Bible study, Christian noted how many people were praying for friends and neighbors they had been talking to about Christ, some of whom had agreed to come to church. *This is interesting*, he thought. *We might have some unsaved neighbors at the Friendly house on Sunday. And if what I'm hearing is any indication of what's happening with the rest of the church, the church building will still be packed. God must be helping us*, he laughed to himself. *The idea to find a way to relieve the pressure of so many new people came at just the right time.*

After their time of prayer, people started sharing. "I was so blessed," said Mrs. Kindly. "When I told my neighbors about the love of God, they were instantly interested. They said they wanted to come to church."

Mr. Outgoing agreed, "My friends also wanted to know all about it. This really caught me by surprise. Someone even said, 'Christ dying to forgive my sins so I can go to heaven seemed so far in the future. I didn't see the point before. But the immediate presence of God! Now that's something worth looking into!'"

"Yes," said Mr. Friendly enthusiastically. "I noticed that too. Sometimes, I go down to the inn for breakfast so I can talk with the other farmers. Somehow, the subject came up and I told them about how God wanted to change their hearts to be more loving, for God Himself to be a present reality that they could experience. And I was surprised at how what I said caught their attention. And I was amazed at their reaction when they heard it meant letting Jesus be Lord in their life. It seemed to have the effect that they wanted to know Him even more." They all wondered what this meant. Finally, someone said, "I think God is doing something in our town and in our little church!"

Christian thought about this. *It seems that understanding the love of God is a big help to people who don't know Jesus so they start getting really interested in Him. That means we need to really be careful. What we say to people about the gospel and how we live our lives every day is going to influence people either toward Jesus or away from Him.* Christian began to feel a little worried. *Maybe how we explain the gospel is like a gateway people go through to enter the kingdom of heaven,* he said to himself. *It's a disaster for ourselves and for people who don't know Jesus if we aren't clear about the love of God. Understanding His love is more important than I thought.*

The next morning, Pastor Caring came riding over to Christian's cabin. It was a cold day, and soon, he and Christian were sitting close to Christian's little tin stove. "Well, Christian, looks like we've got a sister problem to the big problem of how to fit everybody into the church," said Pastor Caring. And then he described how Mr. Evangelist told him that the new believer's class was getting too big, and he wanted to divide it into three parts. "Seems there are some folks who still have questions and they're taking up too much class time," said Pastor Caring. "So I decided to take those folks to a separate class, get to know their questions, visit them in their homes, and do everything I can to help them. But I've been thinking about the third group who are ready to move on."

Christian was a bit puzzled. "But what about the adult class?" he asked. "Pastor Caring paused, and looked serious. "I was thinking of Mr. Knowsalot," he said. "The problem is Mr. Knowsalot tends to go into minutia that only a seasoned Christian could relate to, and the class members he has right now really enjoy that. But…" Christian spoke up, "But what about the brand-new Christians who are moving up from the new believer's class?" Pastor Caring looked at Christian. Then he said, "That's where you come in. I think you'd be perfect for teaching a new class. Being young, you wouldn't intimidate anyone. But you've got some iron in your backbone. No one's going to push you around. You know your Bible. The opportunity is yours if you're up to it."

Christian was quietly looking down and was thinking. Finally, he said, "I don't think I can teach like other people. They seem to get into all the details that are in the Bible. I'm more interested in the main idea. I always want to know the big picture of what God is saying. How He says it is not what I'm too interested in."

"Yes," said Pastor Caring. "I knew you would be perfect. New believers don't need all that detail stuff. What you described is just what's needed."

Christian was still worried and hesitantly said, "I'll give it a try. If I get into trouble, I'll ask for some help."

"Splendid," said Pastor Caring. "I'm there for you if you need anything. What would you like to start with?"

"Well, I've been reading and thinking about Romans," Christian said. "I wrote down some notes about what Paul was trying to do. It's not about details. It's about the main ideas he was thinking."

Pastor Caring thought about the two-inch thick commentary on Romans that sat on his library shelf, but he simply said, "Yes. Romans would be good. Not this Sunday, but the following Sunday, be ready to start teaching the class."

Christian said, "But where can we possibly fit another class?"

Pastor Caring laughed, "No problem! I'm moving everything out of the storage room in the church and putting it in the stable so you'll have a place to meet. Before it gets too cold, some of the men are going to build a shed next to the stable for a permanent place to store things. Finding space is going to become a problem. My new class will be in my library. We're going through exciting times."

"Yes," said Christian. "And we're all being stretched. I'm really going to have to trust the Lord."

Sunday came, and the folks assembled for the Friendly family house church could faintly hear the singing from the church building which was not too far away. This made everyone in the house church sing more lustily. The whole building shook and everyone agreed that they must have been heard even down at the church. Then Mr. Friendly gave a short message on Leviticus 19:34, about being kind to strangers, loving them as you love yourself. "Surely," he said, "we should be kind to strangers. We should also show even greater kindness to those we know." Then because the group was small, some people commented on what Mr. Friendly had said. Afterward, Mr. Friendly held up a piece of paper. "I'm not the only one here who can share something from the Bible," he said. "I would like to see us all take turns." He paused and smiled at the children who were sitting with their parents. "Children," he said. "That includes you, too." He handed the paper to the family nearest him. "Go ahead and sign up."

One of the mothers objected, "But what could a child do?"

Mr. Friendly replied cheerfully, "We're going to set aside some time for the children, because there are plenty of things they can do...sing a song, recite Scripture, do a little skit about a Bible story, talk about a missionary or a hero of the faith, and the older children can recite Scripture with an explanation of what it means and what it means to them."

"Oh, I never thought about that," the mother said.

Mr. Friendly added, "Of course, you may have to help them rehearse at home, but that's good. I think it will bring them closer to our Lord."

The woman's young son, who was sitting next to her, said, "Mother, could I tell about when that missionary, John Paton, had to hide in a tree so the cannibals didn't eat him?"

"Perfect," said Mr. Friendly. "I want to hear that story the next time this church meets." It was on Mr. Friendly's heart that the children should be involved and he was overjoyed that a child had already volunteered.

After church, the potluck dinner went smoothly. There was wild turkey and goose. Christian particularly liked the assortment of pies. He methodically had a piece from each. The children all ate quickly, then bundled up to go play outside. There was a swing in the tree outside the house and the younger kids seemed to be enjoying themselves while the older ones played tag and threw balls to each other. After a while, Mrs. Friendly held a short class for them and the children talked about what our sin cost God. Mrs. Friendly was very talented at explaining things clearly and even the little ones seemed to understand the concept.

Meanwhile, the adults were having a conversation with two of the families who had never been to church before. One of the visiting fathers said, "Everyone here seems to have some kind of joy that I have never known existed. What is it that you have?" A short conversation started where he was offered the same bit of heaven that he was seeing, and people started giving testimonies about their close and loving relationship with God they had, not just on Sunday, but every day. Then the unchurched father prayed and gave his life to Christ, right there in front of everyone. This was an unexpected and wonderful development.

Pastor Caring had called a short meeting that evening for leaders of the house churches which had met that Sunday. "So how did it go?" he asked. One by one, the house church leaders spoke out. Everyone was especially impressed with the conversations that just seemed to happen after dinner. And just like in the church building, the house churches continued after dinner with singing and prayer, but being smaller groups, people felt freer to share what was really in their heart.

Pastor Caring asked, "Do we need to make any changes?" Everyone agreed there was nothing they would change. Then they asked Pastor Caring how it went at church. "We were close to capacity," said the pastor. "We may have to do something more to relieve the pressure of too many people in too small a space."

Mr. Friendly spoke up. "We had a visitor accept Christ. Here's an idea—there's no need to wait before a new believer becomes part of a house church. Even if they haven't finished the new believer's class, send them along. Besides, they should be encouraged to go to a home Bible study from the first day." The leaders all agreed that this would take some of the pressure off. Mr. Evangelist said, "There's about 4,000 people in this town, plus people in farms around. I'd say that maybe two-thirds of them don't go to church. What will we do when they all want to come to this church?" Everyone laughed. Christian thought, *Yes, what will we do?*

---

[1] Matthew 18:18; John 20:23

# 11 ROMANS

Christian set to work to put some flesh on his brief notes. From his conversations with Mr. Confident, Christian knew how easy it was to get the wrong idea of what Paul was saying. *There are some parts of Romans where I'm really going to have to help the class follow the logic that Paul is using,* he thought.

Then Christian looked at what he already had in his notes. Across the top he'd written, "In Christ, Jews and Gentiles should love and respect one another as equals."

*Yes,* Christian thought, *That's what Romans is about…it would be easy to miss that big picture and get lost in details. Romans does talk about the gospel because the gospel is the great equalizer. Jews and Gentiles are lost and guilty. Christ has redeemed both.*

*Some people miss the point of why Paul wrote Romans. They seem to think Paul said to himself, "I'm going to write a theological thesis about the gospel and send it to the church in Rome." I don't think so.* Christian wrote that thought down. *And who is Paul talking to? He says in 1:7 that he's writing to "all who are in Rome, beloved of God," but then he narrows it down and starts mostly just talking to the Jewish Christians.* Christian copied from his Bible, "You who make your boast in the law, do you dishonor God through breaking the law? For 'the name of God is blasphemed among the Gentiles because of you,' as it is written. (Romans 2:23–24)" Then he thought, *Romans was mostly written to Jewish believers. And what he had to say to them was rather harsh.*

Christian stopped working on his notes and began to read. When he got to Romans 4, he was impressed with Paul's emphasis on faith. *Yes, faith,* Christian thought. *So many people have faith in faith. It seems to me that for faith to be faith it has to be in something. And it has to be something you can think about. It has to be in something that can be understood enough to make a commitment to it. And real faith is to take what we have our faith in and make it our own by fully committing ourselves to it!* At that thought, there was a knock on his door.

"Come in!" Christian called, and Steady quickly shut the door behind him. "It's getting cold out there," he said and sat down close to the stove. Christian told Steady about how excited he was that he was going to teach a class. Steady said, "Hey, can I look at your notebook?"

"Only if you'll give me some honest comments," said Christian, handing it over.

Steady read some and said, "Hey, this is good stuff. I wish I were in your class. I think you have the idea."

"Thanks!" said Christian. "And you're welcome to come along. If I'm in over my head, I might need some help."

"You can count on me, then," said Steady, handing back the notebook.

Christian gestured to his Bible, still opened at Romans 4. "You know, in Romans, Paul was writing to people who didn't 'get it' about living by faith. What amazing things would he have said if he were writing to people who did understand living by faith and were beyond that? Someday, I'd like to teach a class where we go beyond what Paul was saying in Romans."

Steady grinned and pointed to Christian's Bible. "You mean, like he did in Ephesians?"

Christian grinned back. "Oh yeah," he said. "I would like to talk about that next."

Steady went on, "But Romans 4 sure says some challenging things about Abraham's faith." Christian nodded in agreement, and Steady continued, "When God promised Abraham he was going to have a son in his old age, Abraham believed Him. Then after a while, Abraham got impatient and didn't live as though it were true. He 'helped God' by having a son with his wife's slave girl. You know what I figured out from that? Any of us could fall into the same trap—we can really believe something and still live as if we don't believe it."

"But when you look at the rest of Abraham's story, it gets a lot better," said Christian. "After more years, Abraham did learn to live as though what he believed were true. In the end, he was willing to obey God no matter what. There was a real lesson that he learned. He had finally learned to trust in God's good and loving character."

"Oh yeah," said Steady. "When Abraham obeyed and started to sacrifice his son, born from his wife who was too old to have children, that was incredible faith, incredible. Abraham had also figured it out that faith includes obedience. I'm even afraid to ask God for faith to do something like that."

Suddenly, Steady jumped to his feet. "Oh, I almost forgot. We had a lot of food left over from dinner. My mom sent me to ask if you wanted to come to supper and help us finish it. I think she meant right now."

"Sure," said Christian. "Your mom is the best cook in the county!" Christian put his Bible and notebook back into the breadbox, put on his rabbit skin coat, and they hurried off into the chilly evening. The almost bare trees cast long dark shadows from the faint sun just dropping below the horizon. There was a warm glow of lamplight from the windows of the Friendly house by the time the boys ran up the porch steps.

As they sat down at the dining room table, Mrs. Friendly said, "It's so good to have you here, Christian. The roast beef won't keep, so we need to eat it all." Christian eyed the large bowl of gravy, the slices of roast beef, and the mashed potatoes. He loved anything with gravy, especially mashed potatoes, and did his share of taking second helpings.

When they were almost finished eating, Mr. Friendly asked about his Sunday school class. Christian said, "It isn't for this Sunday, but the Sunday after that. I'm getting ready now. I'm going to teach Romans, which seems to be about getting a bunch of really different people to love one another. And Paul reasons that since we're all in Christ by grace through faith, there's no reason not to love each other."

Mr. Friendly chuckled, "That's reducing it down to a few words."

Christian replied, "I'm going to try to teach what it actually says, but I don't want to get too bogged down with little details."

Mr. Friendly said, "The way it's usually taught, a great deal of emphasis is put on the gospel and on faith. And when we're all done, we still don't know much about faith. Maybe that's why we keep emphasizing it."

Steady commented, "Christian and Careful and I were fishing last summer, and we decided faith was the fearless part of unconditional love."

"I remember that," said Christian. "We had half a dozen definitions for faith, and that was one of the best."

"I like the way Careful put it," said Steady. "He said, 'Faith is fearlessly obeying God because we believe Him and we love Him.'"

"Oh," said Mr. Friendly, "what other definitions are there?"

Steady said, "Faith is doing what is right without worrying about what might happen. Faith is living as though God's promises are true. Faith is believing God's love can be counted on and really living like we believe it."

Christian chimed in, "I remember saying, 'Faith is just plain ol' trusting each other.' After I said that, I remember Steady saying, 'Faith is being fearless.' Then he said, 'Faith is unconditional love in action!'" Christian put down his fork and grinned at Steady across the table. "And after that, you said, 'God sure was being fearless when He saved me.' Then we all agreed God was fearless for saving any of us."

"Oh yeah," said Steady. "Now I remember. That's when Careful came up with 'Faith is fearlessly obeying God because we love Him.'"

"Then we got back to fishing. By faith, we baited our hooks and let them dangle in the water." They all laughed.

Mr. Friendly said, "Careful's definition is the best one I've ever heard. I think it matches up really well with Hebrews 11 about 'faith is the assurance of things hoped for, the conviction of things not seen.'"

Steady responded, "Yeah, like it says the same idea."

Just then, Mrs. Friendly came in from the kitchen and said, "I've baked a blackberry pie! The blackberries are done for the year, so this will be the last berry pie until next summer. I think it's cool enough to eat now. Would anyone like some pie?" There was a loud chorus of eager replies.

After supper, Christian walked down the dark but familiar path to his cabin. He was glad he had brought his fur coat as the night was cold. Back at the cabin, he was soon under the warm quilts on his bed and fell asleep thinking about Sunday school…and pie and roast beef with lots of gravy.

The rest of the week went by swiftly. Christian was a little bit scared and did according to Paul's commandment to pray without ceasing. Christian's prayer was, "How can I teach this?"

Finally, Sunday morning came, and the class was assembled. There were some older boys and girls Christian's age and some old folks and all kinds of people in between, with every eye looking intently at him. Doing his best to smile, Christian introduced himself, talked about when Romans was written and some background that he had learned from the book of Acts.

Stopping, he asked if the class knew who the Jews were. There was a general nodding of heads. *Whew,* thought Christian. *Looks like Mr. Evangelist did a good job introducing them to the Old Testament and the history of the Jews.*

Then Christian straightened up and said very firmly, "Romans is like a puzzle. There are many ideas that fit together to form a picture. Sometimes, people only see the pieces, and they use those pieces to come up with crazy ideas. So to keep that from happening to us, we'll start with seeing the big picture, why Paul wrote Romans. Then we can follow how Paul uses his ideas to work toward his goals.

"So why did Paul write Romans? What was he aiming at?" Several people leaned forward and looked expectantly at Christian. Though he did feel just a bit intimidated, Christian spoke clearly and boldly, "Romans was written to correct a lack of love and respect between Jewish and Gentile believers. In his letter, Paul goes after two things that were the source of their problems with one another:

"One: the believers in Rome were trying to live righteously by keeping the law. They thought that was what Christians were supposed to do. They needed to get a better understanding of what faith is all about."

Immediately, a low murmuring broke out among the class members and Mrs. Uncomplicated raised her hand. "But I thought we were supposed to keep God's law," she said in a puzzled voice.

Mr. Tenderheart blurted out, "We're supposed to love God and love our neighbor. That's the whole law."

"But it's still a law," said Mrs. Uncomplicated. Steady, who had come to the class, was smiling broadly and was laughing to himself, *What fun. Christian's in trouble already. I wonder how he'll get out of this one?*

After a few seconds of silence, Christian said, "The first and greatest commandment is to love God, to have a real and living and committed love relationship with Him. And the second commandment is that we also commit ourselves to love others in the same way that He loves. But—there is no way we can do any of that on our own. That's the mistake the Roman believers were making. That's why they needed Paul to tell them about faith because faith is the key."

"Wait a minute, son," Mr. Considerate spoke up. He was a big man who lived in town and worked at the lumberyard. Christian had occasionally seen him there carrying enormous stacks of boards on his shoulder. "How is that different from my neighbors who don't believe in God, but they're always doing nice things for people?" Steady leaned back in his chair. Now he wasn't just smiling, he was visibly grinning and stifling a laugh.

"You make a good point," Christian said to Mr. Considerate. "Think of it this way. You and your neighbors may be kind, even loving, but how do you compare with God's love?"

"Well, I guess when you put it that way," said Mr. Considerate, "bringing over a pie doesn't compare with the love of God. But God is God, while we're just people."

"Exactly! And like Paul was trying to say in Romans, that's where faith comes in," responded Christian. "Our faith that God will share His life with us is like a constant prayer that we know He will answer. Faith is fearlessly doing the things in this world that He loves doing, knowing He is with us. Paul is saying to the Romans, 'Living by faith is better than trying to do what's right on our own, trying to do the best we can without Him.'"

Steady remembered that he had promised to give Christian some help. So he spoke up and said, "When we selfishly hold on to doing what's right by ourselves, that keeps God from helping us. Our letting Him help us is something He wants."

Mr. Considerate commented, "So what you're saying is that without Jesus helping, I can't do much more than be a good neighbor. But with His help, the sky is the limit."

"Exactly," said Christian. "But getting there is a learning process we all have to go through."

Steady added, "I remember how hard it was to learn that Christ is all I need. Then came the really seriously hard part—learning to yield myself, being willing to become like He is. Every day, I learn more about how loving Jesus is. And every day, I learn more about how I should act in order to be like Him."

Mrs. Pleasant interjected, "And we learn that He will never leave us, and we can trust Him to make us able to live the way that He wants us to live. But like you said, Steady, for most of us, this takes time."

"I still don't see this. What is it like to have God's help?" Mrs. Uncomplicated asked.

Christian said, "Let me give an illustration: Suppose someone who doesn't like you deliberately drove their wagon through your vegetable garden. He was so anxious to mess up your garden that he turned too quickly and the wagon tipped onto its side. If Jesus is in your heart, how would you react? You would want to love and help the person who did that to your garden. So you come out to the garden and help him lift the wagon back onto its wheels. Miraculously, you're not angry because you're trusting Jesus to act as He would. You're thinking from your heart, 'What does this person need? How can I help him?'"

Mrs. Uncomplicated frowned fiercely and said, "If anybody did that to my garden, I would set the dogs on him! But you talk about how we need to be willing to be like Jesus. For me, that would take a miracle."

"Exactly," said Christian. "It's the miracle Paul wanted the Romans to have. It's the miracle God wants you to have."

"I guess," said Mrs. Uncomplicated. "I guess the bottleneck is me."

Before Christian could respond, Mr. Considerate chimed in, "I like that idea! Jesus and I are able to do together what would be impossible for me to do alone. I can trust Him to help me love even neighbors who are ornery. If that's what it's like to have God's help, that's what I want!"

"And that's where living by faith will take you," said Christian.

Mr. Thoughtful had been quietly thinking. He spoke up and said, "I think I get it. If we're like the Jewish believers in Rome and don't live by faith, we won't be trusting that Christ is all we need. We'll be limiting our love for our neighbor to what we can do without God's help. And as good as we might think we are, in reality, we would be horribly frustrating to Jesus because He wants to be part of our lives. It's like He's waiting for us to live like we believe that He loves us enough to help us."

"Exactly," said Christian. "Now we can go on to the second problem that Paul wrote to the Romans to correct.

"Two: because of their heritage and knowledge of the law, the Jewish Christians in Rome were acting like they were better than the Gentile Christians."

Steady interjected, "It seems that their affection for the law led to pride, and their pride made it hard to love Gentile believers. And what added to the problem was that among nonbelievers, the Jews really were outstandingly more righteous than the Gentiles. They're really good at being good people."

Christian continued, "The Jewish Christians were proud, and

they had reason to be. They were the inheritors of the promises made to Abraham. And they had always been better behaved than their Gentile neighbors. Gentiles were formerly pagans, newcomers, being invited into promises first given to the Jews. So it was natural for the Jewish believers to see themselves a cut above the Gentile Christians. They needed to let go of that and see themselves and the Gentile Christians as both part of the body of Christ."

"Oh, yes," said Steady, still trying to be helpful. "Paul talked about Jews and Gentiles being brought together in Ephesians 2:11–22. He said, 'For through Him (Jesus) we both have access by one Spirit unto the Father' (Ephesians 2:18)."

"Yes," said Christian. "In Christ, both Jews and Gentiles have been raised up to the highest level that we can imagine. And it's all by God's grace, so it's impossible that one can have anything to boast of over the other."

"That's so," said Mr. Farmer. "I think I know what it must have been like. I've been to the city. Those city people think we country folks are unsophisticated, uneducated country bumpkins, and sometimes, they let us know it. They call us 'hay seeds.' Well, I have my opinion about them. I think they're unrealistic, impractical, arrogant, and don't know anything about the real world. Why, they think food comes from grocery stores, and some of them even keep a dog for a pet! I can't even imagine what it would be like to keep an animal that doesn't have a job. It's real easy for people who think differently to look down on one another."

Mr. Thoughtful said, "It must really grieve the Lord when Christians do that."

Christian continued. "The Jewish believers' attachment to the law and their national pride were problems that were related, and the law was an important part of the problems Paul wanted to fix. I counted how many times the word law is mentioned in Romans, 74 times. So Paul had a lot to say about the Jewish believers' attachment to the law. Even so, all of Romans is Paul working toward one single united goal, that Jews and Gentiles should come to love and respect one another as equals. They both received God's grace and redemption through faith in Jesus Christ. So if you were Paul, what would you say to the Romans to help them love each other?

Mrs. Uncomplicated said, "What I have heard today is so wonderful. I had no idea we could be part of God's love for others. And I would tell them that."

"You're so right," said Mrs. Thoughtful. "I would tell them that, too. And I would tell them with Jesus in your heart, you can love God and your neighbors much better than you could by trying to keep the law."

Then Mr. Thoughtful said, "Yes, and I would tell them about how being interested in others, wanting to help them with their problems, is what Christians do. It's not all about you being righteous for yourself."

Then Mr. Tenderheart said, "And it's a message for us too. It's not just for Paul or Pastor Caring to help other people. We can all be like Paul."

Christian continued, "Paul worked toward his goal of helping the Roman Christians love each other by directing his arguments toward three things:

Destroying the Jewish Christians' lofty opinion of themselves.

Breaking people's attachment to the law by talking about faith. (They are saved by faith and are to live by faith.)

And beginning in chapter 11, telling how Jews and Gentiles should love one another as the body of Christ.

"And I see we're out of time. I encourage you all to read Romans this week, or at least read the first few chapters. Let's pray."

After church, Christian sat for dinner at the same table with Mr. and Mrs. Evangelist and their daughter, Evangeline, who was about his age. Mr. Evangelist asked how his first Bible class went. "I was barely able to introduce the book of Romans when our time was up. But we had some good discussions, and that's what I really wanted." Mr. Evangelist nodded. "When I teach the Bible," he said, "I make a list of questions that require some thought about what the Bible is saying. Then I just go through my questions." Christian thought this was a great idea.

Evangeline joined in and asked Christian what he liked about Romans. He said, "I like the way Paul was so fearless, but still tactful and logical when he was dealing with the prideful Jewish believers. He was firm, but gentle. He began chapter 9 with sympathy before doing the hard thing of explaining that God has both the right and good reason to reject Israel. He began chapter 10 in the same kind and thoughtful way. I know that if I were faced with the same situation, I might not remember to be anywhere near so…so…"

"Considerate," said Evangeline.

"Right!" Christian replied. "That's one reason I really admire Paul and I like reading Romans."

Evangeline agreed enthusiastically, and said, "I like the way Paul includes his prayers in some of his letters. It's like he's telling us what's in his heart."

"I agree," Christian said.

Evangeline went on, "My favorite part of Romans is chapter 6, especially verse 8 that says, 'Now if we died with Christ, we believe that we shall also live with Him.' It's like Paul wants to take us beyond any struggles we might be having. He tells us how to live now that we're dead to sin. I like to think about that, especially when I'm having a hard time with something."

Christian and Evangeline discussed this verse in chapter 6 for the rest of dinner. Finally Evangeline said, "I'm not a new believer, but I would like to come to your class." Christian said. "Please do. I want as much discussion in the class as possible, and you would be a great help." Mrs. Evangelist was thinking, *They seem to like each other. He's friendly and outgoing. At the same time, he thinks before he speaks. And yes, I also like this boy.*

That week, Christian was busy doing odd jobs for people in town. Finally, it was Friday and he was walking past the bank on his way home, when he heard loud gruff voices inside. One voice said, "Put it in the sack." Christian stopped, wondering what was going on. Opening the bank door, he found himself looking down the barrel of a gun.

---

Romans 3:28-30, 15:5-12
Romans 4:1
James 1:17
Hebrews 11:1
1 Thessalonians 5:17; 1 Timothy 2:8; Proverbs 15:8; John 14:13-14
Romans 1:16-17

# 12 THE BANK ROBBERY

"You just step right in, son," said the man with the gun. Before Christian could turn and run, the man grabbed his arm and pulled him in so hard that Christian almost felt as if his arm were being torn off. Out of the corner of his eye, he saw several people huddled in a corner. "Get over there," said the man with the gun, poking it into Christian's ribs.

But Christian stood his ground. Looking straight at the gunman, he said, "You don't have to do this. Jesus wants to come into your heart and change you so you will love people. That's worth more than all the money in the world." The robber stared at Christian like he'd seen a ghost. Slowly, he began to lower the gun. Then suddenly, he whirled around and said to his partner, "Let's go. We gotta get outa here."

The other robber said, "Wait! I haven't got all the money yet." But the gunman snatched up the sack and started dragging it to the door. On his face was a strange mixture of shame and ferocity. One look at him and the other robber realized something was up, took the sack, and the two of them left quickly. The sound of horses' hooves went galloping away and they were gone. The bank teller ran for the back door and headed for the sheriff's office, yelling, "The bank's been robbed. The bank's been robbed."

In the meantime, the customers came hesitantly out of their corner, all of them staring at Christian. One of the men asked, "What did you say?"

"I told him the truth," said Christian. "Jesus rose from the dead and offers even robbers to come into their lives and change them to love others as God loves each one of us."

"Well," the man said. "I think you scared him right good." The deputy sheriff came and got a description from everybody and left in a hurry. Christian stepped outside the bank just in time to see the sheriff and a dozen men gallop by all loaded down with guns. Before he could leave for home, the owner of the newspaper came running and got everyone's story.

Later, Christian was telling Steady about it. Steady said, "I wonder if it was Butch Cassidy and the Sundance Kid. I heard all about them. They have a hideout in Wyoming and they come out and rob banks and trains."

Christian laughed, "I don't think so. One of the customers thought I scared them away."

By Sunday morning, Christian's whole class had heard about the great bank robbery and they all wanted to hear about it from him. Christian had to tell what happened. Then he gave a short review of what they talked about the week before: the two problems Paul wanted to solve and the three main ideas he presented to solve the problems.

Then he said, "Paul is juggling a lot of ideas, and they're all mixed together. His argument against law keeping would be easy to follow if it wasn't all mixed up with discouraging the Jewish Christians' superior attitude toward Gentile Christians along with explaining the gospel and living by faith. And Paul is so careful to be tactful. He really loves his own Jewish people, and he tries not to get the Jewish Christians angry with him while giving them a message they don't want to hear."

Mr. Tenderheart commented, "That's fine for them, but it makes it hard for us modern folks to follow."

"Still," said Christian, "it allows us to see a gentle side of Paul, being tactful, right from the start of Romans. He begins by saying good things about his own Jewish people. It was to them Messiah was promised, 'Born of the seed of David' (Romans 1:2–3). Then Paul begins to include Gentiles, 'To all who are in Rome, beloved of God, called to be saints' (1:7)."

"Oh," said Mrs. Uncomplicated. "I didn't know they were all saints." Christian noted Steady's wide grin. But Evangeline, who had been quietly sitting nearby, said to her. "Mrs. Uncomplicated, you are favored by God, His very special person, just like all the rest of us. God loves everyone who belongs to Jesus and He made us all saints. It isn't even possible for God to love you more than the love he has for you right now."

"Oh," said Mrs. Uncomplicated. "You're right. I never thought of that. How could it be any different?"

Beginning at Romans 1:1, Christian had the class take turns reading a verse and telling what they thought it was saying. Then anyone could add to what was said. Finally, Christian chipped in his comments. But he didn't say much because almost everyone related the verse back to things Christian had told them. When they reached verse 14, the class pointed out that Paul describes himself, a Jew, as "a debtor both to Greeks and to barbarians." And when they got to verse 16, they talked about how it related to the reason why Paul wrote Romans. The gospel is "for the Jew first and also for the Greek. For in it the righteousness of God is revealed from faith to faith" (1:16–17a).

When they got to verse 17, it was Mr. Thoughtful's turn. He said, "We're saved by faith in what Christ has done for us. Now we live by faith. I figure that means we put our trust in Him all day long every day."

Mrs. Thoughtful had the next verse. "For the wrath of God is revealed from heaven against all ungodliness and unrighteousness of men, who suppress the truth in unrighteousness." She said, "If you're not even aware of what God says, then He won't judge you and hold you accountable. But everyone knows something about God, and they will be held accountable for how they use the information they do have."

While all this was going on, Mr. Strict, who was sitting in the back row, looked increasingly grim, and didn't say anything. Finally he roared out, "This is a bunch of hogwash. You keep talking about God's love, but what about His wrath? That's His nature too!" Before Christian could answer, Mr. Thoughtful turned to Mr. Strict and exclaimed, "Absolutely not! Look at what God went through so that He could save us from sin. That's proof enough—He wants to avoid wrath. He does everything possible to persuade people to accept His forgiveness. He doesn't want to pour out wrath on them."

Mrs. Thoughtful added, "Besides, suppressing the truth means they had truth to suppress. What is God supposed to do with people who deliberately turn away from Him and prefer to live ungodly, unrighteous lives? I guess you could call it wrath, but I think He's just being fair. It's His nature to be fair while He tries to avoid wrath."

Mr. Inquisitive responded, "There is no question that God does do what the Bible calls wrath. The real question is: 'Does God display wrath because He's forced to by our bad behavior, or is it something He does because that's part of who He is?' So, Mr. Thoughtful, even though I think you're right, I would like to hear you address the real question: are we stronger than God and can force Him to demonstrate wrath even though He doesn't want to?"

"Yes," said Mr. Thoughtful. "God made us able to make choices. So by our willful disobedience, we can force Him to deal with us in an appropriate manner."

"That's ridiculous!" snorted Mr. Strict. "How could we puny humans force Almighty God to do anything?"

Steady said, "If God Himself told us that we can, we should believe Him. Check out Ezekiel 33:11. "'As I live,' says the Lord God, "I have no pleasure in the death of the wicked, but that the wicked turn from his way and live.'" And since many wicked people will not turn from their wickedness, they force God to not let them into heaven. He Himself says He finds no pleasure in doing what He has to do to the wicked."

Evangeline, looking in her Bible, added, "And Lamentations 3:33 says, 'He does not afflict willingly, nor grieve the children of men.' Our choosing to do wrong forces Him to afflict us, which He would rather not do."

Christian, faced with his class possibly disintegrating into chaos, said, "I don't think we have any reason to doubt these verses. But if you have doubts, as we discuss more things in Scripture, we'll be able to understand more about God's character. Let's be patient and see what Scripture tells us." The class settled down again, with a few stray murmurs as Christian continued.

"In Romans 1:18, Paul begins a long, long chain of logic to show that Jewish believers have no reason to feel superior, because sinful Jews have been just as sinful as sinful Gentiles. Among both Jews and Gentiles, there are many who 'suppress the truth in unrighteousness.' So as not to appear one-sided, Paul began by describing sinful Gentiles:

Gentiles know God exists, and God does influence them.

But many refuse to respond to God or seek Him, choosing instead to follow their own selfish desires."

Mrs. Thoughtful added, "Gentiles do know that there is a God. I knew it before I became a Christian. God did help me see He is real."

Mrs. Reader added, "And in Romans 1, God is showing Himself even to people who kept rejecting Him. If God is showing Himself to people like that, He most certainly is showing Himself to everybody else too."

Mr. Inquisitive, the bookkeeper at the bank, asked, "Wait a minute! What's all this nonsense? God's unknowable. We can't comprehend Him."

Evangeline, in an effort to answer his question, said, "I think this verse is talking about something the Holy Spirit does. He uses creation as an example, to teach everyone what He wants them to know about God."

Then Christian spoke up, "John 1:9 says that Jesus Himself 'gives light to every man' when they are born. The light Jesus gives is light about Himself, about what God is like in His character.

That fits right in with Romans 1:19."

Oh," said Mr. Inquisitive, "So Paul is making a case for the idea that God does show something about Himself to everyone— not just Jews, but Gentiles too. I think I can see where Paul is going with this."

Next it was Steady's turn and he read verse 20, "For since the creation of the world His invisible attributes are clearly seen, being understood by the things that are made, even His eternal power and Godhead, so that they are without excuse."

Steady held up his Bible and said, "This verse says every person in the world has a revelation from God they can respond to. And when they respond to that, God can speak to them in their heart and show them more."

Mrs. Reader raised her hand. "In the new believers' class, they said to read the New Testament first," she said. "So I did. I started reading Matthew. What you're saying reminds me of something I saw in Matthew, called the parable of the sower." Opening her Bible to Matthew 13, she pointed to a verse, "I circled it right here in verse 12, 'For whoever has, to him more will be given, and he will have abundance; but whoever does not have, even what he has will be taken away from him.'"

"Yes," said Christian, "that certainly applies to what Paul is saying in Romans!"

Mr. Thoughtful commented, "As Paul describes in Romans 1, some people push God away because they want to go their own way, to do bad things. Then God doesn't influence them as much. But He doesn't just walk away and leave them alone. He doesn't just write them off and ignore them."

"Yes, exactly," said Christian. "What we see in Romans 1 is certainly an example of that. Paul says, 'Because, although they knew God, they did not glorify Him as God, nor were thankful, but became futile in their thoughts, and their foolish hearts were darkened' (1:21). Then 'God also gave them up to uncleanness' (1:24).

"After further pushing God away, they worshipped idols (1:25), and God withdrew even more. 'God gave them up to vile passions' (1:26). But still, God did not withdraw completely. The light was still there."

Mrs. Thoughtful said, "Today, people are not tempted to worship idols or things like that, but we are tempted to do things like gossip. God wants us to stop so He can give us more light and understanding about Himself."

So Christian asked the class: "What can we expect God to do when we insist on doing wrong?"

Mrs. Uncomplicated said, "He won't stop loving us, but He might let us experience the consequences of our sin…that's scary."

Christian said, "Let me summarize Romans 1:18–32. Many Gentiles refuse to respond to God, and when evil people push God away in order to follow their vile passions, God withdraws a little bit, but He leaves enough of His influence that they can be persuaded to repent. And God lets them experience the consequences of their bad choices. Then after that, in Paul's example, if those people do even greater wickedness, God steps back some more. 'Even as they did not like to retain God in their knowledge, God gave them over to a debased mind, to do those things that are not fitting' (1:28).

"Even then, God does not give up. Paul said, 'who, knowing the righteous judgment of God, that those who practice such things are deserving of death, not only do the same but also approve of those who practice them' (1:32). How could such people know that what they're doing is wrong? Simple: God keeps reminding them. And at that time, Rome was a very immoral place. It would not be unusual for the Jews to have neighbors who fit this description."

"I read about that," said Mrs. Reader. "The people who lived in Pompeii were very immoral. In AD 79, the whole city was covered with volcanic ash. And the ash preserved everything so we know how they lived."

Christian continued, "Paul wrote this section not just to show the Jewish believers that he knows there are wicked Gentiles, but to also show that God cares for and is patient with Gentiles, even after they have fallen deeply into sin."

Evangeline commented, "God is so persistent."

Steady followed Christian's summary by saying, "Romans 1:18–32 is sort of like a window where we can look in and see the heart of God. People who say God quickly abandons the wicked are so wrong. They don't understand the depth of His love, 'not willing that any should perish but that all should come to repentance' (2 Peter 3:9)."

Steady, who had been reading ahead, continued, "And Paul wrote in Romans 2, 'Or do you despise the riches of His goodness, forbearance, and longsuffering, not knowing that the goodness of God leads you to repentance?' Look at how much God puts into persuading everyone to change their minds about their sin—the riches of His goodness, forbearance, and all of that. His love is amazing!"

Mr. Strict commented, "If I were God, I would have sent those people straight to hell right from the start. I guess God isn't so willing to do that. Maybe God isn't like me."

Steady said, "You're just thinking what a normal person would think. But we're all learning to trust God to help us think the way He thinks."

Christian nodded in agreement and said, "Here's how I imagine the Jewish believers in Rome would react to what we read in Romans 1. They would be chortling at what they thought was a description of ungodly Gentiles. 'That's right,' they would say. 'Isn't it terrible—the depth of sin into which a person can go? Those Gentiles are disgusting.' The Jews might not even notice how patient and loving God is with sinful Gentiles. Now they were really going to be in for a shock, because Paul went on to making another point, that there are also righteous Gentiles. Listen to his logic."

Christian read from his notes.

Jews aren't the only ones who are righteous.

Gentiles aren't the only ones who are unrighteous.

Both are in need of the righteousness that is from God by faith.

Mr. Thoughtful said, "Yes, I suppose that would make the Jewish Christians start to bristle and frown, but maybe they would also see the value of righteousness by faith."

"Yes, and Paul doesn't stop there," said Christian. "In complete contrast to the people in Romans 1 who pushed God away, in Romans 2, Paul wrote about people who followed what they knew about God and chose to seek Him further, 'Those (both Jews and Gentiles) who by patient continuance in doing good seek for glory, honor and immortality' receive what they seek after, 'eternal life.' 'Those who are self-seeking and do not obey the truth, but obey unrighteousness—indignation and wrath, tribulation and anguish, on every soul of man who does evil, of the Jew first and also of the Greek; but glory, honor, and peace to everyone who works what is good, to the Jew first and also to the Greek. For there is no partiality with God' (Romans 2:7–11)."

"Wait a minute," said Mr. Inquisitive. "What Paul says in these verses is not 'believe on the Lord Jesus Christ and you will be saved?' It sounds like Paul is saying your good works will save you. That's not what Mr. Evangelist said in his class. So what do we make of this?" Christian remembered the controversies he'd had with Mr. Confident and others. *Whew!* he thought. *Mr. Confident taught me one thing: talking about how God chooses the people who will receive saving faith sure gets folks riled up. If I teach what Paul plainly said in Romans 2:7–11, I'm liable to be burned at the stake. But now I have to answer this question. If I'm going to be a teacher and teach things that are useful, I have to talk about it. Maybe I'd better just let the Bible speak for itself.*

While Christian was thinking about what to do next, Mr. Thoughtful spoke up, "Look at this! People are always asking, 'How can someone who has never heard of Christ be saved?' Sounds to me like what Paul is saying is that God looks for people who are seeking Him, and He gives them saving faith to believe in Him."

"I noticed that too," said Mrs. Reader. "This is like the parable of the sower, again. 'Whoever has, to him more will be given.' I read ahead a little, and Romans 2:26–29 says there were even Gentiles living the 'righteous requirements of the law.' It says God was pleased with them. It seems to me, that if God was pleased, He would show them more of Himself to help them live even more righteously."

"It does make sense," said Mrs. Uncomplicated. "And if they never heard of Jesus, they would be judged the same as people in the Old Testament. But we Christians were judged righteous when we were born again."

Then Christian said, "Exactly! What Romans 2:7–9 is saying is that God gives each person what they want, to live forever with Him if they want Him and His ways, or to live forever without Him if they don't want Him and His ways. And He's been doing this right from the beginning." Then he said, "Paul is steadily heading toward his goal, and I need to keep on going too. Let's just read all of chapter 2 and 3, each of us taking a turn reading 3 verses." Christian thought, *Whew! I really didn't know how to explain that difficult idea, but the class explained it so well! I was going to bring in more Bible verses, but I didn't have to do anything.*

After the chapters were read, Christian continued, "For the last half of Romans 2, Paul speaks very firmly to the Jewish believers, but then in the first two verses of chapter 3, he lightens up and says some nice things to them. He talks about the special place Jews have."

Mr. Wise said, "I bet they were pretty steamed by now. It was wise of Paul to lighten up. But he was in big trouble if he didn't explain himself."

Christian said, "And Paul knew he couldn't just say something nice about the Jewish people. He also had to answer their questions. I don't really relate to the questions Paul brings up, but I can see that he was answering objections Jewish believers might have. He seems to be saying that setting aside the law doesn't mean righteousness is also set aside, but it does put Jewish believers on the same level as Gentiles in Christ, both needing grace. In verse 9, Paul clearly states, 'What then? Are we better than they? Not at all. For we have previously charged both Jews and Greeks that they are all under sin.'"

Mr. Wise commented, "I imagine Paul knew quite well that at this point the Jewish believers would still be thinking, 'Sin? Who, me?'"

"Exactly," said Christian. "In 3:10, Paul directs the Jewish believers' attention to their nation's history. In Romans 3:10–18, there are several quotes from the Old Testament. In fact, all of Romans has many quotes from the Old Testament."

Christian was thinking, *Mr. Confident was so sure of himself—almost arrogant, actually—when he quoted two of those verses from Romans 3 to prove that all people are born so messed up by sin that they can't even respond to the gospel. In his make-believe religion, God engineers it so only a few people respond. And they're people preselected before they were born! Mr. Confident was so deflated when I showed him that Paul was quoting Psalms, and I read the whole psalm to him from the Old Testament. I'd better make sure that the class knows it's important to not just take quotes out of context, but go back to the Old Testament and read the whole thing. It sure makes a difference when people see what all those quotes in Romans 3 are really saying.*

Christian looked at the class and said honestly, "I really don't want to talk about this. But I have to make the point that everyone can choose to respond to the gospel. It's only a matter of time before every one of you will run into someone who says, 'All people are born so lost in sin that they don't even have the ability to respond to God seeking them.' The problem is, people who say this like to aggressively push their opinion. At least they're honest about it. They say because God created us, He has a right to be a capricious, evil dictator who is totally unfair! But our God who loves wouldn't tell people to seek Him unless they could. So I have to ask you, what are your thoughts? Does God give everyone a fair and equal chance to be saved, or just a few?"

"That's silly," said Mr. Thoughtful. "We just read how God is more than fair. Those who do not believe are without excuse." The class all voiced their agreement. Still Christian said, "Here's a similar question. Do any of you believe people are born so evil, they cannot seek God in the way that He asks them to seek Him? Please, if anyone doubts the infinite love of God for every person on this planet, please come and talk to me afterward. We can talk about it over dinner. It's so very important to be confident of God's perfect love.

"Let's continue. What Paul is trying to do is simply show that Jewish Christians have no reason to think of themselves as better than the Gentile believers. In Romans 3, he reinforces his argument by laying out evidence that Jews can be as guilty of sin as Gentiles. He takes selected verses from seven places in the Old Testament that show there really is such a thing as wicked Jews. Two of the longer quotes are from the Psalms."

Steady said, "Can we look at a couple of those Psalms in the Old Testament? The Jewish believers who read Paul's quote would know the whole thing, so we should read the whole thing."

"Yes," said Christian. "Good idea. That way we'll know what the Jews knew when they read Paul's quotes."

After reading Psalms 5 and 14, Mr. Thoughtful said, "These Psalms sure look different now that we've read the whole Psalm. They talk about both wicked and righteous people. I'm impressed. It's better to look at the context and not jump to conclusions."

Christian said, "Let's look more closely at Romans 3:11–12, a quote from Psalms 14:1–5, which talks about fools. 'The fool has said in his heart, "There is no God."' Among the fools, since this a Jewish psalm, are Jews. The Jews would get the point: Paul is talking to them.

They are corrupt,
They have done abominable works,
There is none who does good.

"The Bible doesn't begin and end with parts of a Psalm. We need to look at the whole Psalm and also the whole Bible which talks of many people God calls righteous. Even though part of this Psalm says everyone is corrupt, the Bible also says 'Hezekiah… did what was good and right and true before the Lord his God.' And so did Job and many others." Christian continued reading Psalm 14.

"'The Lord looks down from heaven upon the children of men, to see if there are any who understand, who seek God.'"

Christian thought, *When the psalm says "no one seeks God," David doesn't include himself. In so many other places, the Bible talks about people who did seek the Lord. How can anyone not see that?*

"'They have all turned aside, they have together become corrupt; there is none who does good, no, not one.'" Christian stopped and pointed to his Bible. "Notice," he said. "David is still talking specifically about fools."

Steady said, "Even in Noah's time, there was one who did good—it was Noah. I don't understand how anyone can read this and not know this is only talking about wicked fools who think, 'there is no God.'"

Mr. Thoughtful said, "David made it clear at the end of the Psalm that he wasn't talking about himself or people who were righteous. I wish he'd made that more clear as he went along."

Christian continued reading,

"Have all the workers of iniquity no knowledge, who eat up my people as they eat bread, and do not call on the Lord? There they are in great fear, for God is with the generation of the righteous."

Christian thought, *Yes, David's description of evil people is not talking about everyone, or every Jew. When I pointed this out to Mr. Confident, he rather choked on it.*

Christian said, "So there it is: The Bible is not contradicting itself. Only part of the Psalm is talking about the wicked.

"Now let's look at Psalm 5, which Paul quotes in Romans 3:13. In that Psalm, David is talking about his enemies. Some of David's enemies were Jews. David, at the time, made it the focus of his life to be righteous and obedient to God. His enemies did not live that way. He describes his enemies in Psalms 5:9.

'For there is no faithfulness in their mouth; their inward part is destruction; their throat is an open tomb; they flatter with their tongue.'

The psalm ends by saying in verse 12,

'For You, O Lord, will bless the righteous; with favor You will surround him as with a shield.'"

"Yes," said Evangeline. "This is God. He doesn't force wicked people to be righteous. He courts every human being just like a lover does, because that is who He is. He loves us and when we accept His love, He draws us closer to Himself, so He can bless, protect and save us."

Christian said, "We're out of time. Let me close with a summary. In Romans 3:18, Paul wrapped up his argument that there really are some wicked Jews. He did this by quoting what David says in Psalm 36:1, 'An oracle within my heart concerning the transgression of the wicked: There is no fear of God before his eyes.'"

"So why didn't Paul mention any of the many verses that are about righteous Jews?" said Mr. Inquisitive.

Christian answered, "Because that had nothing to do with demonstrating his point he was making from Scripture, that there is such a thing as wicked Jews. But you have brought up a good point. These Psalms are about righteous Jews and wicked Jews. The Jews are no different from the rest of us. Today, Jews and Gentiles both can learn from the psalms David wrote almost 3,000 years ago. Our time is up, so let's pray."

At dinner after church, Christian purposefully went to an empty table. Taking advantage of that opportunity, Mr. and Mrs. Questioning from the class joined him. "So," said Mr. Questioning, "why can't God do as He pleases, fair or unfair? He is the Creator and has a right to do as he pleases."

"I agree," said Christian. Then Evangeline and Steady joined them. "So," asked Mr. Questioning, "what do you believe that is different from someone who says God chooses whom to save before they are born?"

"Of course, God has a right to preselect people," said Christian. "He just doesn't exercise that right." Just then, the ladies announced, "Dinner is ready!" and all conversation stopped till Pastor Caring said grace. Back at the table, after everybody had loaded up their plates and sat down again, Evangeline said, "Here's what I think. Angels are over the throne of God, watching everything He does. Then they evaluate what they see and report their conclusions for everyone to hear. And here's their report: 'holy, holy, holy.'" Pointing to Mr. Questioning, she said, "If you were there among those angels, this is what you would see: You would see God using His whole power, wisdom, and love to do what is best for everyone on earth, unconditionally, without concern for what it might cost Him."

"That's what I said," said Christian, munching on a piece of chicken.

Then Mr. Questioning objected, "Yes, God is in heaven. Yes, He is holy. But we're on earth, and we tend not to be holy. There's no way we can be holy. That's our problem."

"Woah!" said Steady, "it's not just our problem—it's God's problem too. He created us to be His friends, to do things with us. He can't do that if He doesn't solve our unholiness problem. Because He's God, He can solve that problem. And because He is love, He wants to solve it."

Christian said, "God wants to have fellowship with us, to share His life with us. And He longs for us to share our lives with Him. Yes, like Evangeline said, God is holy. That's why God told us in Scripture to be holy, for He is holy. And as Evangeline said, this means that just like God, we are called to use all our strength to do what is best for God and others."

"What? That's impossible! How could any of us ever do that?" Mr. Questioning said incredulously.

Christian smiled back at him and said, "Well, here's what I figured out. First, you need to accept God's love offered to you in the death and resurrection of Jesus Christ, as atonement for your sins. I figure you've already done that, right?" Mr. Questioning nodded.

"Second, you need to understand the difference between how you live and how God lives. Obviously, there's a lot of difference! That means you need to agree to His offer to change you. So you tell Him it's okay for Him to change your heart, to make you able to live a godly life. That way, God can fellowship with you in everything you do, if you let Him." Christian paused and looked straight at Mr. Questioning, before he continued, "I can't minimize this. It's a heavy duty choice. Do you want God to change you to be that kind of person, someone who uses all his strength to serve others?"

"I'm not sure," said Mr. Questioning. "What you say sounds disturbing. I would have to think about it."

"All right, then," said Christian. "The last thing to do is this: don't doubt God's love for you. Expect His fellowship. Expect Him to make you able to live a godly life, where you dedicate yourself to doing what's best for others."

"So what's the catch?" asked Mr. Questioning.

Steady immediately responded, "The catch is that we're sort of slow about learning what a godly life looks like. And then, once we learn what it is, we might be a little slow about agreeing to actually live that way."

"Oh," said Mr. Questioning. "I knew I was supposed to love my neighbor. But doing what is best for them never crossed my mind. That's like you're expecting me to look out for them! Even worse, I'm supposed to look out for them more than I look out for myself! That's outrageous!"

Christian laughed, "Too bad. When you became a Christian, that's what you signed up for. Sooner or later, you will be like that."

"So you think I should make it sooner?" asked Mr. Questioning.

Mrs. Questioning, who had been quietly listening, said, "Yes, dear, I think you should make it sooner…and I will too!"

Christian nodded and headed off to get a piece of apple pie.

---

[1] Ezekiel 33:11
[2] Romans 2:4
[3] Romans 2:6-16; Acts 18:10; Isaiah 49:6
[4] John 5:24; Acts 8:36-37; 16:31
[5] John 5:24, 28-29
[6] Matthew 7:21; John 3:19-21; 5:29; 6:44, 7:16-17; Acts 16:14; Ephesians 2:8-9
[7] John 3:21; Proverbs 3:5-6
[8] Deuteronomy 4:29; 1 Chronicles 16:10; 2 Chronicles 16:9; Isaiah 55:6-7
[9] 2 Chronicles 7:14; Luke 15
[10] Romans 2:6, 11; 1 Peter 1:17
[11] 2 Chronicles 31:20; Job 1:8, 29:12-17
[13] Luke 1:6, 2:25-32, 37-38
[13] John 15:5-15, 17:21; Revelation 21:1-3
[14] 1 Peter 1:16; Leviticus 11:44, 45
[15] Romans 6:19, 8:5, 16; Galatians 5:25; Matthew 7:7-8

# 13 LIVING BY FAITH

Monday morning, Steady came over to Christian's cabin with Saturday's newspaper. Christian, seeing his picture was on the front page, just broke out laughing. Then he read the article. It had everything he said to the reporter, with a lot of embellishments. When he read, "The robber fell to his knees weeping uncontrollably, while his partner had to drag him away," Christian started to laugh even harder. When he finally brought himself under control, he said to Steady, "I think the newspapers sure know how to make a story exciting."

"Yeah," responded Steady. "They want to sell newspapers."

With everyone in town now recognizing him, Christian had an enjoyable week talking to people about Jesus. So the time went by swiftly, and soon he was looking forward to teaching his next class. Sunday morning, he spent more time than usual praying for what the day might bring. He was having so much fun with his class he was afraid he might go off on something and not hear what God was saying. He felt that the most precious thing he had was for God to be with him as he talked to people about Jesus.

When Christian arrived at the church that morning, he saw that already there were horses in the church sheds and wagons parked outside. When he came into his classroom, Christian noticed that people were having conversations and getting to know each other. As the bell chimed 9 o'clock, Christian stood up and said, "Good morning, everybody. Let's pray." Then he started in. After a quick review of the week before, he went on, "Having shown that Jews are no better than Gentiles when it comes to sin, Paul comes to his conclusion in Romans 3:23. 'For all have sinned and fall short of the glory of God.'" Then he asked for comments as to what "the glory of God" might mean.

Evangeline said, "When it comes to 'glorious,' nothing compares to what God is. He's perfect in wisdom and love and everything else. That's His glory. And the 'fall short' part shows that our sin is basically anything we do that's different from God's perfect character.

With God's character as the standard, we have to agree with Paul. Everyone has sinned."

No one wanted to add to that so Christian said, "With such a high standard, we're all guilty. Now Paul is going to talk about the way out of our guilty condition. That way is called 'faith in Jesus.'" Christian paused for a moment and looked earnestly at the class. "I'll tell you what I think. Whenever I hear about all my sin and guilt removed by the blood of Christ, it really makes me feel loved by God. He sees my weakness and inability to be righteous (and yours too), but because of His goodness and love, He counts us righteous through faith in His Son. I can almost feel Him reaching out to me and putting His loving arms around me. His love for every person is without limit. Once we yield to God's love, we find no reason to try harder to be righteous. Instead, trust in His love becomes a way of life in which we do righteous things together with God. Paul is going to say more about this in chapter 6.

"But we're in chapter 4, which Paul begins by saying that he has been writing to Jewish believers, and is still talking to them. It's in this chapter that Paul talks about their heritage. So let's take turns and each read three verses of chapter 4."

After reading the chapter, Mr. Wise said, "Tradition and ritual do not make a person righteous. 'Without faith, it is impossible to please Him.'"

Evangeline said, "It makes me want to live in a way that He is pleased to live with me."

Steady said, "And knowing He loves me, I can fearlessly obey Him."

Christian said, "Faith trusts in His unfailing love, that He will always be with us so we can live righteously, which is different from trusting in how well we keep the law by ourselves. Rigid rule keeping is keeping God at arm's length. It's like saying, 'God, You just tell me what You want and I'll do it. But don't ask me to love You. I want to hang on to my independence.'" After a few more comments, Christian concluded the class time and amid a joyful bustle of voices, everyone headed in for the Sunday service.

The following week, Christian continued, "Now, in chapter 5, Paul takes faith even further. Verses 1–5 say there's a special reward if we patiently keep faith when difficult things come our way. We grow inside so the Holy Spirit can become a bigger part of our lives. As a result, God's love flows from us.

Christian continued, "Romans 5:10, 'For if when we were enemies we were reconciled to God through the death of His Son, much more, having been reconciled, we shall be saved by His life.' First Paul is talking about Christ dying for our sins, and then there's even greater love! God is 'much more,' than ready to unload more and more love upon us. It's like standing under Niagara Falls, only instead of water, it's the love of God. The water just keeps flooding down upon us, and in the same way, the tidal wave of God's love sweeps over us more and more. Do you want more? Here it is, and there's more after that—even more than the love demonstrated to us in the death of His dear Son. And verse 11 tells us this isn't for the future. This is the love He is pouring on us right now."

Suddenly, Mr. Strict shouted, "Hallelujah! When you asked us to be patient, I was determined not to be anything close to patient. But I get it now. I'm ready for the Lord to dump a load of love on me."

Amazed at the change that had come over Mr. Strict, Christian asked, "What happened that changed your mind?"

A smiling Mr. Strict said, "When I became convinced enough to allow myself to really believe God loved me, I felt closer to Him."

Christian said, "Amen. Now that Paul has shown how God is constantly overflowing with love even toward sinners and enemies, and even more so toward those who are His, he considered his readers to be about ready for chapter 6. So let's do it!

"In chapter 6, Paul is still talking to the Christian Jews. He wants them to understand the full richness of righteousness they enjoy in Christ. It has everything to do with the love of God and the grace of God and has nothing to do with Jewishness or the law. It's all about being born again, a new creation. 'Knowing this, that our old man was crucified with Him, that the body of sin might be done away with, that we should no longer be slaves of sin. For he who has died has been freed from sin,' says Paul.

"Romans 6 is very clear: We don't have to sin. That's the point of chapter 6. If we sin, it's because that's what we chose to do. Even as Christians, we haven't lost our ability to sin. Paul has a simple answer to sin in our lives: stop doing it. We are in Christ and we can stop. So why do we still sin? Because we still hang on to selfishness, pride, and lust. But Paul doesn't leave room for excuses. He says: 'For just as you presented your members as slaves of uncleanness and of lawlessness leading to more lawlessness, so now present your members as slaves of righteousness for holiness.'"

"Those sure are strong words!" said Mr. Questioning. "Paul doesn't hold back from laying out the truth."

Mr. Thoughtful commented, "It seems I'm constantly discovering new sins that I do. When I become aware of those sins, I know I can trust Christ to stop, but sometimes, it takes me awhile before I really want to. I think wanting to stop is the challenge." Then he added laughingly, "And I feel miserable until I do."

"And prayer helps," Steady commented, then he added, "Sometimes we need to ask God for help with our 'want to.'"

Christian asked, "Chapter 6 also raises a question, 'If being crucified with Christ means we are dead to sin, then what are Christ-following Jews supposed to do with the law?' Paul answers that question in chapter 7." There was a great rustling of Bible pages as the class all turned to chapter 7 and took turns reading a verse aloud until they had read the whole chapter.

Christian continued, "In chapter 7:1–4, Paul gives an illustration: In the same way that marriage vows are no longer valid after one of a married couple dies, Christian Jews, having died with Christ, are free from the law."

Mr. Uncomplicated said, "We Gentile Christians, who were never given the law, sometimes make the mistake of putting ourselves under it. I've talked to Christians who really believe the rest of Romans seven is talking about them. They read verse 18, 'For I know that in me (that is, in my flesh) nothing good dwells; for to will is present with me, but how to perform what is good I do not find,' and they say, 'That's me. I can't help myself. I just keep on sinning.' But what part of 'Reckon yourselves to be dead indeed to sin, but alive to God in Christ Jesus our Lord' don't they understand?"

Christian said, "That's right. After his example of being free to marry someone else, Paul describes his own experience of what it was like for him before he knew Christ, when he used to be under the law. All that stuff in Romans 7 tells us how he struggled on his own to keep the law. He finishes by crying out, 'O wretched man that I am! Who will deliver me from this body of death?' Then Paul gives his grateful answer, 'I thank God—through Jesus Christ our Lord!'"

Mr. Uncomplicated wasn't done. He said, "Paul would never think of a Christian as a 'wretched man.' Besides, being wretched would not be something Paul could thank God for."

Christian continued, "In 7:25b, Paul says his flesh is still around, but its power is broken, no longer able to take his mind captive."

Mr. Uncomplicated was on a roll. He chimed in, "This isn't hard to understand. We know all kinds of bad things go through our minds. But Paul gives us an answer, 'Do not walk according to the flesh but according to the Spirit.' It's right there in Romans 8:5. You can now rest your mind on the things of the Spirit. So let's all do that. We can stop resting our minds on the things of the flesh because we can. And if we need help, we can ask, and God will help us."

"Amen," Christian replied. "And right now, we have to stop, because our time is up. We'll start here in Romans 8 next week."

It snowed some the following week, and it really felt like winter was coming. When Christian stepped outside Sunday morning, he was greeted by a blanket of white fluff, but not quite enough to make snowballs. Leaving tracks leading to the church, he stopped to stomp his moccasins clean before entering. With the class assembled, he had them read chapter 8.

Christian said, "Romans 8 is beautiful. It's about rejoicing in being set free from the law of sin and death, a freedom that will someday be given to all creation. Verse 9 tells us what our freedom from the law looks like. 'But you are not in the flesh but in the Spirit, if indeed the Spirit of God dwells in you. Now if anyone does not have the Spirit of Christ, he is not His.' It's what we find in verse 16, 'The Spirit Himself bears witness with our spirit that we are children of God.'

Mrs. Uncomplicated said, "We shouldn't trade this for putting ourselves down, or worse, go back to the law or go back to struggling and striving and trying instead of trusting."

Evangeline added, "If I took my eyes off Jesus and just looked at how bad I am, I couldn't even raise my head high enough to see what other people need. And even if I did, I would be so busy criticizing myself that I wouldn't have the confidence to help them. But I've learned to trust the Holy Spirit to help me, especially when I talk to people about Christ. People say to me, 'Oh, Miss Evangeline, how can you be so bold and brave?' My answer is that I have a miraculous life in Christ. I trust. That's where my boldness comes from."

Christian said, "Yes! In verses 9-18 Paul emphasizes the blessing of the Spirit's help with the difficulties in this life as we wait for the 'glory which shall be revealed in us.' I agree with you. Now we're coming to Romans 8:28. 'And we know that all things work together for good to those who love God, to those who are the called according to His purpose.'

Christian looked earnestly at the class. "People take this verse out of context," he said. "They think that 'good' means what makes them 'feel good' in this fallen world. That's not how to treat God's Word." Then he asked, "The verse says 'all things work together for good.' If a baby dies, or your house burns down, or people hurt you, what's good about that?"

Mrs. Pleasant exclaimed, "I overheard someone tell that verse to a poor widow whose husband had just died. I thought it was a dreadful thing to say!" Others agreed.

Steady said, "The way people use verse 28, it almost sounds like they're blaming God for bad things that happen. But the fact of the matter is that bad things happen because we live in a fallen world."

"Looks like a lot of folks have used this verse the wrong way," said Mr. Thoughtful. "But what is the right way? What is this verse saying?"

So Christian began to explain. "Romans 8:28 should be read with verses 29–30 and 31. Notice that verse 29 begins with the word 'for.' This connects it to verse 28. Verse 28 is based on what is said in verse 29 and 30. Then verse 31 is like a climax that leaves us shouting with joy.

"[29]For whom He foreknew, He also predestined to be conformed to the image of His Son, that He might be the firstborn among many brethren. [30] Moreover whom He predestined, these He also called; whom He called, these He also justified; and whom He justified, these He also glorified. [31] What then shall we say to these things? If God is for us, who can be against us?

"See how it works? Once you read 29–31, you can see that verse 28 is about how wonderful our assured place in heaven will be. It's not talking about stuff that happens to us before we die."

Mrs. Reader asked, "This seems so obvious. How could anyone misunderstand it? When you see the word 'for,' of course you'd connect all the verses together! Actually verses 16-39 all connect together and are about the same thing."

Christian paused, not sure how to respond. Finally, he said, "I agree, and I think the reason people isolate verse 28 from verse 29 is that verses 29–31 are hard to understand without knowing what the words mean."

"Oh yeah," said Mr. Strict. "I was talking to Mr. Confident, and he said predestined means God controls everything that has ever happened and everything that will happen."

"I heard it means that before we were born, God planned which of us would be saved!" said Mrs. Uncomplicated.

"Ah!" said Mr. Thoughtful. "Then why would Paul need to persuade anyone about anything?"

*Oh no!* thought Christian. *The class is already going down the wrong trail on this. Mr. Confident's definition of predestination has messed them up already.* So he spoke up, "Whoa, everybody! The word 'predestine' in the Bible has nothing to do with whether or not you will be saved. And it's definitely not talking about God controlling everything that happens. Before repentance, you were predestined to hell. After repentance, giving your life to Christ, your destiny changed. Verse 28 is talking about what for sure will happen after you are saved. Like it says here in verse 29, you will be 'conformed to the image of His Son.' And there are even more places in the Bible that tell us about lots of other things we're predestined to, after we're saved. These things are the 'good' that God will bring out of the mess we're in, and it's for those who love Him and are called according to His purpose. And that purpose is that there will be sons to the Father and a Bride to the Son."

"I read about something," said Mrs. Reader. "We're predestined to be at the marriage supper of the Lamb. I'll bet God knows how to throw a humdinger of a party! How wonderful to able to see Jesus face to face!"

Then Christian looked hard at the phrase "For whom He foreknew…" He remembered how fond Mr. Confident was of thinking foreknew and predestined meant the same thing. *I'd better make sure these folks understand about God foreknowing,* he thought, and spoke out very firmly and clearly, "The other important word here is 'foreknew.' Foreknowledge means the steps God already knows He will take to reach His goal of what is predestined. Once you believe the gospel, God has it all figured out how He will lead you and change you to be Christ like, and all the other things He has predestined believers to have."

Mr. Thoughtful said, "It makes sense that foreknowledge and predestined mean different things. I think I understand the difference. Predestine means the final intent. Foreknowledge is like the steps we took to build the house we live in. A finished house that we can live in isn't the same as one under construction. But instead of a house, those who believe are predestined to God's final intent, for people to live with Him forever."

*I can still hear Mr. Confident's "Ah hah!" when he read Romans 8:29–33 to me,* thought Christian. *It sure popped his balloon when I read John 7:16–17 and Matthew 7:21 that tell the basis God has to choose who gets to have faith in His Son. Those passages all have to do with a choice people make about whether or not to obey God, a choice they make for themselves after they were born. Mr. Confident's jaw dropped like he was about to take a bite out of an apple when I showed him that.*

"Taking off from verse 31, 'If God is for us, who can be against us?' Paul continues with the same thought he began in verse 28. With a vision far beyond today's fallen world, we read Paul's triumphant call, 'Who can lay anything to the charge of God's elect? We are more than conquerors through Him who loved us. For I am persuaded that neither death nor life, nor angels nor principalities nor powers, nor things present nor things to come, nor height nor depth, nor any other created thing, shall be able to separate us from the love of God which is in Christ Jesus our Lord.'"

There were several comments of "Amen!" and "Hallelujah!" from the class, and Christian could see genuine joy on their faces. Holding up his Bible, Christian continued, "But after this shout of victory for those who are in Christ, Paul turns to a subject that made him very sad. We're out of time so next week we'll see what Romans 9 has to say."

---

[1] John 3:16; 1 John 2:2, 4:17
[2] Hebrews 11:6; Romans 1:17
[3] 1 Peter 1:23; 2 Corinthians 5:17
[4] Galatians 6:15
[5] Romans 6:6-8
[6] Romans 6:18-19
[7] Romans 6:11
[8] Romans 7:24-25a
[9] Romans 8:4
[10] John 14:13-14
[11] Galatians 5:24-25
[12] Colossians 1:13
[13] 1 John 3:2; Revelation 21:2-3
[14] Ephesians 1:12-13; 1 Corinthians 2:9-10
[15] Matthew 7:21; John 1:12, 6:44, 7:16-17; Psalms 4:3, 145:18-20
[16] Romans 8:27-39

## 14 ROMANS 9

Monday morning found Christian sitting close to his stove and reading the Bible. Once he was all warmed up, he headed outside and started collecting leaves to cover the asparagus, the rhubarb plants, and the carrots that he had planted to winter over for fresh eating in spring. After heaping up huge mounds of leaves over the plants, he thought about his potatoes. *It'll be a while before the ground freezes,* he thought, *but if I wait much longer, the ground will be too hard to dig.* On a knoll next to his cabin, Christian had dug a pit and made a ladder leading down. He'd put a layer of rocks and a layer of sand on the bottom to give water a place to drain. On top of that, he put an old barrel he found by the railroad tracks. He had also built a lean-to over the top to keep the rain out.

So getting a spade from the shed, Christian started carefully digging up his potatoes. Once he had a basketful, he uncovered the pit and dumped the potatoes into the barrel. After a couple of hours, he said to himself, *I feel so much better. Sitting and writing is hard. I guess I can go back now and do some more work on Romans.* After washing his hands in the river, he returned to his cabin. The warmth put out by the tin stove felt good. He sat down and started reading Romans 9 and thinking about his class on Sunday.

The week went by and the sun rose brightly on a very cold Sunday morning. People's breaths were like mists in the freezing air, and their cheeks were red with cold as they hurried into church. After having the class read Romans 9, Christian said, "Our salvation is so wonderful, but when we turn our attention to those close to us, our family and friends who have refused God's way of salvation, we become very sad. For a Jew who has come to trust in Jesus, this means grieving for their own Jewish people who have turned away and refused to believe.

Now it's time for Paul to answer Jewish believers' questions with great sympathy. By the things Paul says in Romans 9, it seems he takes the position of an advocate for God, answering anticipated objections, even the bitter question of why God would temporarily cast off His people, Israel. With forceful arguments Paul explains God's right to have done this. Paul also explains God's patience. The Jews needed to cut God some slack."

*Here it comes,* thought Christian, *Romans 9, the part where so many people think Paul is saying God is so evil and disgusting that He brings people into the world whose only possible destiny is hell. I'm going to have to slow down and have the class look below the surface and see what Paul really is saying.*

Christian continued, "Paul patiently answers the question, 'Why has God rejected His people?' It's because they rejected God's righteousness that is by faith."

Mr. Thoughtful asked, "Why all this fuss about faith? There's something here I just don't understand. Why did God make faith the way to be saved?"

Mrs. Pleasant said, "I think it's because faith is so much bigger than just a religious thing. Look at marriage. How can you have a loving marriage without faith in each other? And Jesus wants us to have a love for Him that is even bigger still. When we put our whole faith in Him, it's not just words. Our faith is from our heart and tells Him, 'Yes, Jesus, I do want you in my life.'"

Evangeline said, "It's like a suitor courting a bride! God spent fourteen hundred years trying to convince Israel that He loved them, and they should accept His love and love Him in return. So what did they do when He demonstrated His love by sending His Son? They still ignored Him and just kept obsessing over His laws. After all that time, I can understand God's pain as they refused to respond to His love, and He was being true to his character when He sent His Son to die for their sins. It wasn't just God the Son they rejected, it was God the Father. They refused to accept His love for them." Some of the other class members also began to speak up with their own ideas about what Paul was saying.

Listening to all this, suddenly Christian had a horrible thought. *Oh, no!* he almost gasped. *What's God going to do with Mr. Confident and others who limit and even deny His love? Without knowing any better, they use Romans 9 to slander God's loving character. They read Romans 9 and say that it proves God chooses to save or not save people before they are even born! But God is not a monster, creating people so He can roast them in hell. He would do anything to save just one more person from choosing to live forever without Him. That is the whole reason why Jesus came! To say He died for some and not for others doesn't match the love God demonstrated when He gave His Son!*

Christian remembered the people he had talked with about this and said to himself, *They say, "God is love, and He loves me!" Then they talk about God's wrath as though God relishes wrath. No, no, no! Why don't they see that wrath is the only option left after people refuse and reject all of God's love and forgiveness? Wrath is God's last resort, and it grieves Him when He has to exercise it.* Then Christian asked himself the question, *So what is God's wrath? It's God saying to those who have scorned and despised Him, "Thy will be done!" Look at what Paul is saying here in Romans. He's saying that God has given Israel the freedom from Himself that they wanted. Still, God lovingly pursues and even chastens, trying every way possible to persuade them to change their minds.*

The class was still talking about faith and how much God longs for everyone to put their trust in Him. Once it seemed that everyone who wanted to say something had had a turn, Christian said, "Now that we've discussed the value of faith, we can better appreciate why Paul wrote Romans. So let's get back to Romans! In chapter 9, Paul answers a possible objection. How could God even temporarily reject the special relationship He had with His people? Before he gets into the tough stuff that would be hard for the Jews to hear, Paul first softens what he had to say by sympathetically sharing his own pain. With tender compassion, Paul identified with how the Jewish Christians must have felt because God had set aside their nation of which they were so proud.

"Why would God set aside His own, specially chosen Jewish people? Paul had already given the obvious answer: 'Because most of the people had rejected the salvation offered to them through faith in His Son, Jesus Christ, God had no other choice.' But it seems Paul thought a more thorough explanation was needed. He now sets about showing this from God's point of view. First Paul establishes that God has a right to choose which nations He will bless. After all, it was by His choice that Israel, the nation descended from Jacob, was chosen in the first place and it wasn't based on anything Jacob (or Esau his brother) had done."

Christian had the class read verses 10–13, then Genesis 25:21–23 and 33:1–11. Mrs. Reader said, "This is so clear. Of course what is quoted about Jacob and Esau was talking about Israel and Edom." This sparked a discussion about how important it is to understand the context, especially where there is a quote from the Old Testament.

Then Christian had them read Deuteronomy 2:4–6 where God spoke of His protection for Edom even though they were not his specially chosen people to whom He would give the Ten Commandments. And it was through Esau's brother Jacob's descendants that Jesus would come into the world. But much later, Edom sinned against Israel, and God responded to their sin by destroying them as a nation and laying waste their land. The class turned to Amos 1:11–12 and read,

> For three transgressions of Edom, and for four,
> I will not turn away its punishment,
> Because he pursued his brother with the sword,
> And cast off all pity;
> His anger tore perpetually,
> And he kept his wrath forever.
> But I will send a fire upon Teman,
> Which shall devour the palaces of Bozrah.

Christian said, "When God was finished, Edom was as Malachi 1:2–3 described, 'Jacob I have loved; but Esau I have hated, and laid waste his mountains and his heritage for the jackals of the wilderness'"

"Oh!" said Mr. Thoughtful. "It looks like we need to look at the context of every verse, the context of the book it is in and the whole Bible!"

*Yikes!* thought Christian. *Maybe I overdid it with my emphasis on context. But Mr. Thoughtful is right. Lord, help me. What can I say?"* Trusting God to help him, Christian said, "We can't be putting ourselves under the law, even when it comes to knowing what is in God's Word. Seriously, we won't know everything in the Bible in our lifetimes. But there are things we can do. We can talk to God as we read His Word. We can look at context within reason, trusting Him to help us understand what He wants us to understand. And we can take the attitude of someone who is always learning. We don't want to be stuck on a quickly made conclusion but should be open to correction. For myself, I read the Bible looking for things I didn't know before or should be doing. When I find something, I pray about what it means, think about it, and study it further, trusting God to guide me. Like everything else we do, even our reading of

God's Word has to be something we do with Him.

"That's so logical," said Mrs. Uncomplicated. "We learned in Romans we are to live by faith that God loves us enough to be with us in everything. Of course we can trust Him to be with us as we read His Word. And like everything else, we need to do our part by being responsible and diligent as we trust in His love for us."

Christian couldn't help but laugh. He said, "Thank you, Mrs. Uncomplicated. I couldn't have said it better. Let's continue in Romans 9."

"Another comparison Paul makes is from Jeremiah 18 where God compares Israel with a lump of clay. From Israel, God can make something beautiful. Or He can smash down what was beautiful in Israel and make that nation into whatever else He chooses. In the context of Jeremiah, God's point was this: what He does with them depends on them. Therefore, Israel should change their minds and behave in a way that God would want to make them into a beautiful nation. It's interesting that at the time Jeremiah wrote about this, he also felt the pain of seeing Israel rejected by God, as they were about to be deported to Babylon because of their evil behavior.

Mrs. Reader said, "Yesterday I read this chapter, and noticed every verse of Romans 9 is either in the same sentence as the previous verse, or begins with words that connect it to the previous verse. So I think we have to look at the whole chapter as all belonging together."

Mr. Thoughtful spoke up, "But what about verse 22, where Paul begins the verse by saying 'What if'"?

"Well," said Mrs. Reader. "Paul's 'What if?' fits with Jeremiah 18, which the previous verse was referring to. But you're right. That's one place where the connection wasn't immediately obvious, and I did have to stop there and dig a little deeper."

"Thank you Mrs. Reader," Christian interjected. "I hadn't noticed that. This is an example of being too quick to separate verses, and that puts us in danger of missing the whole point of what the Bible is actually saying. The whole chapter is about objections Paul anticipates the Jews still had. Perhaps they would say, 'Hey! God can't do that to us! We're the chosen people. We have His promises.' In verse 22, Paul says, 'So what?' to the Jew's objections. He writes, 'What if…? What if God has a right to do as He pleases with Israel, and treat them as He does other nations?' But did He use that right? Not entirely. If He did, He would destroy them all as He did Sodom and Gomorrah. As proof that Israel earned that judgment, just take a look at Isaiah 1:9–10:

Unless the Lord of Sabbath had left us a seed, we would have become like Sodom, and we would have been made like Gomorrah.

"In Romans 9:29, Paul actually quoted this from Isaiah. He was rough on the Jewish Christians, really letting them have it. They couldn't help but realize that if God had not given Israel mercy, He would have done a lot worse to them than merely cast them off. Sodom and Gomorrah were totally destroyed.

After nine chapters of explanation, Paul was able to say some hard things the Jewish Christians couldn't deny. He wanted them to think, *My attitude was wrong. We're not better than the Gentile Christians after all.* Then Christian asked, "What do you think the Jews would be feeling after reading what Paul had to say in chapter 9?"

Mr. Thoughtful said, "Assuming they agreed with Paul's patient explanation of why Israel was cast off, they must have felt a great sadness."

"Yes," said Christian. "And that's our introduction to chapter 10." After the class read chapter 10, Christian said, "In this chapter, Paul begins by again drawing from his well of sympathy. Then Paul answers what they might be feeling, 'But what can our people do? How can we help them? What is the message for them that we can bring?' That's where Paul tells the simplicity of the way of faith, the way Israel rejected because they were 'seeking to establish their own righteousness.' Paul gives them the tools they need to help their brethren.

"So how can they become saved by faith? Paul answers in verse 9, 'If you confess with your mouth the Lord Jesus and believe in your heart that God has raised Him from the dead, you will be saved.' Then, like any wise Jewish rabbi, he repeats the same idea in verse 10. 'For with the heart one believes unto righteousness.'"

"What does he mean by the word 'righteousness' in verse 10?" asked Mrs. Uncomplicated.

"It's like God is saying the person is on the right track, but is not yet saved...Perhaps my testimony will help. I believed Christ died for my sins and God raised Him from the dead long before I was actually saved. With my little faith, I even prayed. God saw what I had done and said, 'That's right, Christian!' My little bit of faith was something God could work with. Paul calls it 'righteousness.'"

"I see," nodded Mrs. Uncomplicated.

Christian continued, "Verse 10 finishes by saying, 'And with the mouth confession is made unto salvation.' What I did not do right away is what I needed to do to be saved: tell Jesus that He is my Lord. It was when I really did want to turn my back on my sin and for Christ to be in my life that I asked Him to be my Lord and I was saved."

Mr. Thoughtful said, "The word 'Lord,' as in the Lord Jesus Christ, has a lot of meaning."

Christian replied, "When we tell people the gospel, it's helpful to explain the meaning of the word 'Lord.' Jesus is not offering that He should be a tool in their tool box, to be taken out and used as they choose. Rather, Jesus's offer is to be Lord in their lives, changing their character and attitude to become like His. If this is what they want, it certainly is good news. And once they decide and confess Jesus as their Lord, already knowing they need to obey gets them off to a good start.

"We should be saying, 'If you ask Jesus to be your Lord, it means you really do give Him permission to change you, to have a heart attitude to love other people the way He does.'

"We should also say something about the word, 'saved.' Saved doesn't just mean you go to heaven. It also means God saves you from selfishness and bad attitudes that lead to doing wrong. In its place, He puts the ability to value and love others. And He does this with the expectation that this is what you want, and that you will use that ability. It's something you do with Him.' Christian paused for a moment, then he continued, "After saying this we should ask, 'Is this what you want?'

"The invitation is, 'If you knew how, would you want to be that kind of person, the kind of person God wants to live with forever?' So when we tell people how Christ would be part of their life, they can make a more thoughtful, sincere decision to receive Him. And if they have followed what we have been saying, we can even ask, 'What do you think Christ would change in your life?' and that question would make sense to them.

"I think the gospel was a good rabbit trail Paul went on. Then Paul gets back to his main subject he started at the beginning of chapter 9. He reminds them again why God has rejected Israel and quotes what God said to Isaiah, 'All day long, I have stretched out My hands to a disobedient and contrary people.'

"At this point, Paul has accomplished his goals. He has explained how faith in Christ apart from the law puts us in right relationship with God. And by accepting faith in Christ as God's means of making us righteous, Jews and Gentiles are equal. They have both received grace equally. Now they can have unhindered love and respect for one another."

Christian closed his Bible just as the church bell began to ring. Our time is up," he said. "During the week, I encourage you to read chapters 9, 10, and 11 together, and try to follow the flow of Paul's thinking. At first glance, it seems Paul is jumping from subject to subject. So try to get past this and see how these chapters belong together and lead into chapter 12." After a short prayer, Christian dismissed the class.

All that week, Christian, convinced that comprehending God's love was essential to abiding in His love, found himself weeping for the class as he labored in earnest prayer for each person, that they would understand the love of God, not just for Israel, but for them as well. Young as he was, Christian was learning to think and act like a shepherd.

---

[1] Romans 9:31-33, 10:3
[2] Jeremiah 3:12-14; Ezekiel 6:9
[3] Romans 9:1-5
[4] Romans 9:14
[5] Romans 9:29; Isaiah 1:9
[6] Romans 10:3; Deuteronomy 30:11-14; 2 Corinthians 11:3
[7] Romans 10:21; Isaiah 65:2
[8] John 15:9-10, 7:23
[9] Hebrews 5:7; 2 Timothy 1:4

# 15 UNITED IN CHRIST

Sunday came and Christian arrived at the church very early to make sure the room was all warmed up and ready for the class to arrive. As people came in, Christian greeted each one while silently praying for them in his heart. Then he opened his Bible and began, "In chapter 11, we need to feel Paul's anguish because of what has happened to his people. He consoles himself, and the Jewish Christians, by the fact that God has not completely abandoned Israel. In chapter 11, Paul also has some things to say to the Gentiles, because having heard how God has cast Israel aside, the Gentiles might get a swelled head. Paul tells them that the rejection of Israel is only temporary, which should make everyone happy, especially with one another.

"The setting for the first few verses is a time in Israel's history when idolatry and wickedness were everywhere. But God told Elijah He had preserved the lives of 7,000 loyal to Him, though they were but a 'remnant,' a small scrap of what they once were. This was a word of encouragement, that it is in God's plan to always protect some who are loyal to Him until Israel is restored to favor.

"But in the meantime, does this give Israel something to boast about? Or is it something to be thankful for that God did not wipe them out, but gave them grace and saved a few? They can only boast of God's grace that will continue to be given to Israel. Though they are presently experiencing the consequences of their disobedience, God is not finished with His people. When God is finished, Israel will be obedient and a blessing to the world.

"Keep in mind that as Gentile Christians, we have every reason to show respect to the Jewish people. The first Christians were all Jews. It's by their obedience and love for God that they gave us the gospel. We should be praying for the Jewish people. We owe them a debt that we can only repay by sharing back to them the good news of the gospel Jewish believers once generously shared with us. As Paul had done, we pray for their salvation.

"Chapter 12 begins with a simple formula for Christians, Jews and Gentiles to become like Jesus: Give yourself fully to God, be renewed by His Spirit in your mind, live the good will of God."

Mrs. Reader said, "Mr. Knowsalittle was telling some of us about Romans 12:1–2, how important it was that we give ourselves completely to God so He can transform our minds. Then I remembered what you said about reading the context. The very next verse begins with the word 'for.' 'For' means what follows is important and is the reason for what was already stated. Then I saw that the next verse also begins with 'for.' And the verse after that begins with the word 'so.' 'So' means what follows is the point Paul was getting to, going all the way back to Romans 12:1. In the context, we need to have our minds transformed to use our God given gifts to help other Christians, and also to receive help from them. The church is to be like a family."

Mrs. Uncomplicated said, "That is so right. If we don't let God be in what's in our minds, we think all kinds of proud things that keep us from loving one another."

"Whew," Christian exclaimed, "I'm learning from all of you."

Mr. Thoughtful had scanned Romans 12 and added, "This chapter also seems to say that in order to help one another, we need to be humble. In order not to be proud, that would take a transformed mind."

Getting back to what she really wanted to say, Mrs. Reader continued, "I'm really grateful that I've learned to look at the context of every verse. It really makes the Bible come alive."

"Yes," said Christian. "And in the next section of Romans 12, Paul is telling the Romans and us not to be proud, but contribute what we can to one another.

"Toward the end of chapter 12, Paul begins talking about general attitudes within the church, beginning with loving even an enemy. In chapter 13, Paul talks about honoring rulers. In verses 11–14, he expands on the simple formula for how Christians are to live: give ourselves completely to God so He can transform our minds, then live the good will of God.

And do this, knowing the time, that now it is high time to awake out of sleep; for now our salvation is nearer than when we first believed. The night is far spent, the day is at hand. Therefore let us cast off the works of darkness, and let us put on the armor of light. Let us walk properly, as in the day, not in revelry and drunkenness, not in lewdness and lust, not in strife and envy. But put on the Lord Jesus Christ, and make no provision for the flesh, to fulfill its lusts.

"And yes," commented Mr. Thoughtful. "We did sign up for this. Romans is very clear that we should cast off the works of darkness because we can cast them off. Put on the armor of light because we can put it on."

Christian said, "Do you all know what these things mean? If not, we can go back and talk about chapter 6 again." Everyone seemed satisfied, so Christian pressed on to finish Romans. He was already looking forward to teaching Ephesians.

After the class read chapters 14–16, Christian said, "Chapter 14 tells us not to allow food or special days to interfere with our love for one another. In 15:8–16, Paul gives a final word to Jews concerning Gentiles. Paul finishes his letter by talking about his trip to Jerusalem, bringing a contribution for the poor. He then sends greetings and ends with a beautiful benediction."

At dinner that day, Mr. Thoughtful came over and joined Christian, Steady, and Evangeline. He asked Christian, "You seem to have a special interest in making sure we understand Romans 9. Why is that? I think there's something you're not telling us."

Christian laughed. "You are so right! I believe God wants to share His life with us. We're going to be talking about that next week when we start Ephesians. According to Ephesians 3:19, the condition we must meet for God to fill us with the fullness of Himself is that we understand what His love is all about. And the devil does his best to keep us from understanding God's love. I think one of the devil's favorite tools is to get Christians to misinterpret Romans 9. He's quite successful at it, and lots of Christians are really into their misinterpretation, even though it has become like a wall that separates them understanding God's love. And they're very militant about spreading lies about what God is like. They place limits on His love, saying, 'As Creator, He has a right to be mean if He wants to.' I agree that He has a right to do that. But He really is love. He will never lie. And He did say He delights in love. So I want to be sure no one is sucked into a way of thinking that would keep them from living what is called an 'abiding life,' life that is always full of God."

Mr. Thoughtful responded. "I see your point, and I'm looking forward to what you have to say about Ephesians. It's short and I want to be ready. I think I can read it through every day."

Mr. Strict had quietly been sitting next to Mr. Thoughtful and was listening intently. Finally he said, "I get it now. When I allowed myself to think God really is love, I started to expect Him to be part of my life. When I did that I felt myself changing. I...I finally realized that I was creating a god whom I could control. But when I started expecting God to be close to me, loving me, I discovered that He more than met my expectation. I never realized how lonely I was until I started believing God loves me. It was like being born again all over again. Since then, I've been conscious of His desire to be with me. Thank you so much for your patience." For the rest of dinner, the five of them talked about the love of God and what it means to us that He earnestly wants to share His life with us.

That night, Christian was lying in bed thinking about Ephesians when there was a knock on his door. "Who is it?" he asked. There was no response, and the knocking just continued. Christian lit his lamp, dressed quickly, and opened the door. He felt his heart leap in his chest. It was the robber standing at his door. Recovering himself, Christian said, "It's really cold out. Please come in." Christian put some wood on the coals that were still glowing in his little stove. "What can I do for you?"

The robber took a deep breath and said, "For a long time it's been on my mind that I've hurt so many people that I wrecked myself inside. People talk about love. There's nothing in me that relates to that. I could never have a family, people I love. Whatever that means, I wrecked it for myself. When you said Jesus could help me, I suddenly realized I just want to be human. It's as if it came crashing into my mind. I just wanted to get away. But now I've had time to think. So tell me. How do I do this?"

"Jesus changes you so you can obey Him," Christian said quietly. "When people pushed Him around, He reacted by doing what was best for them. Are you sure you want to love other people the way He does?"

"You don't understand," said the robber. "I haven't any choice. I don't want to be what I am anymore."

"Does that mean you would give back to the bank your share of the loot?"

"I don't really want to do that," said the robber, and then he hesitated. "Actually, I've got all the loot now."

"How did that happen?" asked Christian.

"My partner wanted more because I said we should leave the bank before he got everything. We had some words and he went for his gun."

"Oh!" said Christian. But he was thinking, "Does this guy really want Jesus or does he just want to feel better about himself?"

Finally, Christian said, "How about if I give you a Bible verse that tells how to start following Jesus? Then you could think about it and do what it says."

"All right," said the robber.

"Okay," said Christian. "Do you believe Jesus died for your sins?"

"Yes!"

"Do you believe God raised Him from the dead?"

"Yes," said the robber.

"Then here's the verse," said Christian. "Memorize this, 'Whoever calls on the name of the Lord shall be saved.'"

"That's all?" the robber incredulously asked.

"That's enough," said Christian. "The word 'saved' means God takes the selfishness out of your life and replaces it with a true care and love for other people, including bankers. And the word Lord means that you will obey Him. For sure, He will change you so you will give the bank back its money. Knowing that's what will happen in your heart, do you still want Jesus to come into your heart and change you?" The robber made a big toothy grin and said, "When and if He changes me, I'll do that. Like you said, being changed into what Jesus wants is worth more than all the money in the world. But He hasn't done it yet."

"Okay," said Christian. "That verse is God's promise to you. It's all about you talking to Him. It says you have to talk to Him. So can you remember the verse?"

"No problem," the robber said seriously. "'Whoever calls on the name of the Lord shall be saved.'"

Christian said, "You have what you came here for. The rest is between you and God. There's nothing more I can do for you."

Still looking serious, the robber said. "I can't remember ever saying thank you to anybody. But I feel I should say it to you. Thank you. It must be working already." Then the robber slipped out the door and disappeared into the night.

Two weeks went by, and again, in the night, there was a knock on Christian's door. Again, he lit his lantern and dressed quickly. Opening the door, he found a large sack full of money. Looking out into the still darkness, he couldn't see anyone. Christian said to himself, *Tonight there's rejoicing in heaven. Tomorrow there will be rejoicing at the bank.* Taking the money inside, Christian went back to bed wondering what would become of the robber. Praying that God would take care of him, Christian fell asleep.

---

[1] Romans 11:15, 25
[2] 1 Kings 19:18
[3] Romans 11:12, 26-27
[4] Jeremiah 9:24
[5] Luke 15

# 16 MR. FRIENDLY AND MR. EVANGELIST

Mr. Friendly, who served as an usher, noticed some of the new people were arriving late for the church service and leaving early, before the last hymn. Wondering why, he started making a point of intercepting them on their way out, and what he discovered soon led him into earnest prayer. It seemed that the reason why they came late and left early was they were having personal problems and didn't want anyone to notice them. At first, they were hesitant to talk, even to Mr. Friendly, but sometimes he was able to convince them to stay for dinner, where he made a point of introducing them to the kindest and most compassionate members of the congregation.

Eventually, Mr. Friendly went to Pastor Caring and asked for help in getting more people to be ushers. Working alone as he usually did, while he was talking to one person, several others would slip by. "We need ushers who've been a Christian for a while," Mr. Friendly said. "And we'd need to teach them a bit about how to help people with problems."

Pastor Caring immediately contacted the elders, and using their recommendations, a sizable group of enthusiastic church members was recruited. In fact, at the training meeting that Saturday morning, so many eager believers came that Pastor Caring thought, *Wonderful! We've got enough people here that I could even ask some of them to help me with counseling folks. That would be a wonderful ministry for these caring people, and it would be a help to me!* When he suggested the idea at the new usher meeting, Mr. Friendly said, "Great idea! Ushers should also know how to be counselors." There was a murmur of agreement and also of excitement when Pastor Caring said, "All right then—let me lay out the basics of how to help troubled people."

All eyes were on Pastor Caring as he stepped to the front of the room and said, "The foundation for all counseling is this: Love heals most problems. By definition, real love is to do what is best for others no matter what the cost. So when I counsel, I follow a simple formula. Here it is: When people do what's best for others, that is real love, and it will heal their relationships. That's my formula. When children do what's best for their parents, it heals their relationship. When parents do what's best for each other, it gives their children an example of a relationship that works. Real love heals, and real love is all about doing what's best for others. If you use this formula, you won't get too bogged down with the same people with the same problems that never seem to get solved. I've often preached on this, but it seems people have a hard time applying it to themselves. That's where you would come in, helping people visualize what their life would be like doing what's best for others, especially the person they're having difficulties with.

"Here's an example of a family I counseled some time ago. A wife and mother, we'll call her Mrs. Feelings, would find some small disagreement with her husband and her feelings just took over. She would find herself out of control, yelling at him without knowing why she was overreacting. He was a patient man, but sometimes, he reached his limit and yelled back.

"The sad thing was the effect this had on their children. They saw their parents disconnected from one another, so they also emotionally kept their distance. They were not happy children. Separately, I counseled the mother, and I asked her what was best thing she could be doing for her husband. She actually said, 'Never yell at him again.'

"We talked about how her life would be different if she did that, and she reluctantly agreed to simply make her wishes known, then not nag him. Oh, she put on such a sour face when she said, 'Okay, I'll try it.'

"I also counseled the husband following my simple formula. He said, "If she gets into one of her moods, I guess the best thing I could do is think about her feelings and try to help her feel as if I'm with her and everything's going to be all right…Yeah! And I'll do the hug thing."

"Then I talked to the children separately. They said they would run away and hide 'when mother and father talk mean to each other.' We talked about what they could do instead. The oldest boy said, 'I think the best thing we could do for our parents is find some chores to do instead of holing up somewhere.' Then we prayed for their parents. The next time I saw Mrs. Feelings, she said, 'I can't believe my children. Just like you said, they saw my husband and I reconnecting with each other and they began to behave better. We all feel more like a family instead of individuals living in the same house. And I found that I could trust my husband.' Then she laughed and said, 'And by respecting him instead of yelling at him, I usually get what I want. Thank you very much!'"

Pastor Caring paused and smiled at the recollection. "I tell you," he said to the class, "that made my day!"

After the class members discussed the example, an hour had gone by, and the group talked about what to do next. It was decided to meet every week to learn more, ask questions, and talk about what they learned.

Pastor Caring believed in learning by doing. He said, "Keep this in mind: You'll make mistakes. On my way home from counseling people, I regularly realize I said things I shouldn't have said, and often I think of other things I wished I had said. But this is how we learn. It's like learning to swim. You put aside your fears and get into the water."

Some people in the class suggested they start by working in teams of two or three. There was a sigh of relief when Pastor Caring enthusiastically said, "That's fine! Let's do that, at least until you all feel comfortable doing this." Those who wanted to help with counseling formed teams, and after praying, Pastor Caring gave them names of folks who had asked for help. Mr. Friendly scheduled others to help usher on Sundays. There were also a few who wanted to do both.

A week later, when the group met again and shared their experiences (without naming those whom they had counseled), Mr. Forthright said, "With the folks our team talked to, we put the choice right in front of them by saying, 'Do what's best for the other person if you want your relationship to work. If you insist on doing what's best mainly just for yourself, no relationship will work as God intended.'"

It turned out that the other new counselors had done something similar. They saw families being reconciled right there in front of them. Mrs. Tenderheart said, "They started crying and hugging each other and saying, 'I'm sorry.' I was so touched I started crying with them."

The ushers also had stories to tell. Hearing the enthusiastic reports, Pastor Caring and Mr. Friendly rejoiced, and Pastor Caring was especially gratified because he always thought it important to encourage everyone in his congregation to have a ministry. He reflected on how his ministry taught him to truly care for and pray for others.

Pastor Caring encouraged everyone to use Bible verses. He said, "It's okay to say, 'Let's have a short Bible study.' Then you can introduce something from the Bible to talk about. Today, I want to talk about what to do when people have an anger problem. A good passage to introduce would be Ephesians 4:29–32. Angry people often enjoy terrorizing people with their anger and are quick to make excuses for their behavior. They often point to Ephesians 4:26 where it says, 'Be angry, and do not sin, do not let the sun go down on your wrath,' and say, 'See, it's okay to get angry!'" They ignore the fact that their anger is sin and lacks compassion for the other person. They also ignore what it says just five verses later in verse 31, 'Let all bitterness, wrath, anger, clamor (which is loud quarreling), and evil speaking be put away from you with all malice.' And indeed, most of what they say when they are angry is 'evil speaking.' Chapter 4 ends with an exhortation to behave like our Lord, with tenderness and forgiveness. It's impossible to be angry with people while thinking about what Christ has done for us and being thankful."

The timing of Pastor Caring's advice about anger was perfect. Later that day, Miss Molly Dearheart, Mr. Firm, and Mr. Bottomline talked with the Shortfuse family. They all sat down in the parlor and Mr. Shortfuse announced, "We're always getting mad at each other around here. Yellin', yellin'. We sure do have a problem."

Mr. Firm responded, "You folks don't have an anger problem. You have a love problem. If you respond to one another with love, each one of you would do what is best for the other person! But tell me, who was the last one to be angry?"

"It was me," said Mrs. Shortfuse. "I just finished mopping the linoleum in the kitchen this morning when Mr. Shortfuse here came in from the barn and tracked mud everywhere on my clean floor. I snapped at him about it. Then he told me to stop nagging and get over it. It got real ugly from there."

Mr. Firm asked, "So why is mud on the floor more important than doing what's best for your husband?"

Mrs. Shortfuse looked very puzzled and raised a doubtful eyebrow, so Molly Dearheart said compassionately, "You don't have to answer. But what Mr. Firm said is what a Christian does, to do what's best for others and not just think of ourselves. When we were doing wrong, Jesus was thinking about what was best for us. So if at the time Mr. Shortfuse tracked in mud, you were thinking, *What is the best thing I can do for my husband*, what would that have been?"

Mrs. Shortfuse laughed, but her laughter had an edge to it. "I guess I would have stopped to think about how hard he was working out in the barn and how tired he was. I guess I could have nicely asked him to head back into the mud room to take off his boots. Then I could have gotten the mop that was still wet and cleaned the dirt up and thanked him for his hard work he does for us all."

"See," said Mr. Bottomline. "In order to be angry, you had to lay aside God's command to love one another. Love means to do what is best for them, not thinking of yourself. Now, Mr. Shortfuse, what would you have done differently this morning that would be the best thing for your wife?" Mr. Shortfuse said, "I didn't do nothin'!"

Mr. Firm persisted, "Well, other than telling her to get over it, what could you have done for your wife?"

"I suppose I could have helped clean up the mess I made," Mr. Shortfuse said reluctantly.

"Come on," said Mr. Bottomline. "What else could you have done?"

Mr. Shortfuse hung his head down and said, "And I could have given her a hug and told her I was sorry."

Molly Dearheart wasn't satisfied. With a twinkle in her eye, she asked, "Could you have whispered sweet nothings in her ear?"

Mr. Shortfuse began to turn a bit red. Finally he said, "Yeah. I used to do that when we were first married. I don't know why I stopped. I really do love my wife."

Mr. Bottomline said, "I have a verse I would like to share with you, 'And be kind to one another, tenderhearted, forgiving one another, even as God in Christ forgave you'—Ephesians 4:32. This is what we're talking about. Being quick to forgive is a different way to live, and it brings pleasure to God who loves you. Can we all agree to change our minds and start living this way?"

Mr. and Mrs. Shortfuse looked at one another with a softness in their eyes that said yes before their "yes!" was spoken.

Meanwhile, the five Shortfuse children were as quiet as little mice. Mr. Firm turned to them and asked, "You kids need to do this too. You need to do what's best for one another."

They all bobbed their heads up and down and mumbled, "Yes, sir."

Then Molly Dearheart said, "Doing what is best for others, even if it costs you some pain to do it, allows Jesus to be part of your life. This is something He wants. It's what He created you for. Now we're going to pray, and I want each one of you to ask God to show you how to do what's best for one another, no matter what they have done or what it costs you. And then ask Him to help you do it, so you do it together with Him. If you do get angry, stop and pray. Don't give in to your anger. Ask Jesus to help you. It may take a while, but you can get over getting angry. Don't give up and Jesus will help you."

But before they prayed, Molly Dearheart became like a tiger and went after every one of the kids until she was sure they all understood what they were praying for. One of the boys asked, "What should I have done when Larry spit on me?" Miss Dearheart said, "You're in good company. They spit on Jesus. Just stop and ask Jesus to be with you, and say to your brother, 'Jesus loves you and I forgive you.'" Then she made each child pray in turn, their own understanding of what it meant to do what was best for their brothers and sisters. As they prayed, the Holy Spirit seemed to fill the room, as if God Himself was giving His approval. Mr. and Mrs. Shortfuse also prayed and asked God to show them how to do what was best for one another. As the team left, they looked back and saw them with their arms around each other. Molly Dearheart later said, "Seeing that made me feel good all over."

As time went on, the counselors grew in confidence. In situations of ordinary selfishness, they only had to point out an appropriate Bible verse and talk about the love God wanted the person to express by doing what was best for others. If there was something more complicated, the counselors would let Pastor Caring know, and he would take it from there. A few people thought the counselors weren't telling them what they wanted to hear, and some of them even left to go to one of the other churches in town. But those who took the advice to do what was best for others had their relationships healed and their problems solved.

In the meantime, Mr. Evangelist was watching all of this going on and was starting to think that he and Pastor Caring needed more help visiting newcomers to the church. *It isn't right that they aren't all being visited. Some of them know the Lord, but some don't,* thought Mr. Evangelist.

So Pastor Caring announced at church there would be a meeting for those interested in evangelism and visitation. "Come at 3:00 p.m. Saturday," he said. When the day came, Mr. Evangelist was very pleased when eleven people showed up, and he was especially pleased when he saw that his daughter, Evangeline, was among them.

"Whenever we do evangelism," he said, "our main emphasis is the loving character of God. God desires to have relationship with us, and it's into this relationship that we invite people. So give them a chance to tell you about it if they're angry at God about something. Until their objections to the love of God are answered, the unsaved might not want to make any kind of commitment to Him. And the saved need to have confidence in the love of Christ in order to grow in Him."

After spending some time in prayer, the group divided into teams and off they went.

One of the evangelism teams, led by the very experienced Mr. Herald, came to visit Mr. Stuck. As they sat around the kitchen table talking about Mr. Stuck's visit to the church, Mr. Herald finally asked, "If you should die, do you know for sure where you are going?"

Mr. Stuck said, "I hope heaven. But I don't think anyone can know for sure."

"Think about what it means to be ready to go to heaven," said Mr. Herald. "God will have to change you to love others more than you love yourself. If you decide to give your life to Him, He really does come into your life and He changes you to love as He loves. If He didn't change you and you went to heaven, you would probably wreck the place. Do you want Him in your life, making that kind of change?"

Mr. Stuck thought that over for a minute and said, "I guess so. Sounds good." Then he and the team spent some time discussing what Jesus would change and what it would be like if Jesus were his Lord. Finally, Mr. Stuck said, "I want to do this. I want Jesus to come into my life and help me be the person He wants me to be." So the team prayed with him as he asked Jesus to be His Lord.

Mr. Assured then showed him John 3:16 and asked, "When you prayed, was that your way of believing on the Lord Jesus?"

"Yes, it was!" said Mr. Stuck.

"Then what does this verse say that you have?" asked Mr. Assured.

"I have eternal life," said Mr. Stuck.

"So if you die, where will you go?"

"Heaven! I'll go to heaven," smiled Mr. Stuck.

The following Saturday at the 3:00 meeting, Mr. Herald told the evangelism class about how they had prayed with someone to receive Christ. Then he said, "I really feel the power of the Holy Spirit when I give an invitation to receive Christ. It can take many forms. Sometimes I say, 'If you knew how, would you want God in your life, helping you to live in a way that He can live with you?' It seems that when I give an invitation, the Holy Spirit rivets the person's attention on every word."

Mr. Evangelist said, "Just before the invitation, I always ask, 'Do you believe Christ died for your sins and rose from the dead?' If they say they can't believe, I spend more time talking about the change Christ would make in their lives. Then I ask, 'If it were true that God would change you, is that something you would want?' For them to thoughtfully make the decision to say 'Yes—if it were true,' is a step in the right direction.

"After they have made that commitment, I tell them, 'Believing is easy. All you have to do is stop refusing to believe.' I recently did this, and later in the conversation, I asked again, 'Do you believe God raised Jesus from the dead?' The man I was talking to thought for a moment and said, 'Yes!'

"Some people think believing is something that we feel. In actual fact, to disbelieve is a decision. It's not a feeling, it's a choice. When people stop choosing to disbelieve, they often find themselves believing."

Mr. Evangelist paused and then went on, "There are two parts to the gospel. There's what I call the mechanical part: believe Christ died for your sins and rose from the dead."

Mr. Custom objected, "But isn't that what people need to believe to be saved? What more could there be?"

Mr. Evangelist shook his head. "There's also the heart part. People need to believe with all their heart.[4] To believe in the heart is to really want Christ, a real decision of the heart. It's more than just an intellectual belief. God wants to change the attitude of people's hearts so He can have a living relationship with them. So our will and our heart are both involved, not just our minds. Once people are on board with the heart part, wanting from the heart a real relationship with Christ, they more easily understand and believe."

"You mean they have to want the part about how Jesus changes us to be like Him?" asked Mrs. Insight.

"Exactly," said Mr. Evangelist. "We need to tell them what it's like to have Christ, having our hearts changed to be more loving and kind. Once they're on board with that, they find they believe, and their belief is from their heart."

"I can understand that," said Mrs. Insight. "It starts converts off on the right foot. And I also need to be reminded of the change God is making in my life."

"Yes," said Mr. Practical. "If someone is already a Christian, talking about how the love of God changes us would also make for a good visit."

"That's a good point," Mr. Evangelist continued. "A lot of Christians became Christians without knowing what they were getting into, and it has hindered their growth. That is, if they only figure out how to live as a Christian several years after they're saved, it's not the best thing, especially if in the meantime they've picked up habits that exclude Christ from their lives except on Sunday. We need to give people an understanding of what they're getting into right from the start. But if they missed learning how to live as someone who is in Christ, we need to be talking to them about it."

Evangeline, by far the youngest person among them, turned out to be a real asset to the class and her team. When visiting families, the children would identify with her. She had a way of explaining the love of God in a way they could understand. Her manner had a sweetness that gripped people's attention. She could tell anyone anything about the Lord and they would receive it.

Emboldened by Evangeline's example, other young people began to join the visitation teams. They in turn encouraged others to join. As it turned out, being included with adults made them feel quite grown up. For most of them, it was an introduction to serving Christ.

A short time later, Mr. Evangelist and Mr. Friendly began to regularly meet together for prayer and to talk about what they had learned and how they could help each other. Like desperate men, they also prayed for the church. For the present, things were under control, but such an avalanche of new people were descending on the church that it would only be with God's help that they could accommodate them all. Almost every week, they needed a new miracle.

---

[1] 1 Peter 3:7
[2] Colossians 3:8, 14; Ephesians 4:30-5:2
[3] Matthew 22:39; Ephesians 5:2, 28-29; Acts 8:37

# 17 BIBLE SCHOOL

A few weeks later, Christian was at the home church meeting in the Friendly's house. It was communion time, and as the bread was being passed around, he thought about how it symbolized that we are, all of us together, the body of Christ. Looking around at the people in the warm atmosphere of the house church, Christian felt a strong desire to spend the rest of his life serving these people whom he had come to love. *There's so much more I need to learn,* he thought. *Pastor Caring went to Bible school... I'd like to be a pastor too. But where would I ever get money for tuition?*

The answer was very quick. The next day, Christian was offered a job as a helper at the blacksmith's shop. Thinking, *God provides,* he jumped at the opportunity and saved almost every penny he made.

When he was fifteen, Pastor Caring said to him, "You're old enough now. So get going. Write a letter and apply for the Bible school." Christian's heart leaped at the thought and he said, "Yes, sir!" Since he used the church as a return address, the whole church knew about the letter that arrived from the Bible School before Christian did. Yes, he was accepted. Mr. Evangelist was there when Christian opened the letter. Immediately he said, "The elders have already decided to help. Whatever you need, we're going to make sure you have it." When Mrs. Hospitality got the news, she said, "Oh yes, we ladies are going to have biggest sendoff bash you ever saw."

A week later, Pastor Caring rode over to Christian's cabin and began to ask practical questions. "How are you going to get there? Bible School is 300 miles away."

Christian said, "I'm going to walk. Here's my backpack I made out of rawhide."

Pastor Caring's jaw dropped. Then he said, "So what are you going to eat?"

Christian proudly showed him the small oilcloth bags he had made. "This one is full of pemmican for energy. I found some rocks I could use to grind jerky into a powder which I mixed with rendered fat. I lined the bag with waxed paper to keep the fat from getting on everything."

Pointing to another bag, he said, "I also roasted some corn, cut off the kernels, and ground them into powder. To this, I mixed in a lot of sugar and ground cinnamon. I can mix it with water. It will be something I can drink to get me going first thing every morning. And look. I have cheese and dried fish. I also have some jerky to chew on while I walk. Don't worry. Three hundred miles isn't that far."

"Hmmm," figured Pastor Caring, "it could take a couple of weeks. Are you sure you won't run out?"

Christian said, "I don't eat much when I'm hiking. It should be enough food. And I have an old bottle for carrying water to drink. And there should be creeks along the way."

"How are you going to sleep?" asked Pastor Caring.

"Oh," said Christian. "I'll bring a wool blanket. I'll just tie it over the top of my backpack. I also have a rubber sheet to use as a ground cloth."

"But what if it rains?" asked Pastor Caring.

"I hope it doesn't," said Christian. "But if it does, my wool blanket is wrapped in a piece of oilcloth that's big enough to go over me if it gets too cold or it rains. Don't worry, I'm ready to go."

"I see you are," said Pastor Caring. "Just don't go before Sunday. The ladies have something special planned for you. They'd be very disappointed if you'd left already, and so would I."

That Sunday, the ladies outdid themselves. *What a feast*, thought Christian, as he sampled everything. And at the dinner, it seemed like everyone wanted to make a speech. Finally, Pastor Caring stood up. "Christian, we all know how you like to speak your mind. So here's my advice for surviving Bible School. Don't say much in class until you figure out your professor. Some will want you to parrot back exactly what they teach and will not tolerate any creative ideas. Others appreciate creative ideas as long as you can logically defend them. Once you figure out your professors, give them what they want. And the tests—tests are not about what you think, but what they want. In their lectures, note anything the professor emphasizes. If you emphasize that same thing, it will get you an A. Remember, there's a time to learn and a time to teach. This is your time to learn. Take advantage of it and learn all you can."

Pastor Caring was like a father to Christian, and Christian resolved to take Pastor Caring's advice to heart.

Pastor Caring finished by saying, "We want you to write and tell us all about what you're doing."

Christian said, "I will. I promise."

Mr. Friendly offered to store anything Christian wanted to leave with him. Everyone wanted to help. Then they presented him with a pocket watch as a going-away present. The great outpouring of affection got Christian all choked up. It would be hard to leave these people who loved him so much.

Arising early Monday morning and eating a last breakfast of fish from the river and vegetables from his garden, Christian put on his backpack and was off, walking mile after mile. Next morning, he was up at first light. Quickly, he stowed his gear and started to walk. The morning was cold. When he reached the first patch of bright sunlight, he stopped for a breakfast of pemmican, dried fish, and a corn drink. Midmorning and midafternoon, he stopped for a ten-minute pemmican break. Dinner was dried fish and cheese with pemmican. Supper was pemmican with cheese and dried fish. Just before the sun went down, Christian looked for a flat place off the road, where he could sleep under the stars.

This was his routine during all the days he spent walking to Bible School. One night, it rained, and he had to spread the oilcloth over the wool blanket and his backpack. At noon the next day, he spread everything that was wet out in the sun while he ate. After ten days, his long walk was over. He arrived at the Bible School just as the sun was going down and spent his last night under the stars. Feeling tired yet excited in joyful anticipation of learning more of God's Word, Christian fell asleep.

That night, he had a dream. He was standing in a bright sunlit meadow looking up at the sky. Heaven opened and he saw the Lord speaking the promise made before creation, the promise of eternal life.

Eternal life which God, who cannot lie, promised before time began. (Titus 1:2)

In his dream, suddenly an angel stood by him and said, "I'm here to show you things in Scripture in order that you might understand and know God's heart. You know the verse, John 3:16?" Christian nodded. He remembered it well: "That whoever believes in him should not perish, but have everlasting life."

"From before the beginning," the angel continued, "it was God's intent to share His life with mankind, so that He could be in you and you could be in Him. This is what Jesus called 'everlasting life' in John 3:16.

"As you know, the Scripture also calls this 'the mystery which has been hidden from ages and from generations, but now has been revealed to His saints. To them God willed to make known what are the riches of the glory of this mystery among the gentiles, which is Christ in you, the hope of glory.'

"Why would God do this? Why would Christ want to be in you? Because God loves and cherishes you—each and every one of you. No matter how rebellious and unreasonable mankind became, He never stopped practicing His peacemaking efforts, nor did He stop loving and cherishing each of you. Yes, there were times when God had to practice tough love. Like the father in the parable of the Prodigal Son, He often had to let people go find out by experience that the result of sin really is death. But He never stopped wanting every human being to learn from that, repent, and return to Him, though He often had to accept the decisions of those who reject His offer to forgive them."

Another angel came and said, "I've come to tell you a parable. It's about love, too. It's a story about marriage. In Bible times, marriages were arranged well ahead of time by the parents. There would be a betrothal ceremony. Before returning to his own home, the groom asked his bride what kind of house she would like to have, and he would start building a house, usually attached to his father's home. In everyone's mind, they were as good as married.

"It was a lot of work to build a house, and it took a while, but the groom had a firm betrothal commitment. He didn't have to worry that he might build half a house only for his bride to say, 'I've changed my mind.' And she too had things to prepare. She also had a firm commitment.

"When the groom was ready to receive her and begin a family that he could support, he and all his friends would go to her house. Then he with his friends would take her to her new home. Celebration and feasting continued for many days."

The angel paused and looked at Christian for a moment. Then he said, "Consider what is going to happen to you. The apostle John 'saw the holy city, New Jerusalem, coming down out of heaven from God, prepared as a bride adorned for her husband' (Revelation 21:2). The bride is the Church, which you are part of. And the husband is Jesus, who died for His Church.

"Jesus made a promise before time began. You have a firm commitment. He will keep His promise. But as for humanity, His creation, many say in their heart, 'I don't want to be with Jesus.' But for those who do, He has prepared a home. He will come for them with a large company of angels. The celebration and feasting will continue for many days."

A third angel then stood by Christian and said, "The story of Jesus and His bride, the Church, is a love story. It's the story of deep love and unbreakable commitment, a story that is truly beautiful. Allow yourself to feel some of that when you think of the pain He endured for His beloved, the resolute love He has for her. His resolve was tested and did not waver. No other love story can match the drama that has unfolded.

"Do not forget that Scripture leads to this simple truth: The story of man's relationship with God is a love story. It's the story of a promise kept."

Awakened by the dawn, Christian wondered at his dream. Then he prayed, "Lord, I want to join You in Your resolve that we should be Your bride forever." *Today is going to be wonderful*, he thought. And it was.

Though he hadn't been to school for years, Christian quickly adjusted to the academic life of the Bible School. Suspecting that Pastor Caring had something to do with his being admitted, he was determined to do well and not let him down. And so many people from the church were writing to him that, except for Evangeline, he didn't have time to respond to them all. So Christian would answer with one general letter to the church which, like the letters Paul wrote, contained many greetings to individuals.

He also took Pastor Caring's advice and waited to see what kind of person each professor was before speaking his mind. One day, a professor who didn't mind contrary opinions asked Christian for his thoughts on the loving character of God. Christian knew that this particular professor believed Christ did not die for everyone, but only for individuals whom God chose ahead of time, before they were born. After hesitating for just a moment, Christian spoke up boldly and said, "I think God is love, and He enjoys being God. He delights in who He is. He will never pass on an opportunity to love. Jeremiah 9:24 says He delights in exercising lovingkindness on the earth. This verse is saying to me that God will always do what's best for each one of us unconditionally and without reservation. That's what His character is like. That's what lovingkindness means. As for us, we are to trust Him to enable us to have lovingkindness toward others in the same way." The professor suspected the implications of what Christian was saying, but couldn't think of a way to question it. He was an intelligent man, and what Christian said gave him a glimmering of realization that God would not want to treat people capriciously, giving no reason to explain His choice of whom to save and whom to damn. *If I acted in that way,* the professor thought, *I would assign students an A or an F before the exam was given. But I would never do such a thing.* The professor hesitated a moment in his thoughts. *Could it be possible that God doesn't treat people in the way I've been teaching that He does?*

Then the professor asked the class how they would define God's lovingkindness. Christian held his breath wondering what the response would be. Outside class in discussions with other students, he had been talking about the love of God in contrast to the constantly heard refrain, "God is in control." Christian thought, *Saying "God is in control" when bad things are going on, actually makes God look very unloving,. And it takes away our free will to choose.* As Christian waited to see what would happen, he remembered how recently he'd been noticing that he was having more influence on the students than the professors were, and other students were speaking up on the love of God in their classes. So he wasn't surprised when Sensible said, "Love does what is best for others, even if the one who loves has to make a sacrifice. And everyone I know is willing to make some sacrifice for people they love, at least a little bit. But for God, there is no limit to the sacrifice He would make for every one of us. He constantly looks for ways to show kindness even though we don't deserve it. God's lovingkindness is His always using all His resources for our benefit. If God's character were different, there would be no explanation for the giving of His Son to die for our sins." There were a few "Amens!" from the class. *Oh yeah,* thought Christian. *Sensible nailed it.*

Wisely, the professor didn't try to bring in his determinist theology but guided the discussion to a believer's responsibility to exercise loving kindness toward others. In fact, because of the lively discussions, this became Christian's favorite class, and he appreciated how students were encouraged to say what they thought. At the end of the semester, both Christian and Sensible got an A in the class. To Christian's own great amazement, he got As in his other classes as well.

Some time later, there was growing excitement as the Bible School approached its hundredth anniversary. It was a special day with many activities, one of which was a poetry contest. Two days before the anniversary, the weather was warm, and many students were outside studying. As he walked around the campus, Christian saw many of them working on poems. One student had an epic that went on for fifteen pages. Christian had already turned in his own poem. Looking at the ones other people were writing, Christian thought his didn't have a chance. *But I had fun writing it,* he thought. The theme of the poem was his testimony and included his understanding of why God saved him.

On anniversary day, to Christian's complete amazement, the judges awarded his poem first place. A few days later, he was further amazed to see his poem framed and hung in the main hallway of the school.

## *It's All About His Love*

*My heart was cold, weighed down with sin.*
*All I wanted was Christ within.*

*My whole life I gave to Him.*
*I received His desire to forgive my sin.*

*Christ replaced my selfish thoughts.*
*Into my heart His love He brought.*

*A new life in Christ came from above.*
*My precious Lord taught me to love.*

*I now know His reason I should live by His ways,*
*So He could be with me all of my days.*

*Changed for a purpose He made me anew,*
*So He could be with me in all that I do.*

Just then, two students walked up. One said, "How could that have won? The metering is way off. And the wording is awkward. My poem was better. And look how short it is. Mine was three pages. I should have won!" The other student, whose name was Genial, said, "You're right about the metering. And yes, as a poem it's not much. But I have to agree with the judges. What it says is more important than how it is said. I really like the message that the poem conveys." Christian asked what meter meant, which Genial was glad to explain.

After his friend walked away, Genial said, "What I really like about your poem is that it made me think of my salvation from God's point of view. Until I read it, I hadn't realized how much I was trying to do on my own what God wanted to do for me. I liked the last part where God wants us to obey and He changes us so He can be with us. That's a beautiful thought that makes me feel loved." They discussed the ideas in the poem for a while. Christian had found a new friend, and knowing that others were blessed by the ideas in his poem was a great encouragement.

Later that day, there was a big rally. As Christian was standing in the crowd waiting for it to start, he noticed an older student staring at him. Then the man broke into a huge smile, came to Christian, and said, "Remember me?" As soon as he heard the voice, Christian knew. "You're the robber!" he exclaimed. "I have a new name now," said the man. "I'm not Robber any more. My new name is Redeemed." He told how he went from Christian's cabin to a quiet place by the river and prayed for the first time in his life. Then he started to weep because of his sins. "I cried for what seemed like hours. Then I felt as though the Holy Spirit washed it all away and He filled me with joy. For two weeks, I felt that joy and it weighed on my conscience. Finally, I couldn't stand it anymore. I got the money from where it was stashed and brought it to your cabin. Then as I was leaving, I felt the Holy Spirit washing over me again. And now I can love! It's wonderful! I found a church where I grew to understand more about what happened to me. Now I just want to serve God. I'm a senior now. I'll graduate this year." After the rally, they talked some more. Redeemed said, "I'm really ashamed of my past. Please don't say anything about it."

"What past?" Christian responded. Later that night, Christian remembered how he prayed for the robber who returned the money. He looked up and said, "Thank you, Father. Prayer answered."

When summer came, Christian continued to take a few classes and also found a part-time job as a blacksmith in the school blacksmith shop. Nearby farmers made use of his services and he was able to share the gospel with them as he worked. In the fall, he joyfully returned to class and finally, after three years, the newly minted Reverend Christian received a letter from Pastor Caring.

*Dear Christian,*

*I'm feeling my age, and the time has come for me to retire. It's unanimously agreed by the elders that you be called to this ministry. God willing, you will accept.*

*Your friend in Christ,<br>Pastor Caring*

*That's where I belong,* he thought, *and it's not just because of Pastor Caring. There's Evangeline.* At the blacksmith's shop, he repaired some discarded wagon wheels and made a handcart. With Evangeline on his mind, Christian loaded the handcart with provisions for the journey, along with his many books and items he valued. *I won't be able to go very fast. This handcart is heavy,* he thought.

Seventeen days and three hundred miles later, Christian arrived exhausted at his little cabin. It was just as he left it. Curiously, he looked around. His garden was a mess. Still, there were lettuces, tomatoes, squash, potatoes, and some other things that had seeded themselves. In his food shed, the smoked fish were still there. They looked fine. Chewing into a strip of smoked fish, he found there was nothing wrong with it, at least, nothing he could immediately taste. Marveling at how well it was preserved, he headed for the river. Then he found one of his fish traps and set it in the water with the smoked fish as bait. After a short swim, he went into his cabin and collapsed into what remained of his bed. The straw had disintegrated and he had grown so much that his feet hung over the end. It didn't matter. In seconds, he was asleep.

The following morning the fish trap had done its job and Christian had fish for breakfast. After gathering wood and finding some dry moss, he started a small cooking fire with matches he had with him. After gutting and scaling the fish, he skewered it on a forked stick. It didn't take long to cook. Holding the head and tail, he ate the best breakfast he had in seventeen days and thought, *What could be better for breakfast than fresh-caught fish?*

Once the sun was really up and the air began to warm, he went for a swim with his clothes on. This was how he always washed his clothes when he lived in his cabin. Putting on the clean dry clothes he'd saved for the occasion, Christian walked up the familiar path to the church and found Pastor Caring in his library. The pastor looked older and tired. *Perhaps*, Christian thought, *he just needs a vacation*. Pastor Caring's whole face lit up with joy when he saw Christian at the door, and they soon got down to discussing Pastor Caring's recent letter. "You're hired by this church from this minute, and you're going to preach this Sunday. The building you see going up is going to be a Bible School. Your first responsibility is to take charge of that project and guide it to its completion.

"There's something else you may not have known. Interested Christians and pastors from all over have been coming here to see what's happening to this church. They want to learn about it. You'll want to get up to speed quickly as they will want to talk to you.

"I'll be available to help as long as you need me. As you learn what's going on, I'll turn everything over to you. As far as finances are concerned, we have so much money coming in that we don't know what to do with it all. We're supporting a number of missionaries, and we hope the time is coming when we will send missionaries from this church to every corner of the world."

On hearing all this, Christian felt totally inadequate. Then he remembered that in fact, he was inadequate. *It's God's work*, he thought to himself. *God will supply. I will trust in His strength*. So Christian replied both to Pastor Caring and to God, "Yes, sir. I'm ready." Then he said, "Pastor, I'd like to begin each day praying with you. I need to understand from the Lord the vision for this school and everything else that He's given you." They agreed to meet every morning at 7:30 am for prayer. It was arranged that Christian would temporarily live in Mr. Friendly's guest room. A house was being built on the hill behind the church that was to be Christian's own home.

Pastor Caring said, "I've cleared everything from my desk. From now on, this is your library. I'm a semi-retired preacher. I'll leave most of my books here for your use." Pastor Caring then got up and motioned for Christian to sit down in his chair. It was like an official passing of the baton.

Sitting in the chair, Christian asked, "Since there are so many new people, are they all Christians? And what are their needs?"

"They're from all over the area," Pastor Caring began. "A significant number of them are already Christians, which might not be a good thing. They come with all kinds of ideas, and some are resistant to change. The Holy Spirit has been blessing us with

His presence and they're attracted to that. But I'm worried. I'm concerned that people just come for the wonderful experience of feeling God with us and not because they care about really knowing and obeying Him. Our visitation teams are aware of the problem. When they talk to people who are just experience seekers, the teams emphasize God's goal for them to live holy lives. We don't want to find ourselves in a position where the most loving thing God can do is to remove His presence from us."

Alarmed, Christian commented, "You make it sound serious."

Pastor Caring responded, "It is serious. It could lead to our becoming an Ichabod church, having form and routine, but God is not there."

Next, Christian went to see Mr. Friendly. Mrs. Friendly made a big fuss over him and eagerly showed him the guest room where he would stay. Christian asked how the visitation was going, and Mr. Friendly's description was similar to what Pastor Caring had said. Mr. Friendly knew Christian would want to see for himself and gave him the names of new people to visit who were already Christians, so Christian promptly spent the rest of the day visiting. With some people, there was resistance to what he had to share about doing what is best for others. It was like a wall that he couldn't get through. With other visitors, he was able to answer their questions, and they joyfully received the message of God's desire to help them be like Him in loving concern for all other people.

After supper, Christian paid a call on Mr. Evangelist. When he saw Evangeline, he felt like his heart would thump out of his chest. Wondering if how he felt could be seen, he asked Mr. Evangelist about the needs of the people whom he had been visiting. It was the same story. "Christians are coming with an 'it's all about me getting a blessing' attitude, covered with a mound of piousness. They talk a talk that's all about their astounding experiences. I'm so concerned for them," said Mr. Evangelist with a worried tone in his voice.

Christian replied, "I did some visiting this afternoon, and here's what I've been thinking. Somewhere in their deepest intents, every real Christian has put Christ on the throne of their life, where it's not 'all about me' anymore, but it's all about Him. So no matter what I'm hearing from them, in the back of my mind I'm thinking, *Deep down inside, this person has surrendered his life to Christ.* My goal is to reach down and lay hold of that intent, and bring it to the surface so they can see it. But it's hard. I heard them talking today about what God does for them as though it's all about them and I'm praying, 'Yes, Lord, for You it is all about them, and they should be thankful. But how can I show them that for them it's all about You?'" Then with genuine pain in his voice, Christian said, "Even as Christians, they've consigned themselves to a life of empty, vain religiousness from which they cannot escape until they say, 'It's You, Lord. It's all about giving You what you want in every corner of my life.'"

Evangeline mentioned how many of the children had also picked up a trust in an outward Christianity, but seemed to lack the gracious and generous attitude that characterizes a true follower of Christ. She said, "Watching the way children, whom I know are Christians, fight with their brothers and sisters, it's easy to forget they gave their lives to Christ. But I find I can help them by showing them how to pray for their brothers and sisters and encourage them to pray that they will act as Christ would toward their siblings. I couldn't do this if I didn't believe that deep inside, they do want to obey Jesus, which reminds me of this verse." She read from the open Bible on her lap, "'Therefore, from now on, we regard no one according to the flesh.' Who are these 'no ones'? Well, in the very next verse it says, 'Therefore, if anyone is in Christ, he is a new creation; old things have passed away; behold, all things have become new' (2 Corinthians 5:16–17). These people are Christians! And that's how Paul says we should see them."

Then she said wistfully, "But sometimes my heart aches when I try to convey to the children the love Christ has for them, so that they would trust Him and be conscious of His desire to answer their prayers and be part of their lives. But just my talking to them isn't enough. It seems there's a point beyond which they must trust Him themselves."

The Evangelist family and Christian had a time of earnest prayer for themselves, that they would always see Christ in every Christian, no matter what. They prayed that God would give them words to encourage people to love and fellowship with God in every aspect of their lives.

Before Christian left, Mr. Evangelist gave Christian more names and addresses of people to visit. The sun had been down for a while when Christian went to his cabin to fetch his handcart and move his few things into his room at the Friendly's house. He always enjoyed going for a walk in the dark. It was like an adventure. *I suppose*, he thought, *if I didn't enjoy adventure, I'd be somewhere else, seeking comfort.* Then he laughed to himself, *Seeking comfort, what a boring life that would be.*

Then it occurred to him, *We're in the image of God and we have a sense of adventure. I suppose that means God enjoys a good adventure. Come to think of it, for God to live as a man must have been an adventure for Him. And to maintain total abandonment to love for others while on this earth, what an adventure that must have been. It's an adventure we're called to live with Him, each one of us. What a privilege it is to answer that call. And what joy He must have in participating in it. Come to think of it, it's a joy He is sharing with me right now!*

It had been a long day. After chatting briefly with Mr. and Mrs. Friendly and Steady, he excused himself and collapsed into bed. The next thing he heard was a rooster crowing. It was morning already. Being country folks, everyone was used to getting up before the sun. After breakfast, he went to the church office to pray until 7:30 when he would pray some more with Pastor Caring. Sunday would be his first sermon. What should he tell people? Should he be careful and say what people want to hear? Or should he faithfully preach on what he knew God wanted him to say?

---

[1] Col. 1:26–27
[2] Luke 15:11-32; Romans 6:23
[3] Luke 15:1-10; 1 Timothy 2:4
[4] Ephesians 5:31-32
[5] Titus 1:2
[6] Matthew 25:34; John 14:2
[7] Micah 6:8 (Mercy & lovingkindness are often translated from the same word in Hebrew.)
[8] 1 John 2:2
[9] Isaiah 6:8
[10] 1 Samuel 4:21

# 18 CHRISTIAN'S FIRST SERMON

Christian prayed, "What do people here need to know?" It came to him that what people needed was to understand that God wants to be understood. *Why do they need this?* Christian asked himself. *Well, for one thing, in order for us to accept His ways as our ways, we have to know what His ways are, and they have to make sense to us. For that to happen, we've got to understand Him.* Christian paused, reached for his Bible, and said to himself, *Not only that, but people need to trust that as we seek to really know God, Christ in us will supply all we need to embrace His ways as our own and live as children of God, citizens of His kingdom.*

*Then there's motivation. Understanding God isn't something we should seek for our own sake, but for the sake of other people, so we can help them. If we just want to be spiritual for our own sake, we miss the point.* Christian prayed that he would make these things clear.

When Sunday came, the whole congregation knew Christian was home and he was going to be the preacher. The church was filled. There were even people standing. Pastor Christian mounted the pulpit and announced the title of his message.

God Wants Us to Understand Him–He is Love

"For a variety of reasons, there are sincere Christians who avoid trying to understand God. I hear them say, 'God is so far above us, there's nothing about Him that we can understand.' But the Bible says, 'Let us pursue the knowledge of the Lord.' God Himself has said, 'I desire mercy and not sacrifice, and knowledge of God more than burnt offerings' (Hosea 6:3, 6). God even said, 'Let him who glories glory in this, that he understands and knows Me.' Then God lists things He delights in doing because of who He is, and number one on His list is, 'I exercise lovingkindness' (Jeremiah 9:24). This is what we should expect from God who is love.

"Why does God put such high value on our understanding Him? In the first place, our spiritual growth as Christians consists of us becoming Christ-like, godly people. For us to cooperate with, rather than fight against, this process of change the Holy Spirit is making in our lives, we need to know what we are being changed to be. We are being changed to be like God in our thinking, character, and attitude, so that Christ can express Himself in our lives. For this to happen, it is vital that we understand God. As we just read in Jeremiah, knowing and understanding God is glory to us. We tell the world through how we live that God is love and can be counted on to exercise lovingkindness.

"When I walked from here to Bible school, it was a journey that took ten days. But if I didn't know where I was going, it would have taken a lot longer. I might still be out there wandering around. It's the same with understanding God. To avoid wandering around in our desire to be godly, we need to know where we are going. We need to understand what being godly looks like. We need to understand God. Since godliness is God's goal for us, God wants us to understand Him and direct our footsteps to be like Him. But sometimes, the devil puts obstacles in our lives. Here's an example:

"A year or so ago, I had a conversation with a woman who said, 'We cannot understand God.' I objected, 'God can do anything. If He wants us to understand Him, surely He's able to help us do that.' But she simply repeated, 'We cannot understand God!' From her tone of voice, I realized she would rather not discuss it farther.

"Later she confided, 'My son, a pastor who helped people every day, is dead. God could have intervened, but He did nothing!' It had been over a year, but she was still grieving her son. I realized I needed to be sensitive. She was still experiencing a great deal of pain.

"'I know that God is love,' she said sadly, looking away from me. 'I know that He has saved me. But He did nothing, and my magnificent son is dead.' Then I realized what she was seeing. It was as if she were looking at a beautiful tapestry with threads of God's love, power, and holiness. But right in the middle of the tapestry, there was a dirty stinking blotch.

"Then she turned back to me and, referring to our previous conversation, sighed, 'Now you know why I said that we, as humans, cannot understand God.' I was dismayed. At the very time that she needed God most, she was pushing aside her confidence in His love.

"I connected the dots she asked me to connect:

God did the wrong thing and let her son die.

She caught God red-handed being indifferent. She had irrefutable evidence of His heartless behavior.

But being a Christian, she wanted to hang on to what was left of her faith that God is loving and caring.

"Faced with the contradiction that her loving God had behaved in an unloving way, she invented a rationalization that allowed her to live with that contradiction. Her rationalization was: 'We simply cannot understand God or His motives.'

"People often accuse God of a disaster in their lives, making Him somehow responsible. I've been told this is part of the grieving process. I didn't want to judge the inconsistencies caused by the grief she was experiencing.

"I felt for this woman. Her improvised rationalization was a huge drag on her spiritual growth, and it denied her the comfort with which God wanted to comfort her. I began to think, 'If a person objects to how God handled something, it looks like they will try to hang on to both their objection and their faith by retreating into 'we can't understand.' I can see why such a person wouldn't want to know too much about God. The devil has them right where he wants them.

"So where did this grieving woman go wrong in her thinking that got her caught in the devil's net? Here's where she went off track: Instead of seeking to understand God, she chose to live in an imaginary world where she herself determined what God's love should look like. This included the idea, 'God should protect my son.'" Christian paused and looked earnestly at the congregation. Then he said slowly, "But what would she see if she began with the understanding that God is love? With the eyes of her heart, she would look for God's love in the Bible, which tells her what God's love is like.

"What she would see is that we live in a very fallen world. Beginning with Adam, every generation has declared their independence from God. But rather than forcing people to obey Him, God stepped back and, out of love, allowed mankind to see what happens when they live apart from Him. Out of His deep love for us, He preserved the free will He created us with. By allowing us to see what the wrong way we had chosen leads to, He gave us reasons to end our rebellion. With those who repent, choosing to seek Him, He responds to their effort to find Him by allowing Himself to be found. Then, having found Him, they have the Holy Spirit to comfort and give assurance of their forever life with Christ.

It's a life we would think unnecessary if God didn't let mankind see the consequences of being independent from Him."

Christian looked around at the congregation and then continued, "These things are obvious to us simply by looking around at the world we live in, but only if we understand God— that He is love and therefore never fails to love. But sometimes, even Christians forget and start to think, 'Oh no! God doesn't care about what's happening here. He cannot be counted on to do the most loving thing possible in every situation.' They might even say, 'God doesn't love me. I guess I have to muddle through life on my own.' This lapse of faith in the love of God becomes a stumbling block which has a stifling effect on their growth in Christ. They end up plodding along, clutching the few shreds of faith they have left, instead of walking strong and free and joyful in Christ, expressing His love everywhere they go.

"Because I felt for this lady, caught in a net where she could not reach out to her Savior, unable to even consider why God does what He does, I asked myself 'What could have been in her life that set her up to be so ensnared?' In this lady's situation, she insisted that she knew best how God should behave. But why? Perhaps this insistence, which she held so dear, was formed in her attitude even before her son died and was only revealed by his death. Without realizing it, she had set up a false god in her own mind, one of her own making, whose values are in this world and are similar to her own. So she had a reason for not wanting to understand God. He might turn out to be very different from the god she wanted."

Christian said slowly, "Brothers and sisters, this is a temptation we all face. Do we really want to understand God, or do we rather continue on with false gods we create in our own minds? When we face pain and disaster, do we rest in our knowledge of God or do we insist that He set everything right for us, and do it now? We need to search our hearts. Are we willing to wait until Christ returns, or are we set on wanting everything in our world to be set right today?

"Yes, personal disasters often create a temptation for Christians to question God's love, and like this lady, turn their backs on God's goal for them. Instead of wanting to be like Him, they decide that there is a heartless side to God's character, which they want nothing to do with. So what attitude should we have toward the disasters that upset our lives? We should do this: As did the Christians who lived before us, never allow ourselves to be moved from completely believing and trusting God's character of love. The early Christians patiently suffered the consequences of mankind's rebellion so we might hear the gospel and be saved. Yes, and some of them were even fed to lions. Now it's our turn to patiently endure the fallen world we live in for the sake of those around us who are lost, that they too may hear the gospel and receive salvation.

"In the Bible, Joshua and Caleb trusted God while the nation of Israel refused to trust Him. But Joshua and Caleb suffered the consequences of the sin of others, wandering in the wilderness forty years with them. In the same way, we have to wander with the humanity in which we find ourselves. The dryness, difficulties, and suffering we experience are not things we can blame God for. God is love, and He never fails to love. He wants us to understand that. For the sake of others, He wants us to patiently endure the spiritual desert of our fallen world. It's a patience that is not without hope. We look forward to the coming of our Lord and the resurrection in which we will be with Him forever. But in the meantime, we must be patient for the sake of others as we wait for His coming. And because we know and understand Him, we know and understand His desire to be with us forever in a situation where He can release upon us the full measure of His lovingkindness. We can understand that God too is patient for the sake of those who will repent and turn to Him, enduring the contradiction of men. In this too, we must be like Him.

"I can understand that if God always protected Christians from problems, there would be many swearing allegiance to Christ for no other reason than to be protected. As a result, the gospel message would become unclear, and the church would become a place where people believe God is someone they can use for protection while they reject Him in every other way.

"So to avoid this, let's affirm our understanding that God is love, placing that understanding above everything that would anchor our hopes and aspirations to the fallen world we live in. With this sure knowledge, that God is love, our hearts are open for the Holy Spirit to reveal to us more of God's character of love and attitude of love. Let us reach out with our heart and embrace the love that motivates what he does. Then, with eyes that see His heart, we see His desire for people to repent of their rebellion and independence from Him so He can be gracious, loving, and merciful to them.[4]

"More than that, by faithfully seeking to understand God's character of love, we open a door in our thoughts to understand God's ultimate goal, to share His life with us, and for us to share our lives with Him. Then we understand why the Bible tells us to be godly in our attitude and behavior. God cannot fully participate in our lives if we are not godly in how we live.

"As we lay aside everything that hinders us from trusting in God's character of love, it's like walking through a door into a new world of wondrous things on the other side. Instead of resisting the work of the Holy Spirit in our lives, we cooperate with Him. And that's important! God has a lot of changing to do in our lives. As Christians, in our heart of hearts, this is what we want too. But how does it happen? How do we get there without God turning us into machines? He does it by making us partners in the process.

"As we spend time in prayer and in reading the Bible, we see that it's God's nature to have a loving reason for everything He does. He is never callous or indifferent. The difficulties we face in this world should not cause us to question God's loving character. It pains God to let mankind suffer what rebellion against Him is like. He feels the pain we feel because we are in a fallen world. But what is best for that lost world is not that we should be taken out of it, but as salt and light, we are His representatives in it. The Bible tells us to seek the knowledge and understanding of the Lord so we will know how to trust God to help us represent Him.

At this point, Christian leaned over the pulpit, momentarily reaching forward with his hands as if he were reaching out to the people. With a softness and sincerity in his voice, he spoke imploringly, "The more we know about the love of God, the more opportunity the Holy Spirit has to be part of our lives, helping us encourage and strengthen other people. Jesus said, 'For whoever has, to him more will be given, and he will have abundance.' Our wanting to know God so we can help others shows that God has been successful in teaching us His ways.

"If we're thinking we want to know more of God only for our own sake, it shows we haven't allowed Him to make much progress in our lives. If our motive doesn't include others, it's an indication that we're resisting who God is and we don't want to really know Him.

"When we come right down to it, if we think in terms of what is best for those around us (as God does,) it shows that we really have gained something in our understanding of Him.

"We're commanded to be salt and light in the world. When we share the gospel, we're inviting people into a relationship with God. For us to be effective in this, we need to communicate a clear picture of what God is like. We can only do a poor job of doing this if our understanding God is poor. Even Jesus's disciples sometimes fell short. Philip walked with Jesus for three years and Jesus had to say to him,

"'Have I been with you so long, and yet you have not known Me, Philip? He who has seen Me has seen the Father; so how can you say, "Show us the Father"? Do you not believe that I am in the Father, and the Father in Me? The words that I speak to you I do not speak on My own authority; but the Father who dwells in Me does the works' (John 14:7, 10).

"If even Philip needed to be encouraged to understand God, then we can see why Paul was led to pray, 'That the God of our Lord Jesus Christ, the Father of glory, may give you the spirit of wisdom and revelation in the knowledge of Him' (Ephesians 1:17). This is not just for some far-off time. It's something we're to be personally involved in every day. So we should make every effort to understand Him more and more.

"Seeking to understand God instead of retreating from that understanding will lead us to grasp His incredible love, a love that springs out of who He is. Understanding His love, we know He will help us be like Him. This is His goal as well as ours. Following Christ is a miraculous life, with a well of faith in God's loving character from which we draw living water to share with a lost world. Let's pray."

Stepping down from the pulpit, Christian thought, *I wish the Lord would have let me preach a more uplifting sermon.*

What Christian said was the topic of conversation at every table during dinner. Some identified with the lady in Christian's sermon and felt their experience-based world was being threatened. They realized that seeking to understand God would carry with it a responsibility to be like Him. Since they would rather have God serving them, giving them experiences, what Christian said was something they wanted to avoid. Of course, they would never admit that, even to themselves. But Christian hit them where they lived. Fortunately, these self-seeking people were in a minority. When they spoke up about what they were thinking, the other church members pounced on them, quickly exposing their words for what they were. "You sound like the lady in Christian's sermon, wanting God to be what you want Him to be. That's why you don't want to understand Him." Christian heard all this going on and thought, *Well, if my sermon didn't get through to them, no problem! Their fellow church members will.*

During the after-dinner sharing, first one person then another confessed that they had resisted knowing about the love of God because rejecting knowledge about God allowed them to keep their independent attitude, an attitude they knew God didn't want them to have. One woman, after confessing her sin of not wanting to know what God is like because she wanted to run her own life her way, began to cry. Finally, she controlled herself enough to say, "I know I'm wrong, but I don't know what to do." This was followed by what seemed like an eternity of silence.

Finally, Pastor Christian stood up and said, "The answer you're looking for is to make a decision. The reason you don't know what to do is because you don't know how to make a decision that is a true decision you can stand by. If you're serious, reinforce your decision by making a solemn vow to God, a vow that is impossible for you to keep, so that you'll have to really trust in Him. Tell God that you will take every opportunity to learn what His love is like, and tell Him that you trust Him, not yourself, to make you able to keep this impossible promise. Then, make a vow to do what's best for others, loving every individual as He loves them. Are you willing to do this?"

There were no tears now as she contemplated what she was being asked to do. Christian waited. Everyone waited. Slowly at first, the woman began to pray, "Dear God," she said. "I do want to be like Jesus, to do what is best for others. I vow to You that I will never resist knowing more about You again. I'll take every opportunity to learn more about Your love. And I vow that I will love others the same as You do. I will think of others as more important than myself and do what is best for them. And I trust that You will make me able to keep this vow. In Jesus's name. Amen."

The presence of the Holy Spirit filled the room. Then Christian said, "Everyone else who wants to make this vow, please stand up." Slowly at first, people stood up until, looking around, Pastor Christian couldn't see anyone sitting. Looking heavenward, he said in a loud voice, "Let's make this vow together. Father, I vow…" Before he could say more, everyone repeated what he had said. And so it went as Pastor Christian continued. When he had finished, someone began to sing, "The love of God is greater far than tongue or pen can ever tell…" The building seemed to shake as they sang out with joyful fervor the words of this wonderful old hymn.

Christian remembered when he had made that vow many years before and the effect it had on him. He thanked God for everything that happened. Then he silently prayed, "I'm sorry, Lord. I shouldn't have grumped about what I knew you wanted me to say." Christian thought, *This was the Lord's doing. This is totally out of human control. What is He going to do next?*

---

[1] Isaiah 58:6-9; John 17:23-24; 1 John 5:20
[2] Psalms 23, 147:11
[3] Ephesians 3:19
4 Hosea 6:3; Matthew 13:12; 2 Peter 1:8-9

# 19 AFTERWARD

That week, Christian went shopping for a guestbook with a beautiful cover. On the first page, he wrote out "The Vow," followed by instructions that anyone who made this vow could record the fact in the book. Then he placed it on a table in the church foyer. In a short time, it seemed that everyone in the church had signed the book. As new people came to the church, they were told about what it meant and encouraged to make that impossible but faith-based commitment. Best of all, the problem of Christians coming to church only motivated by a desire for experiences became a thing of the past.

The following Sunday, Pastor Christian preached on the meaning of the unconditional, limitless, unrestrained love of God. He made sure everyone understood that it was not a love relationship carried on from a distance. "God is near, seeking opportunity to express His love through you, even for people who want to hurt you. His love for you is unconditional. He unconditionally cares about doing what is best for you, even at a great cost to Himself. So let Him have His way in your life to unconditionally do what is helpful to others, regarding even your worst enemy as more important than yourself. Let Christ be your constant companion, giving Him the desire of His heart by expressing with Him His infinite love to those around you."

After church, Christian and Evangeline went for a walk together. He didn't have to court Evangeline very long. She said she loved him so much it hurt. Christian wasn't quite sure what that meant except that she loved him, and that was all that mattered. The ladies of the church offered to help with the wedding, and a good thing, because the whole congregation wanted to come. The church was filled to capacity. Floral garlands hung from every rafter as Pastor Caring officiated. Evangeline was beaming with joy as her father led her down the aisle. As Christian took her hand in his, he could hardly keep from shouting, "Thank you, Lord!" After the ceremony, there was a reception outdoors on the lawn in the shade of the trees. Everyone wanted to say a word of encouragement or advice to the newlywed couple, but finally, the two of them slipped away and Christian carried Evangeline across the threshold of the house on the hill.

Pastor Caring preached the next Sunday. Christian and Evangeline were nowhere to be found. They had decided to take the train to the next town where no one knew them. Returning the following Saturday morning, Pastor Christian let Pastor Caring know he was back.

Christian soon plunged into getting the Bible School up and running, till it became a well-established institution. Every semester, Christian took the first chapel service. He wanted the incoming students to know what the school was all about. All the new students listened eagerly as Pastor Christian said, "Ancient Greek philosophers put a lot of thought into a doctrine of 'god.' Aristotle called their supreme deity 'the unmoved mover who cannot be moved.' This concept of God stands against the Jewish view of God which sees Him as responding to us and being moved with compassion. Our God loves.

"Mainly through the writings of Plato, the concept of an unmoved mover influenced the early church. Unfortunately, even today this idea has a bad influence on some Christians. Even some of you may have been influenced by a Christian theology which teaches that your life was fixed before you were born, written in the heavens by God, and that God never changes His mind. But our God responds to prayer. Look at what happened to Hezekiah. God gave him 15 more years in response to his prayer. I'll say it again: Our God loves. Our God responds to us.

"And our God created us to have real relationship with Him. The purpose of your education here is to learn how to make the most of that relationship. It's not a rigid relationship, but a give and take relationship of love. Your most important lesson to carry with you when you graduate is to give God the relationship that He wants to have with you, and receive for yourself the relationship for which you were created. Our God..." Christian paused for a response, and a roar of voices rose up, "Our God loves!" Christian smiled, and concluded, "Yes, our God responds. Our God wants relationship. That's what we are created for."

Eventually, the students voted to make the school motto, "Creavit Enim necessitudo," which means "created for relationship."

At first, the Bible School students would board with members of the church, but eventually housing and a dining room were built for them. Out of town visitors to the church could stay there as well. The Bible school had its own chapel where Pastor Christian met with people who came to hear about the wonderful work that God was doing. Christian, remembering his dream about a promise kept, always began his talk with the visitors the same way. "Our first priority is to look at our lives from God's point of view. He created us so He could have real fellowship with us." Christian very much enjoyed talking about the basics of understanding God's love and how people could incorporate that understanding into their lives. He especially enjoyed sharing this with people who had never heard such ideas before. Students and Christians coming to the church for the first time were encouraged to join in these talks and the discussions that followed.

One day, a delegation of pastors from the ten other churches in town came to see Pastor Christian. They were losing members because people were leaving in order to attend Pastor Christian's church. The pastors had hoped that Pastor Christian could do something. Pastor Christian said jokingly, "We have a problem of too many people. Please convince your people to come back!

"Since the Lord has given me a vision for what He wants, and that's what I'm following, I can't stop doing what I'm doing. But I can share that vision with you, if you're willing. That way we'll all be doing the same thing, and no one will have reason to leave your churches. At least, listen to what I have to say. It's a vision to emphasize the love of God. I think you can get on board with that."

The pastors agreed, and Pastor Christian gave them a schedule of the times when he was holding a talk for visitors in the school chapel.

"I want your feedback. If what I have to say makes sense, we can work together. Though we are eleven churches in this town, we can function as one church. We have one Lord and He has one body. If we work together, I think people will find it convenient to come back to your churches. Why should they travel to our church, when yours are probably much more convenient to where they live?

"With the Bible School, we also have a tremendous meeting facility here. If you need a place for a special event, just ask. We'll work out a time when you can use it. Also, we have enthusiastic and dedicated students at our Bible School. I'll make them available to you so they can get practical experience. I am your servant. If you need anything in particular, please ask."

One by one, the ten pastors attended the talks. They enjoyed the discussions where they could speak their minds and returned again and again. Being pastors, their remarks tended to be long, so Pastor Christian had to get a three-minute hourglass help set limits. But overall, the pastors added richness to the experience, and Christian found their questions fun to answer. He enjoyed having them there.

"God wants a living relationship with us. Understanding His love enables us to understand the miraculous life He called us to live," said one pastor. "Yes," said another. "He responds to our decision to live that life. He really does respond. And it's a life free of selfish ambition. It's a life of unselfish love for others."

Pastor Christian was so overjoyed at the reports he was hearing about what was happening in congregations all over town, that he made it a regular feature of his talks to invite pastors' testimonies. The pastors enjoyed helping explain the loving character of God. Each time, the Holy Spirit was evident. Though each time the same things were explained, and almost the same questions got answered, no one got tired of doing it.

The pastors decided to get together at one of the churches in town for prayer every Thursday morning at 6 a.m. Pastor Christian, Mr. Evangelist, and Pastor Caring all attended. Once a year, the whole group had a retreat together and prayed for one another and talked about how they could grow in Christ and work together to reach their communities for Christ. They came to really love one another as they prayed for each other's special needs.

Mr. Evangelist had become so busy in the church that he was asked to come on staff as a pastor. It turned out that Christian was good at the administrative needs of the church. He delegated everything that could be delegated so he could spend more time in prayer.

While Christian was at Bible school the church had built a larger building and turned the old one into classrooms. Now, the new church building also became too small. The church property was once a hundred sixty acre homestead, so there was room to build on and expand. Besides building a bigger church, the members worked hard to build a huge fellowship hall. Then they built more Sunday school classrooms. But the church was growing so fast that soon all of this still wasn't big enough for everyone to fit into. Every building was constantly in use, and people were required to meet at least one Sunday each month in a house church.

How to have a congregational meeting was still a problem. "What can we do to decide who can be a member here?" was a debated topic. Finally, the church elders decided that to be a voting member, a person must have attended church services 10 times, be a true Christian, saved by faith, and they had to agree to the doctrinal statement, make "The Vow," and sign the book. They also had to attend a new member's class where the character of the church was carefully explained. But there were still so many voting members that it was impossible to fit them all in one place at once. In the end, they had two meetings. The idea was to combine votes on whatever was voted on. One year the meeting was in June, outdoors so everyone could be there. It didn't work. Though speakers shouted as best they could, not everyone could hear. The older members in particular complained so much that Christian decided not to try it again.

Meanwhile, the visitation teams worked like a well-oiled machine and made every visitor feel very welcome. Members who needed help and encouragement were blessed by them as well. Pastor Evangelist held Saturday meetings for the visitation teams where they were given pointers on how to get new people up to speed as to what kind of church this was and what activities they could join.

Pastor Evangelist also taught the evangelism class at the Bible School. Besides the Bible School students, many from the church were taking his class. He was a strong believer in learning by doing, so he formed teams from his class to do door to door evangelism. Every Friday night and Saturday afternoon, an army of evangelists went into town and the surrounding countryside. Pastor Evangelist was so good at teaching how to share the gospel that despite their initial trepidations, soon everyone felt confident. And their confidence soared even more as they saw people at church whom they had led to Christ.

Though Pastor Caring was officially semi-retired, he still liked to be involved. Every morning he met with Christian and also taught a couple of classes at the Bible School. Since Christian had come on board as pastor, Pastor Caring had been able to rest. Now his energy was back and he could do more of what he enjoyed, which was serving others.

Although Mr. Confident was visited often by Pastor Christian,

Pastor Caring, and the visitation teams, he never changed his mind. He did admit, however, that he was impressed with the presence of the Holy Spirit in the church meetings. But no matter what Scripture was laid before him to prove that God responds to us in love and does not control everything that happens, Mr. Confident had three standard answers. "It's an analogy," "It's a mystery," or "It's an anthropomorphism." Exasperated, Pastor Christian challenged him to name one verse in the entire Bible that was not an anthropomorphism. Mr. Confident's reply was "There are too many to count." Even more exasperated, Christian finally asked, "How can you tell a verse that is not an anthropomorphism from one that is?" Mr. Confident admitted that the way to tell was whether or not it matched his theology. He eventually conceded "Well, maybe there are other explanations for these verses, but I still think my interpretation is the right one." And he just could not bring himself to believe that God loved everyone unconditionally in the present, or that everyone could choose to repent and be saved.

When he had a chance, Pastor Christian would go to town to do some prayer and evangelism. He would sit on the bench in front of Mr. Helpful's general store and pray because that was a spot where everyone in town would eventually pass by. Introducing himself, he would ask people if they had time to talk. Then he would ask if they wanted to take God up on his offer to change their heart. The whole town knew Pastor Christian did this. People found him interesting to talk to and very few objected. As soon as Christian's children were old enough, he would bring them along to join in the prayer and sharing the gospel.

Pastor Christian also went to the town jail. One day, he walked in and said, "Howdy, sheriff. You got any customers?"

"Oh yes," the sheriff replied. "Go right on in. We brought Mr. Drink in last night to sleep it off. He got pretty rowdy."

Mr. Drink was sitting on the bunk with his head in his hands as Christian knocked on his cell. "May I come in?"

Mr. Drink said, "Okay," and Christian entered through the unlocked door.

"I'll get right to the point," he said. "Christ offers to change your life. How do you think He would change you if you took Him up on His offer?"

"I have no idea," said Mr. Drink.

"He would change the attitude of your heart so you would value other people more than you value yourself. That includes your family and the people you hurt by your drinking," Pastor Christian responded. "When your drinking hurts them, do you even feel it?"

Thinking it would put Christian off, Mr. Drink said, "Not a bit."

"That's right," said Christian. "You really have hardened your heart. God's offer is to take the hardness out of your heart, take all the selfishness away, and replace it with a heart that loves and cares for other people. That includes your family. Isn't this what you want?"

Mr. Drink started to snap back an answer, then suddenly he became silent. Finally he said, "Yeah...sometimes it does bother me."

Christian asked, "How would your life be different if Christ came into your heart and changed you?"

"I'd stop drinking," said Mr. Drink, staring at the floor.

"Anything else?" asked Christian.

"I lie," mumbled Mr. Drink. "I tell my family they're important to me. Then I go and do things that hurt them."

Christian asked, "Is there any reason why you would not give your life to Christ right now?"

Mr. Drink looked up, staring at him. "Whoa!" he exclaimed. "You don't mess around, do you?"

"If you really want to stop drinking," Christian fired back, "Christ will give you the power to stop. And He's someone you can talk to. It's a relationship you enter into with Him where He's your friend whom you can trust. He'd also be your Lord, the one you obey. He'd be right there all the time, in your life. So you need to make a real decision that you want Him in your life, and that you will accept His help to do things God's way. Is this what you want?"

Mr. Drink responded, "I guess if Christ comes into my life I've had my last drink, huh? Okay, Pastor Christian. I'm with you. You're right."

"I'll help you, if you want," Pastor Christian said. "I'll say a prayer of asking Jesus into your life. You say it after me, but remember you're talking to God." Mr. Drink agreed, and after leading him in a sinner's prayer, Pastor Christian said, "The proof that you really meant what you just said will be that you show up at church on Sunday. Sunday school starts at 9:00 a.m. There's a special class for new Christians. I'll see you there."

And Mr. Drink was there. So were his wife and children. Week by week, it became obvious that love had become the strongest characteristic of Mr. Drink's life. When his bad attitudes, carousing, and selfish ways were taken from him, it left a giant empty hole, a hole that Jesus filled with His love. In fact, eventually God changed his name to Mr. Love.

Love. That's what it's all about. Finally, there was a community of Christians who both understood and knew how to live in the full measure of God's love.

And sensing the love around him, Mr. Confident, though not willing to let on, was beginning to soften. But he had no idea how God could not have planned everything that happens.

At Sunday dinner, he went to sit with Pastor Christian. Part of him wanting to be convinced, he opened with a question he genuinely didn't understand, "So, why wouldn't God want to know everything, even the future?"

Christian said to Mr. Confident, "Since there truly are three Persons in the Trinity, to be Persons at all, They each have a separate will, and God has free will within Himself. Since God can be creative, He specially would enjoy being creative with the love He has within Himself."

Mr. Confident then said, "Of course, God has free will. He is God. But that doesn't mean we have it too."

Christian shook his head. "God created us in His image. He has free will, so He would give us free will too, and we obviously do have it. We have free will so we can love Him with all our heart. I don't know exactly how it works, but that's how it is. Seems like it's pretty obvious that he made us able to be creative in our choices, just like He is. So let me ask you a question. Does the Father know everything, the Son know everything, and the Holy Spirit also know everything?"

Mr. Confident responded, "Yes, They each know everything."

Christian leaned forward and said earnestly, "Being love, They would defend each other's uniqueness. Being a person requires uniqueness in thought and will. The idea of merging them into a one mind, where each knows all the thoughts and choices of the others for all eternity, would distract from their uniqueness as well as being a conversation killer. Wouldn't their love for one another deter them from doing that?"

Mr. Confident rubbed his head. "You make it sound like I don't think there's a Trinity. Why can't They each know everything?"

Christian asked, "Since God is eternal, how could every detail be known? Eternal means there is an endless future, just as there was an endless past."

Mr. Confident opened his mouth to say something, but nothing came out. He dearly wished that he knew what to say. Finally, he drew on his old standby, "It's something about God we can never understand, because we're only human. It's a mystery."

Christian thought, *There's not one verse in Scripture that supports such an imaginative idea. The mystery is why anyone would believe it.*

A few months later at the Sunday dinner, Mr. Confident again sat opposite Christian and asked, "You haven't been by my place for awhile. Have you given up on me?"

With a twinkle in his eye, Christian said, "Yes, I have. Now I just pray for you more fervently."

Mr. Confident said, "Last night, a raccoon unlatched my chicken house door, grabbed a chicken, and was making off with it. I heard the ruckus and came to the back door with my shotgun. Just before he was out of range, I let him have both barrels, which made him drop the chicken. So there I was, freezing in my night shirt, dressing a chicken in the washtub, thinking, "For all eternity God planned for that raccoon to come and kill this chicken. And here I am, with my own hands I'm living the plan of God that cannot be altered in even the smallest detail. It was His plan that I have chicken for breakfast this morning."

"Just curious," said Christian. "Before creating Satan, did God know everything Satan was going to do? And was it God's plan that he should do those things?"

"Of course," Mr. Confident said, looking very smug. "Everything that happens is according to what God had planned to happen. Of course, God knows what He had planned. How could it be otherwise?"

Christian sighed, "If I follow your logic, God's plan for Satan and all that Satan did came from God's heart. That would mean everything Satan did was also an expression of who God is. You end up making it sound like God and Satan are one and the same. Do you actually believe God and Satan are the same?"

Mr. Confident was very silent. Pastor Christian could see his jaw drop and his tongue move around in his cheek, something Mr. Confident did when he was thinking. Finally, Mr. Confident said quietly, "I have no choice. That's the logical conclusion that my thinking should take me, but I don't want to go there. For once, I don't have an answer."

For a minute Mr. Confident was silent. Then he said, "What you've been talking about sounds like nonsense. I just don't see any alternative to believing God knows and controls everything."

Then, looking thoughtful, he added, "On the other hand...if there was an alternative, it would answer something that bothers me. If God knew that Lucifer had a weakness for pride, then why did God make him so beautiful and strong? He even gave Lucifer a really prestigious job. I mean, you can't go much higher than cherub, adorning God's throne! So why did God put him there? Why didn't He make Lucifer ordinary looking, and him give a humble job serving others? That way, pride wouldn't tempt him, and we wouldn't be in the mess we're in. I'm still a little bothered that God planned all this. But I've learned to accept it...sort of."

Hesitating for a minute, Mr. Confident sighed. Then he continued, "Part of me wishes you were right. I understand that what I believe diminishes God's love. And saying that as Creator He can do as He pleases doesn't really change that. But logic tells me there's no alternative to what I've always believed."

Smiling, Christian replied, "In just three verses, I can show you an alternative." Opening his Bible, he said, "The first verse comes from Paul's description of love in 1 Corinthians 13:7: Look at this. It says that love 'believes all things, hopes all things.' That means if you love someone, you trust them. Even if somehow you could know their future choices, you wouldn't want to, because that would mean you were choosing not to trust them. And to carry around a lack of trust for someone you want to love would diminish your love for them. If we apply this to God when Lucifer was created, God wouldn't want to look into Lucifer's future choices. Rather, because Lucifer was created perfect, God would choose to believe all things, hope all things by trusting Lucifer. (Ezek 28:14-15) And Paul tells us this is what love does."

Incredulous at what he was hearing, Mr. Confident's mouth flopped open. So Christian turned the pages of his Bible and continued. "The second verse is Isaiah 43:25. God said:

'I, even I, am He who blots out your transgressions for My own sake; and I will not remember your sins.'

"This brings up a question. Why would God want to blot out our sins, even the memory of those He has in His mind? Well, it says here He does it for His own sake! What does that mean? I figure it's because it's no fun for God to even have the memory of our sin in His mind. What an ugly thing to have to think about! And if it's sin we repented of, there's for sure no reason for Him to have it in His mind. So here in Isaiah, He's saying to people, 'Please repent, so I can blot out your sins and never have to think of them again. Then I can just love you and be close to you, which is what I would much rather do.' So if that's how God feels about our past sins, then it makes sense that He wouldn't want to look at our future sins either. He wants to just love us and trust us right now."

Now scratching his head, Mr. Confident puzzled, "I can't think of another explanation of that verse right off, but I'm still not convinced. So what's your third verse?"

"It's one you're familiar with," Christian continued. "You probably memorized it in Sunday School, 1 John 1:9." Mr. Confident nodded and quoted,

'If we confess our sins, He is faithful and just to forgive us our sins and to cleanse us from all unrighteousness.' (1 John 1:9) Yes, I know that verse!"

"Well," said Christian, "when we repent and confess our sin, God forgives, cleanses, and treats us as though we will never do that sin again. Look back at all the sins you've confessed to God. He isn't still holding them against you. Do you think He looks ahead at your future choices to see what you will do, or does He trust you to not do those sins again?"

"Of course He knows I will do them again, and so do I!" exclaimed Mr. Confident. "I have a sin nature. God certainly knows that I will sin. If I were God, I would never trust me not to sin."

"Whoa," said Christian. "Let's look at 2 Corinthians 5:17." He quickly turned to it in his Bible. "See here? It says you're a new creation in Christ. It says nothing about old stuff still hanging around. And besides, the whole concept of a sin nature didn't come into the church until the fourth century, mainly through Augustine."

Mr. Confident looked dubious, but Christian continued, "What happened in the Garden is Adam wanted to expand his knowledge to include evil, so he could be independent from God and choose what was right for himself. So God stepped back from Adam and Eve just enough to give them the independence they wanted. This is the condition we inherited from them—*nothing more.*

"Now, because we all know evil as well as what is good, we

make our own choices. And we often choose to include evil in what we choose. Then, every choice to sin has an effect on us, making it easier for us to sin again and again. So if there is a sin nature, it's something each person created for themselves. We can't blame Adam for that. And even with the effects of sin happening in every one of us, we can still repent, and we can still make good choices. You see that all around and every day. That's why in 1 John 1:9, God does such a cleaning and forgiving—He's setting us up to be people He can trust. And He does trust us. He doesn't want to be snooping and looking at our future. He loves us. And when we ask, confessing specific things like what we are told to do in 1 John 1:9, God changes us to be able to not do that sin. And seeing our willingness, God has more of us that He can participate in with us. If tempted to do that sin again, we do the right thing together with Him. As Christians, that's how we live and grow to maturity in Christ"

Mr. Confident said, "Well, you're right on one thing—1 John 1:9 has to mean something. I can't dismiss it as though it doesn't exist. So after I confess, God trusts me until I sin again…Okay, God believing and hoping instead of snooping ahead looking at our future choices is an alternative. I'll give this some thought."

Christian suggested, "I think you would do well to ask God what He thinks."

Mr. Confident responded thoughtfully. "I will. I promise."

Evangeline, Mrs. Confident, and two farmers with their wives sat down at the table and the conversation shifted to raccoons and chickens. But Mr. Confident was still thinking, *Yes, that is what love would do. God would have trusted Lucifer and Adam to remain perfect, just as they were created.* Looking around he thought, *There's real joy here. The evidence is all around me. Fully trusting that God is perfect love changes people, and gives them joy. I need to lay my stubbornness aside and ask God what He thinks."*

---

[1] 2 Kings 20:5-6
[2] Hebrews 10:25
[3] John 17:21-23
[4] Luke 22:42

# APPENDIX A - CHRISTIAN EXPLAINS SCRIPTURE

## ROMANS 16:25

"Now to Him who is able to establish you according to my gospel and the preaching of Jesus Christ, according to the revelation of the mystery kept secret since the world began."

Christian said firmly, "This verse was not written to make a doctrine about God living in timelessness. Romans 16:25 was written to aid in establishing us in Christ. We are given the assurance that God's plan for mankind, established before sin came into the world, was not frustrated by our sin.

"The Romans 16:25 mystery of what God planned from the beginning is Christ's union with His people, His bride. This union could have taken place without mankind falling into sin. The gospel, or 'good news,' is that the union God planned will take place in spite of Adam's sin. It is through us that this mystery is revealed to the angels. It's a mystery fully revealed in Revelation 21 as the marriage of Christ to His bride, the people of the New Jerusalem."

## 2 TIMOTHY 1:9

"God, who has saved us and called us with a holy calling, not according to our works, but according to His own purpose and grace which was given to us in Christ Jesus before time began."

Christian continued, "There are people who read into 2 Timothy 1:9 what they imagine the passage of events was like before our time was created. But the verse does not define eternity as some sort of non-time. Whether or not there was a past, present, and future before God planned for and created the beginning of our time is not mentioned. So the intent of this verse is not that we should invent explanations of what eternity is all about. The point of this verse is that God's original intent, the relationship He planned to have with mankind before time began, is now revealed in us who have received the Holy Spirit through responding to the gospel which was preached. From the moment of our salvation we were joined to God forever.

"This verse says it is a holy calling to be the objects of God's purpose. What is that purpose? Just the same as is meant by 'mystery' in Romans 16:25, which is that there will eventually be a marriage of Christ and mankind. This was God's plan from before creation. If man had not sinned, perhaps our Bibles would be only four chapters: Genesis 1 and 2 and Revelation 21 and 22. Our works have no influence on this ultimate purpose because God planned it before we were born, before sin came into the world, before creation, before our time began.

## ISAIAH 46:10

God said, "Declaring the end from the beginning, and from ancient times things that are not yet done, saying, 'My counsel shall stand, and I will do all My pleasure.'" (Isaiah 46:10)

"Some people say this verse proves God makes everything happen that does happen, even what you had for breakfast. But it doesn't say God chooses to know everything. This verse only says that He can say in advance what He Himself is going to do. To a lesser degree, you and I can also declare things we plan to do, although unlike God, we may or may not be able to carry out our plans.

"Isaiah 46:10 is the culmination of God telling the Jews what He plans to do and comparing that to the uselessness and helplessness of an idol. God is active on the earth, guiding history to its ultimate conclusion. Idols can't do that. What God plans, He has the means to carry out. Idols don't have the means to do anything. God can declare to us what He will make happen. Idols can't declare or make anything happen. Whatever God says will happen, for sure that will happen."

## OTHER OBJECTIONS

Mr. Confident came running up cackling like an old hen. "Gotcha! Look at this." Opening his Bible, he pointed to Jesus's prayer in John 17:9, "I pray for them. I do not pray for the world but for those whom You have given Me, for they are Yours."

"See," Mr. Confident crowed, "Jesus prayed only for the elect, not for the whole world. Admit it. This proves I'm right!"

Christian couldn't help himself and just started to laugh. After he recovered enough to talk, he said, "Jesus's prayer only applies to people who have already believed! According to verses 6–8 and also verse 12, Jesus was praying for protection for the 11 disciples He had personally taught. In verses 11 and 15, Jesus asked His Father to protect them from evil so they would be members of one another.

"Then in verse 20, Jesus includes those who will believe on Him because of their word. It's perfectly logical He would pray for those who choose to believe on Him."

Deflated, Mr. Confident said a meek, "Oh." Then he straightened up, once more determined to prove he was right. "So explain this," he said:

## 1 CORINTHIANS 2:14

"The natural man does not receive the things of the Spirit of God, for they are foolishness to him; nor can he know them, because they are spiritually discerned."

"See," said Mr. Confident. "The natural man could only mean a non-Christian, and they cannot understand the gospel."

Christian patiently began, "Some people assume the natural man can only mean a non-Christian, and take it out of context. This verse says he's unable to understand anything spiritual. But that's not a Scriptural assumption. Just look at the context."

"Huh?" said Mr. Confident. "What context?"

Trying his best to be patient, Christian said, "In the context of 1 Corinthians 2:14, the problem Paul is addressing is that the Corinthian Christians were trying to use worldly wisdom to come to spiritually wise conclusions. We should all agree that they can't do that. The spiritually foolish conclusion they came to is that following their favorite leader was more important than their love for one another.

"So Paul had to remind them in 2:14 that the self-centered or natural man's wisdom is the opposite of the Holy Spirit's wisdom. Talking to Christians, not non-Christians, Paul continues to address the same problem in chapter 3. There he says the same thing: carnal Christians using their carnal wisdom just don't understand godliness.

"So how do you explain the fact that the verse says 'natural man?'" Mr. Confident sneered.

"So you think you got me?" said Christian.

Mr. Confident looked like he was about to dance a jig. "Haw, haw. I got you now," he said.

"Since you're saying it's all about what is meant by 'natural man,' there's something you might consider," said Christian. "This same matter of Christians foolishly using worldly wisdom is also discussed in James 3. James used the same Greek word, translated 'sensual' in James 3:15 as is translated 'natural' in 1 Corinthians 2:14. Considering that James is discussing this very subject, using the same Greek word, and is clearly referring to Christians, 1 Corinthians 2:14 is not a verse that proves that there are non-Christians who have not been given the ability to seek God. The only things 1 Corinthians 2:14 and James 3:15 prove is that Christians can have worldly thinking and behave badly, themes that recur more than once in 1 Corinthians."

Dejected but not defeated, Mr. Confident said, "Christians have the Holy Spirit in them. Paul wouldn't tell Christians they're thinking like natural men."

"It's not an uncommon theme," said Christian. "Romans 12:1–2 is also dealing with the same problem as 1 Corinthians 2:14. Paul writes to the Christians in Rome,

"'I beseech you therefore, brethren, by the mercies of God, that you present your bodies a living sacrifice, holy, acceptable to God, which is your reasonable service. And do not be conformed to this world, but be transformed by the renewing of your mind, that you may prove what is that good and acceptable and perfect will of God.'

Christian loved talking about Romans, so he added for good measure, "After digressing to address Gentiles in Romans chapter 11, Paul goes on in chapter 12 to tell all the Roman Christians not to allow prideful self-centeredness to direct their thinking. In contrast to self-centered thinking, it's by yielding themselves to God as a living sacrifice that they give the Holy Spirit something to work with. Then He transforms their minds, the very thing the Corinthians needed in order to love one another in the same way that God does.

"This is a lesson for us. We should not let self-centered wisdom interfere with yielding ourselves wholly to God. Our yielding ourselves gives Him opportunity to transform our minds, in order that we may be able to fully believe and lay hold of the love of God for one another unhindered by any selfish thoughts."

The corners of Mr. Confident's mouth began to droop. Then he said, "Okay, but I ain't done yet. Try and explain away the plain meaning of Isaiah 64:6."

## ISAIAH 64:6

"We are all like an unclean thing, and all our righteousness like filthy rags."

"See," said Mr. Confident. "This verse proves that no one can choose to repent and turn to God for forgiveness."

But Christian loved reading Isaiah and knew this verse very well. "Wait a minute," he said. "This raises the question, who is the 'we' Isaiah talks about? From Isaiah 63:7 to the end of 64 Isaiah was confessing the sins of Judah, not all mankind. He mentions that they have gone into idolatry. He describes them as a rebellious people. And God sure makes it clear that one of the reasons for His anger was they were self-righteous about their idolatry."

"So show me," demanded Mr. Confident.

With Mr. Confident looking over his shoulder, Pastor Christian turned to Isaiah 65:3 and said, "This is God speaking. God said they were: 'A people who provoke Me to anger continually to My face; who sacrifice in gardens, and burn incense on altars of brick; who sit among the graves, and spend the night in the tombs; who eat swine's flesh, and the broth of abominable things in their vessels; who say, "Keep to yourself, do not come near me, for I am holier than you!" These are smoke in My nostrils, a fire that burns all the day' (Isaiah 65:3–5).

"God is about to punish their wickedness by stripping them from the land and shipping them off to Babylon. God sent Isaiah to try and convince them to repent, to change their ways so He won't have to do that to them. He's not saying that mankind has no free will and are hopelessly lost in their sin. Isaiah is saying Israel has used their free will to make wicked choices." Christian finished by saying softly, "So you see, Isaiah 64:6 addresses their insistence that they were righteous while living clearly unrighteous lives. They are encouraged to use their free will to repent."

"Hurrumph!" grunted Mr. Confident. "Let's see what you have to say about Ephesians 1:4–5."

Turning there, Pastor Christian read the verse.

## EPHESIANS 1:4–5

"He chose us in Him before the foundation of the world, that we should be holy and without blame before Him in love, having predestined us to adoption as sons by Jesus Christ to Himself, according to the good pleasure of His will."

Mr. Confident nodded and smugly raised an eyebrow as he looked at Christian. "Can't be more clear than that!" he said. "God predestined us to salvation from the beginning of creation."

Christian smiled back at him and said cheerfully, "I believe we can agree that God planned from before the foundation of the world that God would adopt us, his specially created humanity, to not only be his sons, but to be a bride for Jesus, His Son. This was predestined. But since sin has come into the world, there will be a large portion of humanity who will not participate in what was predestined.

"The question is, who are those predestined? There are two possibilities.

Individuals chosen from before the foundation of the world, or
Anyone who has joined the predestined bride for Christ.

"Look at verses 12–13. 'That we who first trusted in Christ should be to the praise of His glory. In Him you trusted, after you heard the word of truth, the gospel of your salvation; in whom also, having believed, you were sealed with the Holy Spirit of promise' (Ephesians 1:12–13).

"When we believed in Jesus, we were sealed. That is, we joined the predestined adopted sons of God, like in John 1:12, "As many as received Him, to them He gave the right to become children of God, to those who believe in His name." I think what has you confused about Ephesians 1:4-5 is you misunderstand the actual meaning of the word 'predestined.' It means the end result, not the steps that bring about that result. We became predestined by joining what will be the final result, predestined adopted sons.

"It's like boarding a train. Before we get on the train, we're not predestined to go where the train is predestined to go. But when we get on board, then we are. By trusting in Christ, we got on board with whatever God has predestined for Christ's bride. So the context of Ephesians 1:12–13 defines the 'us' in verses 4–5 as those 'having believed,' just as in John 1:12 they are defined as 'as many as received Him.'

"If you step back, look at the context of the whole book of Ephesians, and ask, 'Why did Paul write this?' it becomes clear that Paul's purpose in writing Ephesians was to talk about what we are predestined to. Paul encouraged the Ephesians to get involved, to make it their aim to go where God was taking them. Ephesians was written to deepen our faith in the outcomes to which God is taking us.

"Every time 'predestined' shows up, in Ephesians or any other place in Scripture, the emphasis is on what is predestined, the end result."

"So what about 1 Samuel 15:29?" said Mr. Confident.

## 1 SAMUEL 15:29

"The strength of Israel will not lie nor relent: for he is not a man that he should relent."

"This proves God never changes His plan which was in place before creation, a plan that even existed throughout eternity," Mr. Confident challenged, with a dogged determination in his voice.

Christian responded, "Let's look at the context. What is it that God is not going to lie or relent about?"

Christian had Mr. Confident read the whole chapter 15. Then Mr. Confident said, "Saul disobeyed God, so God fired him from being king. God won't relent of having fired him."

Christian responded, "I don't agree. But let's say you're right. So look at verses 10–11. God said, 'I greatly regret that I have set up Saul as king, for he has turned back from following Me, and has not performed My commandments.' Then in verse 23 Samuel said to Saul, 'Because you have rejected the word of the Lord, He also has rejected you from being king.'

"Your interpretation of the verse under consideration, verse 29, is that it says God is not going to relent of having relented of making Saul king. For God to say He will not relent of having relented doesn't really prove that God does not relent. If anything, it's proof that God does relent. (1 Samuel 15:11, 35, KJV)

"But I don't think that's what verse 29 is talking about. I think verse 29 is about Saul's reacting with an attitude of excuses. Saul thought what he did was a small disobedience that could be overlooked, even pardoned. (15:13, 25) Then Samuel said what was recorded in verse 29.

"What God will never relent of concerns His righteousness. He is not a man to overlook Saul's rebellion, stubbornness, and the rejection of the Word of the Lord, as the context indicates Saul expected Him to do. God's judgment on Saul might have been different if Saul acknowledged his sin, truly repented, and asked for forgiveness. (Psalm 32:5) But that was not the attitude of Saul's heart. God is not a man that he should relent of His righteousness and overlook Saul's stubborn, rebellious attitude."

"So what about Numbers 23:19?" persisted Mr. Confident.

## NUMBERS 23:19

"God is not a man, that He should lie, nor a son of man, that He should repent. Has He said, and will He not do? Or has He spoken, and will He not make it good?"

Christian immediately responded, "This isn't saying that God does not change his mind. It is saying that He does not tell lies! 'Has He said, and will He not do? Or has He spoken, and will He not make it good?' And again, the context helps make this clear. What was the situation that caused God to say He would not 'repent' or change His mind?

"Look at what was happening. Balaam was hired by the king of Moab to curse Israel. But acting as a prophet of God he blessed Israel instead. Numbers 23:19 was part of the blessing. The verse goes on to say God had commanded Balaam to bless Israel because there was no iniquity or wickedness among them.

"So at Balaam's suggestion, Moab sent harlots into Israel's camp to entice the men to sin (Revelation 2:14). The plan worked and God lifted His blessing. Then 24,000 of Israel died of the epidemic God sent among them (Numbers 25:9). So God did indeed repent of blessing Israel when they ceased to obey Him. This incident proves that God responds to us in the present, and He will never compromise or repent of His principles of holiness as a man would. But Balaam's blessing had nothing to do with God predestinating anything."

---

[1] Colossians 1:27
[2] Ephesians 3:9-10
[3] Revelation 19:7
[4] Titus 3:3-5; 1 John 5:19
[5] Romans 8:5-9
[6] Ephesians 4:22-24

# APPENDIX B - VERSION CONFUSION

Sometimes different versions of the Bible say opposite things. But by doing a little research, we can identify which is correct. Psalm 139 is an example.

## PSALM 139

Psalm 139 as quoted in modern translations is often cited to show we have no choice about anything because God causes everything to happen. But the main point of Psalm 139 is that God is everywhere, and He sees everything. It has nothing to do with God planning every detail of the psalmist's life.

Verses 13–16 can seem confusing. For example, verse 13:

"For You formed my inward parts; You covered me in my mother's womb." (Ps 139:13 New King James Version)

Some people take this to mean that before we were born, God was literally shaping us inside our mother, and this includes having birth defects. Following their logic, whatever caused the birth defects is part of God's plan. As an example, God would have to have both planned for and caused some mothers to take drugs during pregnancy so certain individuals would have certain kinds of birth defects.

If we compare the Hebrew word for "inward parts" with other places it is used, most of the time, it refers to the invisible inner person, where emotions are. It rarely means actual inward physical parts like kidneys or stomach. So in Psalm 139, the psalmist could be describing God looking at his unique invisible inner person and giving God credit for creating his unique personality. This makes sense. We know that the inner person of John the Baptist was given before he was born, and that others, such as Samson and Jeremiah, were called by God before they were born. Therefore, I do not think that Psalm 139:13 can be used to justify a doctrine that God is responsible for birth defects or any other physical characteristics we inherit from our parents.

[14]"I will praise You, for I am fearfully *and* wonderfully made;

marvelous are Your works, and *that* my soul knows very well.

¹⁵My frame was not hidden from You, when I was made in secret, *and* skillfully wrought in the lowest parts of the earth.

¹⁶Your eyes saw my substance, being yet unformed and in Your book they all were written, the days fashioned for me, when *as yet there were* none of them. (Psalms 139:14–16, NKJV)

From the beginning of the psalm, the theme is that God is everywhere and sees everything about us. Verse 15 says, "My frame was not hidden from You, when I was made in secret." Nowhere in Psalm 139 does God take an active, causative role. He is only there to observe and record what He sees. To emphasize this, the Psalmist mentions twice that God was there to see what was forming, not to actually form it.

Verse 16 is often translated in a way that gives a false impression as to what is written. To understand the sense of the verse, it's helpful to look at it a phrase at a time. I quote from the King James Version because that translation of this verse is more faithful to the Hebrew.

"Thine eyes did see my substance, yet being unperfect."

God was watching and observing. He was not forming or creating.

"and in thy book all *my members* were written."

The Hebrew does not specify what the "all" is. The KJV inserts "my members," and to me, that is the only translation that makes sense. God is watching the growth of an unborn child, so it makes sense that He records what He is watching.

For grammar purposes, the KJV then inserts "which," referring to the members/parts of the baby's body as it is formed, "*which* in continuance were fashioned." "Which" has nothing to do with the child's future life. And it's an amazing thing that God can see everything about us even when we were hidden in our mother's womb.

Some translators render "in continuance" with the word "days." Why is this? Because the Hebrew here is the word "Yom," which is usually translated "day" and means a period of time. Just as in English, "yom" can mean a specific twenty-four–hour day or a time in history. The context always makes it clear which one is meant. For example, "yom" (day) is translated as "time" in sixty-four places in the Old Testament, as in Genesis 26:8, "when he had been there a long time," or Proverbs 25:13 "in time of harvest."

It seems obvious to me that the "yom" (day/time) referred to in Psalms 139:16 is referring to the time of gestation, the nine month period that a baby spends in its mother's womb, when it is hidden from view to everyone—except God.

"when *as yet there was* none of them."

What is the "them" here? The KJV translators obviously thought "them" referred to the parts of a developing baby's body. A paraphrase could be, "when I hadn't finished forming and wasn't born yet." Only modern translators drag in the idea of the number of days in a person's life after he is born, with all its accompanying baggage of predestination. Even if what a modern translation says is faithful to the original Hebrew, it would only concern a person's lifespan, how long the person will live, not the individual choices they will make during that lifespan. Hurrah for the KJV translators! They didn't load their translation with their theology, nor did they assume they knew what was uncertain, but with the use of italics, they passed on to us any uncertainty as it is expressed in the Hebrew. They allowed us to look at the context and come to our own conclusion. Here's how they translated the passage:

[13] For thou hast possessed my reins: thou hast covered me in my mother's womb.

[14] I will praise thee; for I am fearfully *and* wonderfully made: marvellous *are* thy works; and *that* my soul knoweth right well.

[15] My substance was not hid from thee, when I was made in secret, *and* curiously wrought in the lowest parts of the earth.

[16] Thine eyes did see my substance, yet being unperfect; and in thy book all *my members* were written, *which* in continuance were fashioned, when as *yet there was* none of them. (Psalms 139:13–16, KJV)

The translators of the KJV obviously concluded that these verses were a description of God watching an unborn baby develop inside its mother. This has nothing to do with God somehow predetermining our lifespan or causing us to be born with some sort of birth defect. Birth defects are inherited from our parents. So why did the psalmist limit his amazement to the nine months of pregnancy? It's because he was making the point that if God can see all there is about him when he was hidden in his mother's womb, he can certainly see all there is about him after he was born. The whole purpose of Psalm 139 is to show that God is everywhere and sees everything. Nowhere does it speak of predestination. Psalm 139 comes to a great climax at the end, with these words:

"Search me, O God, and know my heart; Try me, and know my

anxieties: And see if there is any wicked way in me. And lead me in the way everlasting."

The psalmist asking God to search his heart is consistent with the rest of the psalm. He's saying, "You see everything; now look in my heart too, and show me if anything is not right, so I will be able to follow Your leading in my life." There's nothing here to say that the psalmist's life is somehow predetermined. Quite the opposite. The psalmist is asking God to guide him to make a change for the better in his life.

## REVELATION 10:6

"And sware by him that liveth for ever and ever, who created heaven, and the things that therein are, and the earth, and the things that therein are, and the sea, and the things which are therein, that there should be time no longer." (KJV)

This is a verse that's unclear in the KJV, leading some people to say time will not exist after the described event takes place. People have told me they expect time to end, and then we will enter eternity with God. I admit I don't know what they're talking about, particularly when they start talking about how past, present, and future are simultaneous. The only explanation I have been able to get from them is that there will be no time, and everything happens at once. The reference I've been given is Revelation 10:5–6. In the New King James Version, it reads:

"The angel…swore by Him who lives forever and ever, who created heaven and the things that are in it, the earth and the things that are in it, the sea and the things that are in it, that there should be delay no longer."

The last phrase in the King James Version reads:

"That there should be time no longer."

So it seems some people are looking at the King James Version and making the assumption that time will end. As is often the case, the meaning becomes clear by reading the context. In this instance, we only have to read the very next verse.

The next verse, Revelation 10:7 says,

"But in the days of the voice of the seventh angel, when he shall begin to sound, the mystery of God should be finished, as He hath declared to His servants the prophets." KJV

"Finished" means that there should be delay no longer. That is, time is up. It's time to stop playing with your toys. There is no doctrine about eternity in Revelation 10:6.

## PASTOR CHRISTIAN'S FINAL THOUGHT

Pastor Christian, reflecting on all that had taken place, and how simple it is to truly follow Christ, as individuals and as a church. *It's only obscured by other things that we wrongly think are important,* he thought. Then he said out loud with fervor, "God created us to share His life with us, a fellowship we should value as much as He does. And valuing His fellowship, our decisions, how we live, everything about us will be according to our understanding of His ways. We have no higher priority than to walk with Him. When we get to heaven, every life will demonstrate the love of God. But we're to do this now, with total abandon. We're called to show the world living, breathing evidence that God is love."

---

[1]Psalms 7:9
[2]John 17:21-23

# BOOKS BY WILLIAM G CHIPMAN:

### Satan's Masterpiece—And The Way To Freedom
An easy to read account (with many Bible references) of how Satan's web of deceptions weakens Christians, but the truth about God sets them free.

### Finding Truth
This is a novel that will make you think! Amid bears and bank robbers, the story is mingled with Scripture as a young orphan is used by God to transform a church. Against heavy opposition he leads the congregation into the Christ-centered life God intends for all believers.

### Seven Principles To Growing Enduring Love
How to bullet proof your marriage and grow your love more with each passing year.

### The John Muir Trail in 8 Days-With Hints for Seniors
Starting with training, gear, food and permits walk with the author as at age 75 he does 210 miles over 10 High Sierra passes. This is a good read for people planning to hike the John Muir Trail.

### Journey into God's Ways
Told as a story, the title says it all. Deep in our hearts we all want to walk closer to our Lord. This is a resource for every Christian.